STAFFORDSHIRE

The King's England

A New Domesday Book of 10,000 Towns
and Villages

Edited by Arthur Mee

in 41 Volumes

Enchanted Land (*Introductory Volume*)

Bedfordshire and
  Huntingdonshire
Berkshire
Buckinghamshire
Cambridgeshire
Cheshire
Cornwall
Derbyshire
Devon
Dorset
Durham
Essex
Gloucestershire
Hampshire with the
  Isle of Wight
Herefordshire
Hertfordshire
Kent
Lake Counties
Lancashire
Leicestershire and Rutland

Lincolnshire
London
Middlesex
Monmouthshire
Norfolk
Northamptonshire
Northumberland
Nottinghamshire
Oxfordshire
Shropshire
Somerset
Staffordshire
Suffolk
Surrey
Sussex
Warwickshire
Wiltshire
Worcestershire
Yorkshire—East Riding
Yorkshire—North Riding
Yorkshire—West Riding

NOTHING like these books has ever been presented to the
English people. Every place has been visited. The Com-
pilers have travelled half-a-million miles and have prepared
a unique picture of our countryside as it has come down
through the ages, a census of all that is enduring and worthy
of record.

THE LADIES OF THE VALE AT LICHFIELD

THE KING'S ENGLAND

STAFFORDSHIRE

Beauty and the Black Country

EDITED BY
ARTHUR MEE

With 180 Places
and 107 Pictures

LONDON
HODDER AND STOUGHTON
LIMITED ST. PAUL'S HOUSE, E.C.4

First published October 1937
Fifth impression January 1951

Printed and Bound in Great Britain for Hodder & Stoughton, Limited,
by Richard Clay and Company, Ltd., Bungay, Suffolk

The Editor is greatly indebted to
SYDNEY WARNER
for his valuable help with
this book

For the pictures to
SIDNEY TRANTER, ART EDITOR
And to the following :

Messrs B. T. Batsford, Ltd., W. Bullock, Country
Life, Fred Crossley, J. Dixon-Scott, G. C. Druce,
E. Elcombe, Herbert Felton, Harold Hooley, Photo-
chrom, J. Simnett, H. J. Smith, W. F. Taylor,
J. Valentine & Sons, and to the L.M.S. Railway,
and the Wolverhampton Development Association.
The pictures on pages 69, 121, and 189, are from
the volume of Incised Effigies of Staffordshire, by
the late Andrew Oliver

PICTURES OF STAFFORDSHIRE

Where the pictures are not on or facing the page given they are inside the set of pictures beginning on that page

vii

Beauty and the Black Country

THOSE who know Staffordshire only from its reputation in the papers may be apt to place a black mark against it as a traveller's county, for the Black Country lies within its borders, and its Five Towns, now known as Stoke-on-Trent, form a great industrial area which grew up too fast for beauty to have its fair share in shaping it.

But it is true that the 686,901 acres of Staffordshire contain as pleasant and peaceful a countryside as we find anywhere in England. In the north the moorlands of the Pennine range come in with all their wild beauty, falling away into the less rugged grandeur of Dovedale and the dales and valleys of smaller streams carving their ways through the limestone. South of the county lies Cannock Chase, an expanse of 30,000 acres of heath relieved by birch groves which remind us that here was a wide forest hunted by kings, high-lying country from which the waters flow in all directions to feed the River Trent.

Between the moorland and Cannock Chase lies undulating country through which the rivers flow slowly, the typical country of the dairy-farmer, not in any way monotonous and rolling up to the borders of the Pottery towns.

Staffordshire, therefore, has much to delight the lover of wide open spaces, and though, with her 1,440,000 people, she is eighth in population but only eighteenth in size among our counties, there are great areas thinly peopled, for the busy towns contain three-quarters of her population.

The most lonely country in Staffordshire is the moorland north of Leek. Here walls of native stone take the place of hedges, and the grouse, the lapwing, and in summer the curlew, break its great silences. Mow Cop, crowned at 1091 feet by a ruined castle, is on the border of Cheshire and famous as the site of the camp meeting at which the Primitive Methodist Society was born two years after Trafalgar. East of Mow Cop lies Biddulph Moor, the source of the Trent, and in a valley beyond, surrounded by well-wooded hills, lies the beautiful Rudyard Lake on whose shores Lockwood Kipling asked Alice Macdonald to be his wife; they called their son after the place and so made its name renowned throughout the world. This lake is two miles long and its greatest width is over 400 yards; actually it is the reservoir for the canal dug to link the Mersey with the Trent at the close of the 18th century. Perhaps it is odd to think that Kipling was named after a reservoir.

A few miles east the ridge known as the Roches cleaves the sky at a height of over 1600 feet, the southern corner dropping to form one side of the beautiful valley of the River Churnet on its westward course. Its valley is completed by the Morredge, a long hill rising less abruptly to 1500 feet, but from Merryton Low, standing out 1603 feet high at the north, we look over the moors from which all the streams flow east to feed the Dove on the county boundary.

It is the Dove's famous tributary, the Manifold, which first gathers these streams together as they make their way through moorland rising 2000 feet and higher. This is the country which it is hoped will form (with part of Derbyshire on the other side of the Dove) England's National Park. All England knows of lovely Dovedale, half of which is in Staffordshire, though Derbyshire has the chief fame of it, but the valley of the Manifold, and the valley of its biggest feeder the River Hamps, are less known, in spite of their wilder beauty and the ever-changing views which their frequent windings give us.

One dramatic little thing has happened here in our time, helping forward the idea of the national park. Even the little railway here has been transformed into a public walk, and we may saunter at will where until not long ago the trains of the LMS would run. A great fortune had been spent on the

Leek and Manifold Light Railway (not less than £68,000) but the line failed, and now the rails have been pulled up, a track of limestone blocks has been laid down, and the steel highway is a walk where no wheels other than a bicycle's may come.

From its source near the hamlet of Flash in the extreme north of Staffordshire the Manifold flows south, gathering from the moors small streams like the Blake Brook. At Hulme End its valley becomes impressive, though hereabouts are the remains of the deserted Ecton copper mines, which yielded such wealth in the 18th century that the Duke of Devonshire is said to have built Buxton's famous Crescent from the profits of a single year. At Wetton Mill is a rock with some caverns (Nan Tor), and then come the bold rocks known as Darfur Crags, perhaps the most striking in the valley. Often in summer the Manifold here disappears underground, but when it does flow it soon comes to the Redhurst Gorge, famed for Old Hannah's Hole, a cleft from which a prehistoric urn has been recovered.

Remains of prehistoric man in far greater variety have been taken from Thor's Cave, an opening in a cliff towering over the valley. It is entered through an arch like the doorway of a Norman cathedral, and, within, two pillars of rock support the roof of the cave. Here in the middle of the 19th century a village schoolmaster found flint arrowheads, bone combs, bronze brooches and bracelets, iron adzes, Samian ware, and a Roman coin. Thor's cave had evidently been inhabited for centuries. Below it, nearer the river, is a smaller cave, called Radcliffe's Stable because Farmer Radcliffe hid his horse in it so that the horse should not be seized to carry one of the Pretender's Scotsmen toward London.

At the base of Beeston Tor, a limestone crag towering above the scene where the Hamps adds its waters to the Manifold, is St Bertram's Cave, in which Saxon jewels and coins of King Alfred were discovered not long ago. This cave, named after the saint who lies at Ilam close by, was evidently a place of hiding from Danish marauders.

The River Hamps, like the Manifold, runs underground when summer comes to this limestone wonderland. It has risen among the lonely Morredge Hills, and for the last two miles of its course lies under the shadow of Soles Hill, 1100 feet high, now happily belonging to the National Trust. The lovely Throwley estate, with its ruins of the Jacobean Old Hall, are bounded by this hill and the River Manifold, winding its way on to pass through the lovely grounds of Ilam Hall, also belonging to the National Trust. It was here that Johnson and Boswell came to see the river emerging from clefts in the rock after its course underground. Dr Johnson declared that the waters could not belong to the Manifold, but the gardener assured him that he had tested the phenomenon with floating corks.

Passing close to Ilam's church, with its Saxon churchyard crosses, the Manifold flows into the Dove, where it emerges from its famous Dale.

A few hundred yards from its source below Axe Edge in Derbyshire the River Dove has formed the boundary between that county and Staffordshire as it twists and turns in its deep valley. Beresford Dale, a narrow ravine taking its name from the Beaver's Ford at its lower end, has been immortalised in Izaak Walton's Complete Angler. It is in the second part of that book, the part his friend Charles Cotton wrote, that we find the description of the Pike Pool with the needle rock which Viator declared was " one of the oddest sights he ever saw." Viator's host replied that young Mr Izaak Walton was so pleased with it as to draw it in landscape, in black and white, in a blank book he had at home. That home, Beresford Hall, lay hidden among the hills not far away, but all that can be seen today are a ruined wall and doorway.

The Fishing House built on the river's bank still stands to remind us of these two friends, whose initials are twined on a stone over the doorway. A companion stone is inscribed Piscatoribus Sacrum, 1674, but the friends little thought, as they stood watching the craftsman cut these words, that this delightful building would be sacred down the ages to thousands who would rather hold a good book than a fishing rod.

Charles Cotton loved this little paradise, where he was born in the troubled days of Charles Stuart, and, weary of town life and its unpleasing traits after the Restoration, he would come here to rest and write and meditate, fishing with his older and wiser friend. In his poem The Retirement he writes of his native stream:

> Oh, my belovèd nymph, fair Dove,
> Princess of rivers, how I love
> Upon thy flowery banks to lie,
> And view thy silvery stream
> When gilded by a summer's beam.

Through much wilder scenery the Dove next flows by Wolfscote Dale to reach (at Dunge Bottom) land which, for many miles on one bank or the other, now belongs to the nation. At Milldale is the narrow Viator Bridge: "Why! a mouse can hardly go over it; tis not two fingers broad," says Viator.

Some two miles of exquisite loveliness now accompany the Dove—the Dovedale painted so often by the artist and sung by the poet. The Staffordshire side equals the Derbyshire side in beauty, though it is from Derbyshire that we see most of its glory. Pinnacles of rock and limestone cliffs add quaintness and strength to the lovely scene: Ravens Tor, the Pickering Tors (one looking like a lion), Ilam Rock, and Tissington Spires. Caverns also give a touch of mystery to the Dale.

Bunster Hill and its Derbyshire rival Thorp Cloud mark the end of the vale, and the river winds onward through a wider valley. On its banks stands Mayfield Church with the grave of Olivia Byron Moore, daughter of Thomas Moore, who in Mayfield Cottage here wrote Lalla Rookh and the familiar poem beginning

> Those evening bells, Those evening bells,
> How many a tale their music tells.

Below Rocester, where on a hill are traces of a Roman camp, the Dove is joined by the Churnet, which comes through a valley rich in woodlands from Cheddleton to Alton. The pinnacles of Alton Towers, as they rise above the trees, and a modern convent on a rock not far away, recall the scenery in the valley of the Rhine. Beyond Oakamoor (where copper wire is made) no road runs up the Valley, though from Froghall there is a canal with its towpath. The Churnet Valley is an ideal place for a Nature Reserve, and near Oakamoor one has been established on 250 acres of Hawksmoor Wood and Eastwall Farm, where under the protection of the National Trust the birds and beasts and wild flowers of the county will flourish undisturbed.

It is in the dairy farmer's country of gentle hills and valleys that the tributary streams of the Dove now flow gently, and none bigger than the Tean joins it before it adds its waters to the Trent at Newton Solney, a village on the Derbyshire bank. The Trent is Staffordshire's longest river, rising at Biddulph Moor and tumbling down the moorland to flow through the Pottery towns, which, however, have to use the canals for their water-borne goods. Joined by the River Lyme, whose name is linked with the Newcastle on its banks, the Trent washes away any stains it may have received in the beautiful district of Trentham.

The story of Trentham reveals one of the evils of the industrial 19th century. Here lived the Leveson-Gower family, Dukes of Sutherland, who gained great wealth from the canals and railways. The Duke of 1840 commissioned Sir Charles Barry, architect of the Houses of Parliament, to rebuild the hall in the vast deer park through which the Trent flows, and a great building like an Italian palace arose; but as the years succeeded the river became more and more polluted, and in 1905 the family left the hall for good. The pollution is now abated and the magnificent deer park is public pleasure-ground.

The Trent has now fallen 800 feet and on its journey across England to the Humber it will fall only 300 feet more, so that its flow is gentle henceforward. At Meaford Hall on its banks

6

above Stone the famous Admiral Jervis, victor in the fight off Cape St Vincent, was born, and Shugborough Hall near Great Haywood, ten miles on, was the birthplace of the famous admiral Lord Anson, who made a voyage round the world which added much to the knowledge of his time.

Often would George Anson have crossed the long bridge spanning the river whose waters have just been increased by those of the Sow, which on its 18 miles from Broughton has passed through Eccleshall and Stafford and gathered up the River Penk and the Meece Brook. The bridge has 14 arches now, but in Anson's day it had 42, having been built over meadow and river by the Earls of Essex for huntsmen on their way to Cannock Chase, which is still as wild as ever here. The bridge is over a hundred yards long, but only four feet wide!

This Essex Bridge is perhaps the quaintest bridge in the county, but the longest and the finest crosses the Trent at Burton, having a length of over 1400 feet and a width of 50. On its way between these two bridges the Trent has received the Little Blithe, the Swarbourn, and other small streams from Needwood Forest on its left bank, and on its right (as if to help it to become a wider boundary between Staffordshire and Derbyshire) the River Tame, which gives its name to Tamworth, one of the most important towns in England a thousand years ago. The Tame is a native of Staffordshire, rising near Wednesbury and forming the county boundary for a few miles above Tamworth.

The Trent is thus the river into which most of the rain falling on the county finds its way, to be carried to the North Sea, but as the Pennines are the chief water-parting in the north of England, and have thrust a moorland spur into Staffordshire, we find a few streams making their way west. Perhaps the most interesting of these is the little Dane, which prattles along the northern boundary and then makes its way to the River Weaver, and so into the Mersey. The Tern, on the other hand, for many miles dividing the county from Shropshire, is a tributary of the mighty Severn.

Except the Trent for the mile or two between Burton and the boundary, none of the rivers of Staffordshire are navigable for boats of any great size. This fact, and the forests, and the remoteness from the sea, made Staffordshire one of England's Cinderella counties for centuries, to be transformed almost within one man's lifetime into one of the most prosperous of all by the development of her coalfields. Even in 1801 less than a quarter of a million people lived here.

Prehistoric man did not settle here in great numbers, though the half-dozen hill forts he has left are in strong positions. Kinver Edge, 500 feet above the sea with magnificent views over the Cotswolds, the Malverns, and the Shropshire hills, is National Trust property, almost on the southern boundary of the county. On Byrth Hill above Maer is the site of another big camp, and not far away, near Mucklestone (the most westerly village in Staffordshire), stand two prehistoric stones known as the Devil's Ring and the Devil's Finger.

The most important work of the Romans here is in three roads, Watling Street remaining to this day as one of the widest and best as it cuts almost in a straight line from east to west on the way to Wroxeter. Icknield Street, a direct route from Derby to Worcester, crosses Watling Street at Wall, and here is to be found one of our most perfect Roman baths. It is national property, and close by is a museum in which we see the Roman objects found here. Through the Potteries runs another Roman road, linking Chester with Little Chester, the forerunner of Derby, and along it we come across such Roman names as Chesterton, Rocester, and Uttoxeter, where in the market-place Dr Johnson stood bareheaded in the rain, when he was 70, to do penance for a sin of his youth in refusing to help his father at a stall, a penance in which he showed something of the old Roman reverence for filial duty.

It was two centuries after the Roman legions had trod these roads that Christianity came this way. The English had been slow in settling here, trickling in up the Trent valley and becoming known as the Mercians. Their powerful King Penda was the foe of Christian Northumbria, but his sons, converted to the new faith, brought missionaries home, and among them was the saintly Chad, who founded the see of Lichfield. For a few years at the end of the 8th century the see was raised by the Pope to an archbishopric, an honour due to the influence of King Offa, whose name appears on our maps, where there are still remains of Offa's Dyke, built to keep out the Welsh. Around Tamworth, where he had a palace and a mint, remains of another dyke made by Offa can still be seen. But of even greater interest in this town are the ditch and mound of its castle, for the castle was built by Alfred's warrior daughter, Ethelfleda, "Lady of the Mercians" and conqueror of both Danes and Welsh, and here she died after having made it possible for her nephew Athelstan, brought up at her court, to acclaim himself King of All Britain, just one thousand years before the crowning of our George the Sixth. Stafford also was founded by Ethelfleda.

No church built by Chad or his Saxon successors still stands, but we can still admire the elaborate carvings on churchyard crosses (Checkley has three), some fashioned before the coming of the Danes and others later. From a wall in Enville church look down a Saxon bishop and a Saxon priest, and on the font at Ilam are carvings of men and beasts which many attribute to a Saxon craftsman.

Norman churchyard crosses, imposing in their size and enriched with elaborate detail, stand at Armitage and Wolverhampton, while dragons stand out from stones at Ipstones on the Moorland and Kingswinford on the border of the Black Country. There are fine Norman fonts at Armitage, Bradley, and Pipe Ridware, but to appreciate Norman work at its best we should go to the Priory church at Tutbury with its superb doorway, and to St Chad's at Stafford, with the magnificent nave that Orm built, recording the fact proudly in an inscription on a pier of the tower.

The iron hand of the Conqueror fell heavily on Staffordshire, for its inhabitants had made common cause with the north in rising against him in the early years of his reign, and had paid the consequences. As a result we find in Domesday Book a record of only about 3000 male inhabitants and hardly a mention of a church. During the next hundred years both churchmen and laymen must have entered the county in large numbers, for by King John's time every village had its church, and monasteries were being established in profusion.

Of the buildings raised by the great religious Orders, only Lapley Church and Tutbury are used today, having become parish churches at the Reformation. A graceful arcade, the west front, and part of the tall transept of Croxden Abbey's church, 90 yards long, form the only monastic ruin of any grandeur in Staffordshire, the 15th-century tower of the priory church at Ranton claiming the next place; but of the famous abbeys of Burton, Hulton, Rocester, and Dieu-la-Cresse hardly a stone remains in position, though they are to be seen in the walls of churches and farms.

Lovers of medieval architecture, however, will find many beautiful examples of this period in this county which held to the Gothic tradition even till Stuart times. The most perfect of all, of course, is Lichfield Cathedral, which with its reddish stone seems to reflect for ever the rays of the setting sun. Its three spires are a unique feature in this country, and careful hands have replaced stone by stone all those which time or vandal hand has spoiled, with the result that the cathedral appears today as it did to its builders six or seven hundred years ago. While the choir is 13th century, the nave and the lady chapel are 14th, perhaps the most perfect example of that rich style in all England.

In Weston-on-Trent church, and in the tiny chapel at Coppenhall, is beautiful work of the earlier period, while Clifton Campville, with its graceful spire, is an excellent example of 14th-century building. The noblest church of the 15th century is St Peter's in Wolverhampton, which has rich panelling on its tall central tower and, within, a beautiful stone pulpit carved when the church was new and unique in the county. The finest oak pulpit, dated 1611, is in another big town, Wednesbury, and the pulpit, reading desk, and the pew in which Izaak Walton would often sit at Alstonfield, form a splendid group of wood-carving of Charles Stuart's day.

Timbered houses are rare, but the High House in Stafford and the five-gabled Haselour Hall near Harlaston are delightful survivors from Shakespeare's day, and from the same time come the gatehouse at Tixall and Wootton Lodge, famous for its surrender to the army of Parliament without a stone being hurt. It was through Tixall gatehouse that Mary Queen of Scots passed to captivity in a house no longer standing, having met with the same fate as the houses at Tutbury and Chartley, her last prisons before Fotheringhay.

Holbeach House at Himley recalls the desperate end of the Gunpowder Plot conspirators who sought to kill Mary's son King James. One of their number, Stephen Littleton, lived in its predecessor and in front of its fire a dozen of them tried to dry their own gunpowder after it had become wet when fording the flooded River Stour. An explosion wounded some of them, and all were either killed or captured the next day.

Littleton was not the only famous ruffian associated with Staffordshire. There are Gilbert Giffard, who spied on Mary Queen of Scots, and perhaps concocted some of the letters that sent her to her doom; Jonathan Wild, son of a Wolverhampton wigmaker; and William Wood, ironmaster of that town, who was branded as a coiner and counterfeiter in Dean Swift's famous Letters. Wood was the great-grandfather of Mary Howitt, a girl of Uttoxeter, who with her husband William wrote familiar verses of the trees and flowers and birds of Staffordshire. So two centuries before had written the Staffordshire youth Richard Barnfield of Norbury, whose most famous lyric, *As it Fell Upon a Day*, was long attributed to Shakespeare. To Charles Cotton we have already paid tribute, but in Shallowford we can visit the cottage of his friend Izaak Walton (now a museum) and remember that he left his farm about it to the poor of Stafford, where he was born.

As the county town was the birthplace of Staffordshire's Grand Old Fisherman, the city of Lichfield gave to the world the Grand Old Talker, Dr Johnson. We see him carved in stone (a poor king all unworthy of his fame) gazing on the old house in which his father sold books, and we meet him in spirit in many other haunts in this city—the Three Crowns where he stayed with Boswell, the Friary, and the Upper and Lower Stowe Houses, where he visited friends of a lifetime when he came back in his old age. It was in the neighbouring hamlet of Edial that Johnson set up as schoolmaster with David Garrick as a pupil, both having attended the grammar school at Lichfield, where yet lingered memories of Joseph Addison, who had become a pupil when his father was made Dean.

A pupil at Lichfield earlier still was the saddler's son Elias Ashmole, the antiquary. His native city is almost as proud of the silver cup he gave it in 1666 as Oxford is of the collection we know as the Ashmolean. Ashmole took the King's side in the Civil War, but one of his bitterest foes, Thomas Harrison, was the son of a farmer of Newcastle-under-Lyme, and it was Harrison who brought Charles Stuart from Hurst Castle to take his trial in Westminster Hall, and who called him a "man of blood." Arrested in his Staffordshire home at the Restoration, he showed on the scaffold a cheerful courage which greatly astonished Mr Pepys.

Three years after Harrison's death another humble-born native of the county, Gilbert Sheldon, youngest son of a Stanton farmer, was made Archbishop of Canterbury. A noble and generous man, he built the Sheldonian Theatre at Oxford. Another charitable figure of that century was Thomas Guy, who went to school at Tamworth, lived as a miser and passed to his immortality as an astonishing philanthropist.

We now come to two names which are closely associated with

the conversion of a big area of Staffordshire from agriculture to industry, the names Wedgwood and Dudley.

On the tomb of Josiah Wedgwood in Stoke, below his bust by Chantrey, we read that he converted a rude and inconsiderable manufacture into an elegant art and an important part of national commerce. Thomas Toft and others had been making pottery in the villages now covered by Stoke, and a Dutchman, Philip Elers, had settled near Burslem, bringing chemical knowledge from the Continent. To a factory at Fenton, where Thomas Whieldon was producing improved and decorated earthenware, Josiah Wedgwood went as a partner in 1752. He revolutionised the industry and 15 years later began his great works at Etruria. Josiah was not only a supreme craftsman but a business genius as well, and he arranged for Brindley to bring the Bridgewater Canal by his works.

So the district became the centre of the pottery industry and the Five Towns (Stoke, Hanley, Burslem, Tunstall, and Longton) thrived exceedingly. In 1910 they federated (with Fenton) under the name of Stoke-on-Trent, which now has a population of 274,000 and many other industries in addition to its 300 potteries, for coal, ironstone, and limestone lie about its soil as well as potter's clay.

Staffordshire has another extensive coalfield in the south as well as that in the north, with iron available to found great industries. Her vast forests were used as fuel by the earlier workers in iron; indeed the use of charcoal did not cease until the middle of the 18th century. But in 1619 a young man named Dud Dudley was summoned from his studies at Oxford to take charge of his father's ironworks at Pensnett in Worcestershire. He experimented with coal and secured such good results that his rivals drove him from the county. He set up a furnace at Himley, and another at Askew Bridge, near Sedgley, where he established a British record of seven tons of pig-iron a week. Dudley, however, was a pioneer before his time, and it was not for a hundred years that coal came into its own. Then above the coal measures arose those busy manufacturing towns which gave the name of the Black Country to this area, each town specialising in some branch of hardware—chains at Cradley, anchors and pumps at Tipton, bits and bridles at Walsall, traps and keys at Wednesfield, locks at Willenhall, tinplates at Bilston and Wolverhampton, tubes, axles, and stoves at West Bromwich, lighthouses and their equipment at Smethwick.

Everywhere we see the winding gear at the pitheads, the great chimneys belching smoke and sparks, the ugly slagheaps, and the gigantic factories. Busy streets, innumerable railway lines, and a network of canals fill this crowded region, yet it has its quiet places and memorials, which we would not pass by.

Walsall has its statue of Sister Dora, and West Bromwich the Old Oak House, now a museum; Wolverhampton, biggest town of all, with 140,000 people, has a splendid Art Gallery and other public buildings of distinction, while she has laid out 200 acres of parks and open spaces and is building garden suburbs which will make her one of the most attractive towns in the Midlands. At its gate is Bushbury Church, very much as George Borrow describes it in Romany Rye, and a mile beyond is Moseley Old Hall, in which Thomas Whitgreave hid Charles the Second during his flight from Worcester. In the churchyard of Brewood lies Colonel William Carlos, who supported the king's head as he slept in the Boscobel Oak, which is just over the border in Shropshire.

Staffordshire is indeed a county with a rich store of memories, with a past as well as a present and a great future. We may hope the famous Horn Dance will be danced in September for many a year to come at Abbots Bromley, that the Crooked House at Himley will long amuse the passer-by, and that the natural beauties here abounding will be fostered and guarded by all who come this way.

The Sad Story of a Primeval Park

ABBOTS BROMLEY. Little changes here. All the winter its curfew tolls the knell of parting day. Its delightful black-and-white timbered houses are old; older still is the grey-roofed market cross on its seven wooden pillars; but oldest of all is the Horn Dance, for which the little town is widely famous.

Once part of the religious festivals and now part of a September fair, it is danced by 12 people: Robin Hood on a hobby-horse, his Maid Marian, a jester, a boy with bow and arrow, two musicians, and six men wearing ancient reindeer horns. The dance is believed to mark certain rights of the townsmen to privileges in Needwood Forest, which, hunting-ground of John of Gaunt and a long line of kings, spread here with a circumference of 25 miles, and was governed by laws of terrible severity. The vicar still holds the dance "properties," for in old days a forest right won was important to priests and laity alike, meaning food and fuel.

Although much of the church is new it keeps its 14th-century arcades, and on a wall is a brass portrait of John Draycote, who saw the county divided in its loyalty by the Wars of the Roses. The dance was already old to him, and he would have been less surprised than we were to find its accompaniments, the hobby-horse and the antlers, in a chapel here. All about stretched the forest, and even after the ravages of the Civil War a census showed 47,000 great trees, said to exceed in size and value those of any other forest in England.

Bagot's Bromley, a mile away, was one of the ten parks within the forest bounds. Only the wet moat remains of the manor in which the Conqueror found the Bagots established. The Normans entered them in Domesday Book as taxable owners, and here they stayed for the next eight centuries, ancestors of the Earls of Stafford and the Dukes of Buckingham. One of their guests, it is said, was Mary Queen of Scots on her sad journey to Fotheringhay.

An obelisk in Monument Field tells of their departure in 1811 for Blithfield, two miles off; but a Bagot had already made that journey

15

early in the 13th century, to marry the heiress and establish the line which after 600 years still has there a Lord Bagot at its head.

On visiting the park at Bagot's Bromley, with its ancient herony of 26 nests and its famous herd of goats, we found trees which must have been two or three centuries old when the census of the forest was taken for Charles the Second. Among them were Beggar's Oak, with branches spreading 48 feet from the bole; the Squitch Oak, with a perfect crown 60 feet above the ground; and Bagot's Walking Stick, rising as a majestic column of 70 feet before throwing out a branch.

There was once a Lord Bagot who, riding a poor horse in this magnificent domain, was asked by a friend why he did not sell £50,000 worth of oak, which he would never miss. "The Bagots are not timber merchants," he said. But it was tragic to find these trees, the Walking Stick alone excepted, under sentence of death when we called, and with them the woods and plantations, rich in beech, ash, and Spanish chestnut, in all nearly 20,000 trees with half a million cubic feet of timber.

A grievous thing it is when taxation strips an Englishman's castle of the Old Masters on the walls, but a bitter tragedy it seems when it strips our woodlands of Nature's Old Masters.

Three Generations

ACTON TRUSSELL. The little Penk glides through it, with only one more village to water before its 20-mile adventure ends in its union with another river. The little stream suits the village, where everything is on a small scale, the church not excepted, as small today as 600 years ago, save for the 16th-century tower. Much is changed since then, but something remains that the priest would see when, at the end of an hour's good walk from Stafford, he reached here to serve what was then a chapel of St Mary's Priory.

When a renewal of the ancient fabric became necessary last century the proud little parish summoned to the work one of the greatest of church builders, George Edmund Street, who gave London its Law Courts, and he turned to this tiny task from his most romantic work, the Crimean memorial church at Constantinople. He left what he could, preserving two fine original windows rich with tracery. There is some beautiful modern glass, with nine scenes from the life of Christ.

The Enchanting Waters of the Dove

Charles Cotton's Fishing House
IN LOVELY BERESFORD DALE

A Pastoral Scene near Stafford

Thor's Cave and the Manifold Valley

There is an alabaster tablet which brings to mind a family of Staffordshire poets. It is to Arthur Alsop, who was curate of this church and the allied church at Bednall from 1878 to 1880, serving under his father James Alsop, who was vicar here from 1867 until his death in 1880. On the death of James, Arthur Alsop served as vicar until his death in 1928 ended a faithful ministry of half a century.

The tastes of the two accorded perfectly: each was a devoted servant of his parish, and each loved literature; each, after preaching, catechising, and christening, after comforting the sick and succouring the needy, would retire to his study and his slippers, and there let imagination flower into poetry.

Arthur Alsop saw his hopes crowned when one of his four sons, Philip, in turn proved a poet too. We may read more of these three generations under Bednall.

The Poet's Song of Home

ADBASTON. "Dear native Adbaston, remote from care," wrote its own poet, and remote it remains—its next village five miles away, its nearest station seven.

Snug among trees at the end of a shady lane where a monastery once stood, is Ellerton Grange, a farmhouse which has its place in the poetry of this countryside. The village was not too isolated for the Normans; here they built their church, and here, in the 15th-century church of today, are two of their deeply splayed windows, one on either side of the 13th-century chancel arch. It is possible that the building of the arch was witnessed by some of those who slept under the 13th-century coffin lids built into the wall.

The oldest memorial in the church is a medieval tablet with the figures of Reginald Bradocke in a flowing robe and his wife in a tight-fitting gown and a horned headdress. A wooden tablet tells us of William Wakeley, who died as the village Methuselah in 1714, a very old man—125 according to the register, though we need not believe it.

The porch has its modest place in the literary history of the county, for in it, in 1797, Charles Bowker Ash sat down as a boy of 16, stirred by ardent love of this village to write his first elegy. Half a mile away is the brick farmhouse where he was born and left father-less at three years old. By turns actor and surveyor, and ever a great walker, visiting every town of note in the country, he had always a song in his heart, and two volumes of poems he published in 1831 pleased and appealed to Coleridge.

The piece best remembered here is naturally that in which he chanted the beauties of his native village, declaring:

> *In thy sweet vales a balsam I could find*
> *When nought on earth could calm my troubled mind.*

He saw the landscape changing, but not all has gone. The rushes he loved on the moor are still a summer glory, and the old grange has yet the rustic charms that so endeared it to him.

The Village Crusader

ALDRIDGE. It still has in its keeping two stone figures of men who walked about these lanes 700 years ago, one perhaps the founder of the church, one certainly a crusader. They lie under arches, Nicholas the priest in his robes at the chancel arch, and Sir Robert Stapleton the crusader at the tower arch in his knightly mail, with sword and helmet and lion defiant on his shield as when he fought the Saracens.

The church in which they lie has been made new, but its splendid tower is mainly 14th century, and the arcades of the nave have echoed to the praise of nearly 20 generations. Here we came upon the memory of a parson (Edmund Tongue) who preached for half of the 18th century in this Jacobean pulpit; and in the churchyard is the grave of one who sang in the choir for 60 years, William Prescott.

The Pathos of a Lonely Island

ALREWAS. For ages it has been famous for its baskets, and we found villagers busy at their age-old task, as deft with their osiers as the women with their needles. The Trent runs past and the Grand Junction Canal runs through, and her waterways, her trades, and her treasures give a special charm to the village life of Alrewas. Not least enviable of the village's possessions are the delightful thatched black-and-white cottages.

There was a Saxon church here when the Normans arrived, and in it, they say, Lady Godiva worshipped. It has gone, but its successor has a medieval tower and we still come in by its simple doorways the Normans used. The Norman arches of the south arcade, rising from towering octagonal piers, are slightly pointed.

The font has been here 500 years, and worthy of honour it is, a fine example of Gothic fancy, guarded by four grotesque heads, perhaps a medieval device for scaring witches away. The chancel, which had already seen two centuries of services when the font was carved, has a modern clerestory to light it. In the chancel is a wall painting showing a bishop with an attendant carrying his mitre, and an angel with a trumpet. The stone reredos has a pathetic Crucifixion, showing the two robbers.

The height demands a noble roof, and here is one of the 16th century, with fine timbers carved with clustered leaves. The chancel screen has parts of an older one worked into it, beautiful with roses, the pulpit is of Charles Stuart's days, and there is one 17th-century stall. An old ironbound chest has three locks.

Two brass tablets keep alive cherished memories, one of Henry Kent, whose 60 years of faithful service ended in 1916, the other of Clara Selwyn, a young mother who died on a lonely Pacific island in 1877. She was the wife of a much-loved curate here, John Selwyn, who, son of the first Bishop of New Zealand and afterwards of Lichfield, came to England as a boy and developed at college into a magnificent oarsman, with no thought of church work. A return to the scene of his father's labours, however, roused him to a noble determination, and he gave his life to the people of Polynesia. It cost him his health and his young wife her life. Crippled and broken, he yet proved a great master of Selwyn College, Cambridge, where his influence remained long after his death, and here in Alrewas he is remembered for his curate days, when this fine Cambridge athlete preached on Sundays and on Mondays taught the lads to swim.

The Home of Charles Cotton

ALSTONFIELD. It has for its setting the splendid scenery of the Derbyshire border, with the winding valley of the Dove at its feet. Six great barrows house the dead who peopled the valley in the Bronze Age; and Saxon and Norman relics serve as stepping-stones across the later centuries.

The manor with its tall chimneys is now a farm, but has on it the initials of John Harpur, who built it in the year before the Armada. There are the remains (a doorway and fragments of walls) of Beresford Hall, where Charles Cotton lived 300 years ago, writing his poems, translating Montaigne, entertaining Izaak Walton; and here is the famous Fishing House the veteran angler saw his young friend building.

Under its 15th-century tower, with a great yew by the gate, is the church to which they came, the church described by Cotton when he wrote the second part of Izaak's Complete Angler. "What have we here, a church?" cried Izaak as he first saw it, adding, "As I'm a honest man, a very pretty church!"

In the churchyard, where lie an old stone coffin and an abandoned font, is set up a fragment of a Saxon cross with a serpent's head. In the porch is another fragment with the most ancient portraits in the village, two Saxons at prayer, one wearing a short skirt with a belt and sword. A third Saxon stone, carved with plaitwork, is built into a wall, and there are remains of three coffin lids in the north porch.

The Normans spared the Saxon crosses; the men who remade much of the church in the 16th century left the doorway and the chancel arch the Normans built. They left also the 14th- and 15th-century arcades. The church is rich in fonts, for there is another veteran indoors beside the modern one.

Among the 17th-century seats is Cotton's own canopied pew, beautifully panelled, and carved with flowers, grapes and sea-serpents, with the green paint put on by an 18th-century vicar. Cotton and Izaak would often sit in this pew, listening to sermons from this two-decker pulpit, handsomely decorated but with a text so economical that it makes us smile, for it is

Be faithful &c., and I will give thee a crowne &c.

We can picture the two famous friends walking from the church back to lovely Beresford Dale, and imagine the talk of Ben Jonson, Michael Drayton, Sir Henry Wotton, and the rest. Never was Walton happier than when here; never would man more fully share the rapture with which Cotton wrote of the beauties of the river:

O my beloved nymph, fair Dove,
Princess of rivers, how I love
Upon thy flowery banks to lie.

Brothers of the rod, they fished these waters with the ardour that fires their writings. Here is their tree-shaded Pike Pool with its lichened pinnacle of limestone rising from the water, a spectacle which so excited Walton that, describing it as one of the oddest things he had seen, he returned to the Hall and made a drawing of it in one of Cotton's books.

Many times he was here; the invitations he received and his answers to them are part of English literature. Cotton has pictured something of their simple life and habits:

> *How sweet are all things here!*
> *How beautiful the fields appear!*
> *How cleanly do we feed and live!*
> *Lord! what good hours do we keep,*
> *How quietly we sleep!*

The little Fishing House is trim and sound. The pyramid roof was not complete in time for Cotton to see it, but together they sat here; a stone above the doorway is inscribed with their initials.

The Immortal Friends

IT was a strange conjunction, the old London linen-draper born ten years before the death of Elizabeth, and an aristocrat nearly forty years his junior, a traveller, a man versed in the classics, and a master of modern languages, in whose father's house had gathered such literary giants.

It would have shocked the humility of Izaak Walton to be told that the brilliant young scholar who affectionately called him his father was to ensure his immortality by their friendship, even though he did, in ten fruitful days, write the second part of the old man's Complete Angler. As Walton's friend, Cotton's name will live in men's affections as long as the book is read.

But Cotton's fame is undying by virtue of his own performances. He was a true lyrical poet, as well as an inexhaustible jester, parodist, and creator of burlesque. Above all, he gave us a translation of Montaigne that is a masterpiece. We venerate Florio's stately version, for his was Shakespeare's introduction to Montaigne, but that of Cotton is a triumph of rich and racy English. He loved and understood the Gascon genius, and his work was a delight and recreation to him, as its reading is to us.

He inherited encumbered estates, was always impoverished, and had often to flee from his creditors to the seclusion of the hills, yet in spite of his travels and troubles he wrote untiringly translations, burlesques, essays on gardening, poetry, and finally his inestimable Montaigne. Born in 1630, he died in London in 1687 and was buried at St James's in Piccadilly.

The Valley of Enchantment

ALTON. It is like the magic of Prospero, with something of the cloud-capped towers, the gorgeous palaces, the solemn temples, in its dreamland setting.

With a silent sea of pines behind it, the stone-built village begins where the rocks end, above the lovely valley of the Churnet. On one hill above the water, where a Norman castle stood, is a 19th-century convent, looking on its precipitous rock like a Rhineland castle, 300 feet high; on a height crowning the other side of the valley is Alton Towers, the fairy-like palace in its peerless grounds. Ruined castle and lordly pleasure-house alike were homes of the Talbots; the two link 800 years of history.

The Talbots are not the only great names remembered here; before them were the Furnivals and the Verduns. It was Bertram de Verdun who first came riding up the valley eight centuries ago to build his great castle on the brow of the hill. Then, a man of law and war, he founded Croxden Abbey for the peace of his soul, joined Richard Lionheart's Crusade, and died in the Holy Land.

In later days nine Furnivals were lords of the castle, among them Gerard, who died at Jerusalem in 1219, Thomas the Hasty, who fell at Crecy, and John, whose heiress married a 15th-century Talbot, and so carried the castle and village into the possession of that family.

They did not at once settle at the castle, but John Talbot, the famous Earl of Shrewsbury, so long champion of our arms across the Channel that they called him King of France, stayed here occasionally, bringing to the hilltop fortress strange tales of a girl in white armour named Joan, who had repulsed him from Orleans, and taken him, hero of 40 battles, prisoner at Patay, the first reverse to an English army since our triumph at Crecy. He no more doubted her being a witch than did Shakespeare, who makes this stout Talbot so great a figure in his play of Henry the Sixth.

Two more centuries of Talbot ownership passed, and then the castle was knocked to pieces in the Civil War. All that remains is a round tower with part of a wall. Divided from it by the old moat stands the chapel of the convent, built by Pugin last century. Its alabaster reredos has eight finely carved saints in canopied niches; and its oak roodscreen, richly decorated with roses, has two angels with the Madonna and Child.

Of the church Bertram de Verdun saw there remains only one Norman arcade, but the tower was up when the Talbots came 500 years ago; and the font bowl has for four centuries borne their arms. The modern pulpit has a fine carving of Peter before Christ.

It was at the close of the Hundred Years War that the Talbots established themselves at the castle; it was near the end of the Napoleon wars that they colonised the other side of the valley. In 1814 John Talbot, the 15th Earl of Shrewsbury, came this way. From the centre to the circumference all he saw was his, the ruined castle, the lonely hill on which rabbits had converted a prehistoric settlement into a warren, and an old house named Alton Lodge. Like Kubla Khan in Xanadu, he forthwith "a stately pleasure-dome decreed."

Taking 600 acres of wilderness, he spent the last 13 years of his life in changing it into an earthly paradise, and when he died his nephew carried on and completed the wonder of it all. For more than a century Alton Towers has been one of the most famous of English houses, visited by hundreds of thousands of sightseers. Until 1924 it remained a home of the Talbots, but it is so no more.

The grounds are unexcelled for beauty, laid out by the 15th earl and "Capability" Brown. The earl saw as saplings trees that are giants today. He planned and visualised, and his successor extended his planning, and today we see here one of the great sights of our countryside, a wonder of woodlands with shady paths and winding ways, great yew arches, an army of firs and beeches, sparkling lakes, fountains, and waterfalls, sudden peeps of lofty towers above and between the trees, and gardens of delicate loveliness and exquisite colour in summer.

There is a Chinese temple, a handsome bridge over a lake among cedars, a pagoda on a delightful island, and a cottage which was once the home of a blind Welsh harper. The Flag Tower, a four-storeyed

8

8

stone structure 90 feet high, looks out over the glories of the Stafford-shire hills and the romantic beauty of Wales. The grand conservatory with its seven domes shines above seven terraces descending to the river's brim, suggesting to the eye the hanging gardens of ancient Babylon. Set in the heart of all this loveliness is the copy of a Greek temple with a bust of John Talbot, its inscription truly recording that he made the desert smile.

The magnificent battlemented house he built proclaims its title of Alton Towers by its many towers and turrets; and the family name (Talbot meaning a hound) is announced at the entrance by two armorial Talbot hounds, each with a gilt banner.

An arch above the broad flight of steps brings us under a lofty tower to the entrance hall; and two doors 18 feet high open to an Armoury 300 feet long and lighted by windows glowing with painted glass. The great picture-gallery has no longer its Old Masters, but the fine oak ceiling, resting on corbels with the Talbot dogs, is itself a treasure.

Beyond is the Octagon, a sculpture gallery like a cathedral chapter-house, its wonderful roof supported by a beautiful central clustered pillar with a floral capital. In old festal days carriages were driven along the great stone corridor and turned round in this noble chamber, a strange spectacle for the Talbot bishops gravely looking down from the rich lancet windows. In the Talbot Gallery, about 100 yards long, are 80 shields of arms. In the early 18th-century glass in the library are portraits of Gilbert Talbot and his wife, and in the music-room a delightful bay window is beautified by angels, with fine figures of David and St Cecilia. The dining-hall, a magnificent lofty chamber, has an immense window with a superb view over the hills.

In the chapel, built by Pugin, is a charming east window with figures of the Four Evangelists, and a painted reredos with statues of four Englishmen, Augustine and Becket, the Confessor and St Chad, with delightful figures of angels appearing here and there. The Black Prince, in armour and mantle, dignifies a window of the great drawing-room.

All is splendid in design and execution; we do not wonder that the fascinated Disraeli made it the Muriel Towers of his novel Lothair.

Something is a little changed from the original plan. The first owner's copy of Stonehenge is still in the grounds, but the shot-tower and cannon he placed in a position to command the entrance are no more. He began his work in a militant age, the year before Waterloo, but he mellowed with the progress of it all, and left, not a fortified manor, but a palace of delight. Rarely has it been given to two men, the earls who began, continued, and ended all this, to bequeath to posterity so fair a heritage of beauty and splendour.

Staffordshire is famous for its potteries and its coal mines, but it has here one of the wonder houses of the kingdom, and gardens won from the wilds which, for loveliness and diversity of appeal, are hardly surpassed by any private estate in Europe.

The Rival Knights

ARMITAGE. With the Trent flowing at its feet, it has something of Rome underground, from which it has dug up spears and weapons of brass; it has a Norman church made new, and it looks in one direction to a modern priory and in the other to an ancient manor linking it with events in Shakespeare.

The church, crowning a rocky hill, has been rebuilt in Norman style in our own day, but has its 15th-century tower, a Norman font with 14 grotesque heads, and other relics of its Norman past. Screened by six venerable yews in the churchyard is a magnificent Norman cross, about ten feet high and enriched with fine carvings. The doorway is carved with quaint animals.

Among the memorials is the alabaster portrait of Captain Arthur Samson, the rector's son who, after winning the Military Cross, fell while leading his company in action. Half a mile away, with its century-old iron bridge crossing the river with one span of 140 feet, is Handsacre, from which we have a fine view of Cannock Chase. Among its trees stands the ancient brick-and-timbered manor, with water still in the moat, and the doorway still remaining from what was once an oratory.

From here in 1403 rode out Sir William Handsacre at the head of his retainers, intending to enrol with Hotspur and Douglas on their march to join Glendower in his war with Henry the Fourth. At the same time his neighbour Sir Robert Mavesyn headed a contingent to fight for Henry, and the rival knights met by the Trent, where they fought a battle ending in the death of the lord of Handsacre and the march of the victor to Shrewsbury, where he and Hotspur perished on the field.

In a charming setting at Hawkesyard, a mile or so from Armitage, is a new priory, founded in 1894, with a college, a library, and a church that is a little gem of architecture. Under the vaulted roof of its beautiful chantry, rich with tracery, lie the founders, Josiah Spode and Helen Gulson. The stone chancel screen, pierced by graceful iron gates, is finely carved with many figures, and there is a handsome stone reredos with 39 saints and monks gathered about a statue of Christ. The chancel has 26 canopied choir-stalls, but the greatest treasure here is the rare organ-case, beautifully carved with foliage and four delightful cherubs. Formerly one of the glories of Eton College, it is a masterpiece of Grinling Gibbons, a prize of which this little place may well be proud.

The Black Slave on an English Tomb

ASHLEY. Its church has been remade, but its 17th-century tower remains, with arches on three sides. An old yew in the churchyard is 12 feet round.

There is a brass tablet to David Kenric, a village boy who fought under the Black Prince, and a wonderfully preserved alabaster tomb of Thomas Lord Gerard, who died a year after Shakespeare. He lies under an arch, a knightly figure in armour and ruff, with his wife, two sons, and six daughters. Attending them is a figure who might have come from the pages of Ivanhoe, the devoted black servant who died far from the land he loved after faithfully serving his master and mistress.

A beautiful Chantrey shows us the fine figure of Thomas Kinnersley, who rests on his arm, lifelike, as he must have looked in the days of Trafalgar and Waterloo; and another wall monument has three delightful angels in memory of another Thomas Kinnersley who followed him.

The modern work of the church includes a fine gilded oak reredos with a Madonna and Child, beautiful in carving and colour, an Annunciation, and delicately carved figures of eight Fathers of the Church.

One of Ashley's rectors was John Lightfoot, the man who had Milton's tutor among his masters at Cambridge, and was a student of unsurpassed diligence. In order to be uninterrupted by domestic distractions he bought the field next to the rectory, and in it built a little study, a parlour, and a bedroom.

There he worked far into the night and slept in his little cubicle, completing the studies which made him the greatest Hebrew scholar of his age. He left in 1642 to take his stand for the Parliament, but so great was his fame that at the Restoration he became vice-chancellor of Cambridge University, of which he was deemed one of the brightest ornaments.

The Days of the Black Prince

AUDLEY. The Romans who built its Ryknield Street and had their camp two miles away left untouched the coal the hillside village mines today. Froissart, knowing as little of Audley as the Romans knew of its minerals, unwittingly gave it abiding fame in those immortal pages where the age of chivalry closes in a blazing sunset. In the church is a twofold link with his story of the Black Prince and his bravest knight at Poitiers.

Only the 14th-century tower remains of the church of those days, with part of the wall of a medieval chapel, a 16th-century aisle, and a Jacobean font. The rest of the fabric is modern, including the fine east window, which has on either side statues of Peter and Paul. In the chancel floor are tiles in imitation of the old ones at Tintern Abbey.

The chief treasures of the church are in brass and marble. A tombstone on the chancel floor has the figure of a vicar in cap, ruff, and surplice; he is Edward Vernon, founder of the grammar school in 1612. A portrait brass shows us Richard Abnett, his successor.

In a niche below a window is the quaint plaster figure of an armoured knight, only 15 inches high, a midget hero who may have drawn a bright sword for Queen Elizabeth.

But it is an older brass and an older tomb that are the romance and glory of this place. The brass, with a Norman inscription, has the armoured figure of Sir Thomas Audley, son of the towering hero of Poitiers, the baron who vowed that no man should eclipse him in valour, and was given the post of honour in front of our army on the day of the battle. Froissart tells us that when the day was won the baron was carried, gravely wounded, to the tent of the Black Prince, who stopped and embraced him, saying, "Sir James, I and

27

all the rest of us deem you the bravest knight in this battle, and to increase your renown I retain you for ever as my knight."

Here, it is said, sleeps one of the men who carried him from the field to his tent, Richard Delves, lying on an alabaster tomb in the chancel wall, his arms missing but his armour intact, a lion still at his feet. He was one of the four squires summoned to his tent by the heroic baron, who then and there divided among them the pension given to him by the Black Prince.

The Rise of a Cottage Boy

BARTON-UNDER-NEEDWOOD. Here is a peep of George Eliot's Loamshire, ever young in natural beauty, old in story and possessions.

It lies in the Trent Valley, a picture of charm with farms flourishing about it and looking up to a fine Tudor church whose history is like an act from a miracle play.

One of the rare examples of a church begun and completed in one lifetime, it was the gift of John Taylor, the most illustrious native of the village, one of triplets born to poor parents here and rising to wealth and eminence which enabled him to bestow the church as his blessing on the place which gave him birth.

Much today is as he knew it when he left his modest home here to help Henry the Seventh and Henry the Eighth to govern England, and to deal as an equal with the haughtiest potentates in Europe. Here is still the curious three-sided apse he gave the chancel, and in it is a window with some of the glass he provided, showing a Crucifixion with crudely-shaped Apostles, splendid with rich blues, greens, reds, and purples.

The arch in the chancel wall was probably designed to receive his bones. His initials are with the four shields over the nave arcades, and his coat-of-arms has three infant heads, his own and those of the two little brothers who came with him into the world to startle his impoverished father and mother.

On the site of Barton's church stood the cottage where John Taylor was born. For a quarter of a century Henry the Eighth found him a trusty servant, making him spokesman at meetings of foreign envoys, himself delivering speeches Taylor had written, and taking him with him to the Field of the Cloth of Gold. He was at

Henry's side when he met the sovereigns of France and Spain. Between his embassies Taylor had an important part in State affairs. A practised lawyer, equally at home in civil and ecclesiastical law, he was made Master of the Rolls, and was succeeded in that office by the famous and infamous Thomas Cromwell.

Thomas Becket Comes Home Angry

BASWICH. Chiefly known to the world, perhaps, as a place which helps to fill our salt-cellars, it is linked with moving and tragic events in our history.

Bordering the little River Sow is a farm on which we see an ancient stone wall, two Norman doorways, parts of windows, and remains of monastic buildings, the last relics of the 12th-century priory founded by Richard Peche.

Peche had an all unwilling share in the events leading to the murder of Becket. In the absence of the fugitive Primate he countenanced by his presence the coronation of the eldest son of Henry the Second, and, as coronations were the prerogative of the Archbishop of Canterbury, Becket came home indignant, excommunicated Peche and all the prelates concerned, and so virtually signed his own death warrant.

In the year after the murder Peche went to Canterbury to woo the priests to renew the services in the deserted cathedral, and as a personal atonement he built his priory here and dedicated it to the man he had offended. To this day the farm is called St Thomas's. When he came to die Peche directed that he should be buried in the priory, and somewhere here he lies.

Another notable figure who here sought shelter for his bones was Robert Ferrers, Earl of Derby, married at Westminster as a boy of nine to a seven-year-old niece of Henry the Third. He grew up to challenge his royal uncle by standing with Simon de Montfort for public liberty, and sat in our first Parliament, but he was outlawed and dispossessed of his estates. Broken and impoverished, Derby turned his weary eyes to the priory, and here he mingled his ashes with those of its founders.

In the church on the hill above the little Penk, standing in a churchyard beautified by 16 fine beeches, two things have survived which the unfortunate earl may have seen: the tower and the chancel arch of the 18th-century church were possibly a century old a his death.

The most remarkable feature of the church today is a pair o huge double-decker pews raised on pillars in the chancel, one for the squire with a fireplace in it, the other for his servants without one Here the squire sat during winter services cosily making the best o both worlds, while his domestics shivered in dutiful obedience To make a staircase from his pew to that of his servants the squire cut through the 16th-century tomb of John Fowler and his wife There is an old pulpit which has a reading desk, and a quaint gallery

A Poet of the Great War

BEDNALL. The little church, made new last century, has one striking feature, a fine west window with 25 figures. Among them are saints and Apostles, Aaron, Moses, Abraham, and Isaiah is company with Solomon, the two Augustines, and St Cecilia.

The vicarage was the home of the young Staffordshire poet Philip Alsop, whose father and grandfather ministered here from 1867 to 1928. Both were writers of verse, and Philip's father lived to see moving poetry born of the fine spirit of his son. When the war called, young Alsop, fresh from Oxford, joined the army and it was while sitting in the trenches before an attack on the Somme that he wrote these brave lines:

> If I go home
> With my life's work done,
> Since His mercy's great
> May I have no fears,
> And my friends no tears.
> May I find the gate
> Through the golden sun
> When I go home.

Happily the poet was spared and came home to England. James Richard Alsop, his grandfather, who died vicar here in 1880, was something of a character, claiming descent from a Norman family of Alsop-en-le-Dale in Derbyshire, and we have a picture of him conning over the sermons he had preached, finding them very good and publishing the best, and then sitting down to write little poems still remembered, full of kindly feeling, and likening simple well-doing to the unconscious beneficence of flowers, which, without senses themselves, "delight the sense of others." Surprised he would be to know that there are scientists today as well as poets who think that flowers have senses.

The Oak Arcades

BETLEY. Once a market town to which buyers came across the border, it is now a village which markets elsewhere.

Green grow the rushes round its pretty mere, in whose water we may stand with one foot in Staffordshire and one in Cheshire.

Betley Court is a big modern house snug behind its high wall. Old Hall, a charming gabled and timbered 17th-century building on a hillock, with great elms and sycamores to grace it, was long the home of the Egertons.

To them the village owes much of its 17th-century clerestoried church, with an 18th-century tower. In it kneels the alabaster figure of Ralph Egerton in the ruff and long cloak of Shakespeare's time, with his wife in a ruff and a tight-waisted dress, her daughter behind her. It was the next Ralph Egerton who rebuilt the chancel soon after the death of Queen Elizabeth.

A beautiful peace memorial window has scenes of a church interior with the congregation at prayer; the taking of the Sacrament before battle by a wayside cross, with a wrecked cathedral in the distance; and a realistic Red Cross hospital with surgeon, nurses, an orderly, and a wounded soldier. In the tracery above are badges of the regiments of the Betley men.

The most remarkable feature of the church is the use to which its timber has been put. There are few churches like it in this respect. Not only is the interior of the clerestory, like the fine roof, of oak, but also the beautiful pointed arches of the nave arcades, while eight splendid oaks, their trunks hewn into octagonal pillars, carry the whole, an impressive and charming picture.

The Wonderland Made From a Swamp

BIDDULPH. It has one great house fallen into ruin and another in a scientific fairyland made from a swamp. It has an ancient tomb with legends of the centuries gathered about it. It has memories of crusaders and the mystery of the moor, the stark Biddulph Moor rising 1100 feet and giving birth to one of our longest rivers, the Trent.

Beginning its 170-mile journey here in the weird silence of the waste, the Trent winds grandly down to green and pleasant lands, on by towns and hamlets and half a hundred bridges, and we are reminded that when hot-blooded men were riding from Staffordshire five centuries ago, some to fight for Hotspur and some for Henry the Fourth, the fiery Percy and Edmund Mortimer, dividing the kingdom before they had won it, decided to straighten the river hereabouts. It is Shakespeare who tells us. "See," cried Mortimer, whose share was affected by its course :

> See how this river comes me cranking in,
> And cuts me from the best of all my land
> A huge half-moon, a monstrous cantle out.
> I'll have the current in this place dammed up,
> And here the smug and silver Trent shall run
> In a new channel, fair and evenly.

On the edge of the moor is an ancient burial-place, an impressive monument of unhewn monoliths which the people call the Bride-Stones, carrying on the legend that a Viking, having married a Saxon maid in the village, was slain with her soon after and buried here.

We may believe that Crusaders who had fought the good fight lived to return to their native Biddulph, for at the church are coffin-lids engraved with crosses, swords, and battle-axes. They form seats around the walls, looking on the churchyard with an octagonal cross which must have been set up not long after the last Crusader sheathed his sword.

The oldest possession of the church is the Norman font. Centuries have passed since the grey sandstone altar-rails were carved, and in old Flemish glass one of the windows has the Wise Men, Gabriel bringing the good news to the Madonna, with Our Lord, Abraham, and Isaac. A beautiful 15th-century monument to William and Mary Heath has figures of Christ and angels.

What we have called a scientific fairyland is here called the Grange, a hospital for cripple children run by the Lancashire County Council. It occupies the magnificent grounds transformed from a swampy moorland last century by the horticulturist James Bateman, who became famous for his lectures, his orchids, and his gardens. Here he laid out a Chinese garden, an Egyptian garden, and a Wellingtonia avenue which attracted many pilgrims in his day and are still

Alton   **The Village**

Alton   **The Beautiful Gardens of Alton Towers**

A Path by the Wall

A Graceful Tudor Doorway

ALTON TOWERS

remarkable, a wonderland of beauty and novelty with pyramids of yews and plantations of pines.

By a fine box avenue and a ravine with a stream running through it stand the ruins which were once the home of the Biddulphs. Built in the reign of Elizabeth from stone quarried on the estate, the house was among the fairest in the county, until the Civil War brought tragedy and ruin. The Biddulphs were Royalists, and there is no sadder tale than that of the misfortunes attending them.

The Brave Man Who Begged for Bread

WHEN the Royal Standard was unfurled at Nottingham the Biddulphs drew the sword for Charles. John Biddulph, owner of the hall, fell at Hopton Heath; his son Francis, a man in the early twenties who was already married and the father of children, committed the defence of the hall to Lord Brereton, and himself joined the Cavaliers fighting in Cheshire.

Lord Brereton deemed Biddulph Hall more defensible than his own home, Brereton Hall in Cheshire, and so brought with him here his wife and little child. The Parliamentary force sent against the hall was commanded by his uncle Sir William Brereton, who, finding it impossible to overcome the staunch garrison without artillery, brought up from Stafford a great gun called Roaring Meg. Constructed in time of peace, the hall was not intended to withstand bombardment, and Brereton the nephew, fearing for the lives of his wife and child, surrendered, and the hall was reduced to a ruin to prevent its again becoming a Royalist stronghold.

With his home destroyed, Francis Biddulph was soon denied the need for a new one, for he was taken prisoner when Chester fell to the Commonwealth, and was confined for two years at Eccleshall Castle. On being released, an outcast from his birthplace, he settled with his wife and children on a farm at Rushton.

His means still admitted of his maintaining a Roman Catholic priest and an Italian governess for the education of his children. The governess, locally famous for the beauty of her voice, and long remembered as Singing Kate, was the first of the Biddulph household to be attacked by the Plague of 1648. Biddulph rode 40 miles through the night in quest of a doctor, and wherever he called he left the deadly disease behind him. Death claimed poor Singing

Kate and some of the children, and terror caused his home to be shunned as a pest-house. Supplies became unprocurable, and the unhappy man had to go like a beggar to Congleton to beg for food.

Ruined and heartbroken, he turned from the county, leaving behind the wreck of the beautiful home in which he was born, and the Rushton farm where disaster in full tide had overwhelmed him. He made his way to London, where later his son John was married, but as to Francis himself the record fails, and we do not know his end.

A Father of the Iron Trade

BILSTON. Bilston comes into Domesday Book, and was a market town for centuries before industry came to blacken this countryside.

One of its sons was John Wilkinson, who has been called the father of the South Staffordshire iron trade. Born in 1728 at Bradley (on the outskirts of the town), he set up the first charcoal furnace for smelting iron ore and made other experiments as well as a fortune. His sister married the immortal Joseph Priestley, the discoverer of oxygen, and after a Birmingham mob had destroyed Priestley's property he was able to give his brother-in-law substantial help. Wilkinson died at Bilston, and they laid him to rest in an iron coffin at his seat near Ulverston.

A bronze tablet on the wall of St Mary's Vicarage tells of another famous son of Bilston, Sir Henry Newbolt, who was born here in 1862. Who does not know his Drake's Drum, which has rung out on a thousand patriotic platforms and in ten thousand schools?

In St Leonard's church is a memorial to a lady who died in 1836 and is said to have been descended from "three children of King Edward the First"; and there is a tablet reminding us of a very dark hour of the town. It was in 1832, when an epidemic of cholera broke out; 742 people died in six weeks. The nation raised £8000 to alleviate the distress, and £2400 of it went to build and endow a school to give free education to 450 orphans.

The Storied House and its Monuments

BLITHFIELD. With a noble old hall, a church with many monuments, and memories of one of our oldest families, it has stirring stories to tell.

Beautifully set in the Blythe valley, the grey stone home of the
Bagots stands among stately cedars, splendid old oaks, and glowing
thickets of rhododendrons. Restored a few years after Waterloo,
it is impressive as the cradle from which sprang a long line of men
linking us with events significant in our history as far back as Crecy.

One of the Bagots fought at Crecy and another at Poitiers. Another
rides through Shakespeare with mischief in his wake and dread
in his mind. A Bagot fought at Agincourt; one helped Henry the
Seventh to his crown at Bosworth Field; another shared the rout of
Charles at Naseby. They have witnessed repeated changes in our
dynasty, and the passing of nearly 30 rulers of England, but ever a
Bagot has succeeded a Bagot, and here they are today, delighting
in this grand old home with its many great chimneys, its pinnacled
doorway, and its host of windows.

Joining the hall is the clerestoried church in which so many of
them lie. At its gate stand a great beech and two yews beneath whose
shade generations of Bagots have passed to worship, to wedding,
and to burial.

In the churchyard is a cross as ancient as the Bagots themselves,
its modern shaft carved with a ship, some birds, and a crowned lion.
Under an arched recess in an outer chancel wall is a tomb on which
lies Alfred de Blithfield who preached here 700 years ago, a century
before the tower was raised. The font looks old enough to have
served in his day.

In the 13th-century chancel is 14th-century glass, some with ivy
and oak pattern, and one light with a border of lions. The sanctuary
window has modern glass showing ten beautiful figures of Christ,
and in a tower window shine 16th-century portraits of the three
wives of Sir Lewis Bagot.

The fine woodwork includes not only 40 medieval benches and a
15th-century screen beautiful with acorns and roses, but one of the
most surprising things we have seen in a church. We have come
across many storied altar-stones, some of them lost, buried, and
converted to alien uses, but here, strangest transformation of all, is
an altar table which has been part of a farm bedstead! It is of oak,
finely inlaid with roses and foliage, and is a handsome addition to
the ancient chancel.

The monuments are naturally the main interest here. In the

35

chancel floor are the Tudor figures of Francis Aston with his wife and son; but it is by the Bagot tombs that we linger.

The earliest is the Tudor tomb showing the finely preserved figure of Sir Lewis in a tunic, with armour on his legs and the full figure of two of his wives and the head of the third. On a table tomb lie his son and his son's wife, the son wearing a tabard and the wife belted gown. A beautiful sculpture of 1596 is that of Sir Richard lying in armour with his helmet above him, his wife in a tight-waisted robe beside him.

Nearly 20 generations of Bagots have been lords of this village and the record of the family is truly a little volume of English history.

A Family in Domesday Book

EARLY in the 14th century, when feudalism was shaking the throne of Edward the Second who had knighted him, Ralph Bagot crossed the two miles separating his home from that of the heiress of Blithfield, married her, and established here a family which has since lived at the hall without a break.

Like their famous oaks, they were tough and enduring, men bred to knightly feats, who figured in the great battles of the Black Prince, of Henry the Fifth, and on the stricken fields where the Stuart cause was lost.

By that time their name was lastingly inscribed in sinister characters on immortal pages of our literature. Sir William Bagot was, with Sir Henry Green and Sir John Bushy (Speaker of the Commons) the malevolent force behind the throne when Richard the Second entered on the course which brought him to his doom. Bagot was especially esteemed at the Court, and it was from his house and in his company that the king rode to the lists at Coventry where Bolingbroke and Norfolk were summoned to meet in mortal combat.

Shakespeare gives us repeated flashes revealing the intimacy of the relations between the sovereign and his subject. After the suspended combat, Richard, seeking to justify Bolingbroke's banishment, describes in his picture of the exile's ride through London how

> ourself and Bagot
> *Observed his courtship to the common people.*

One of the four men to whom Richard left control of the kingdom on sailing to Ireland, Bagot escaped the fate of his associates when Bolingbroke returned denouncing Bushy, Green, and Bagot as

The caterpillars of the Commonwealth
Whom I have sworn to weed and pluck away.

Frantic at the bad news awaiting his arrival from Ireland, Richard breaks off his soliloquies to enquire for Bagot and the others; but Bagot was already a prisoner in the Tower, from which he was released at the end of the year, to lapse into obscurity.

Queen Elizabeth gave the Bagots their baronetcy in 1590, and 190 years later the sixth baronet was created a peer, and the house produced, in the second baron, the man who was to write the family annals. There were now two bishops in successive generations. Lewis, brother of the first baron, a school-fellow of the poet Cowper, was successively bishop of Bristol, Norwich, and St Asaph, filling the three sees in nine years, and holding the last till his death.

A notable Bagot in Empire history was Sir Charles, who, beginning his career at 26 as Under-Secretary for Foreign Affairs with Canning, went to Paris as ambassador after the fall of Napoleon; then to the United States, where he had the distinction of establishing the neutrality of the Great Lakes, so that not a gun has since menaced either side of them. Next he was Ambassador to Russia with a difficult Tsar on the throne, and passed to the Hague, where he helped to create an independent Belgian nation.

He crowned his career in Canada, arriving there in 1841 when conditions were in a perilous state of flux. He won the sympathies of English and French alike, and by tact, good-nature, and patience, brought into being responsible self-government in the Colony. Lord Stanley disapproved the Governor-General's policy, and practically broke Bagot's heart by his censure; but history has vindicated Bagot. His health collapsed under the disappointment, however, and he died in Canada in 1843, a British warship bearing his body back to England.

From William's Conquest

BLORE. Overlooking and sharing the natural loveliness of Dovedale, it has a splendour and beauty of its own to show and a stirring tale to tell.

Blore Hall, a grey stone house now a farm, with medieval windows and traces of its moat about it, was long the home of the Norman Bassets. Flanked by splendid elms and stately sycamores, the churchyard has a fine old yew, above which rises the 14th-century tower of the 15th-century church. In the floor of the nave are the brass portraits of William Basset and his wife in the dress of the 15th century, he wearing a long cloak, she her cloak and veil.

Many Bassets sleep here, and in their chapel is an immense canopied tomb, raised in the 17th century by Elizabeth Basset to her father, whose inscription proudly describes him as a courtier and soldier, "witty, handsome, good, valiant, unparalleled, of pure blood from William's Conquest." William Basset lies in armour, his wife in a long gown, a ruff, and a flowing headdress; with them is the armoured figure of Elizabeth's first husband, Henry Howard, son of the Earl of Suffolk, and two figures of Elizabeth herself in Van Dyck costume, one in mourning for her mother, and again kneeling in grief for the death of her husband.

Two years later she married William Cavendish, Duke of Newcastle, and passed to the glories of Welbeck, where she shared in two receptions of James the First marked by such splendour as was said to have had hardly a parallel in England. For these visits Ben Jonson wrote two masques, Love's Welcome at Welbeck and Love's Welcome at Bolsover.

The 16th-century chancel screen, with traces of its original colour, has fine iron gates, and is adorned with roses; the screen before the Basset chapel is splendid with grapes and roses. The oak benches and choir-stalls have been here 400 years. In a chancel window is 15th-century glass of Christ wearing the Crown of Thorns, and of St Anne teaching the Madonna.

BLORE. The county's second place with this name, it is a hamlet near the Shropshire border. Here in what is known as Buckingham's Field, began the adventure which gives the district its little niche in historical romance. It was here, when fleeing from the Battle of Worcester, that George Villiers, second of the evil Dukes of Buckingham, fell from his horse and broke an arm. Taken to Armsdale, he was sheltered and nursed by a kindly woman in a cottage which still stands. Before he had recovered Commonwealth soldiers arrived seeking him, but the ready-witted woman saved the duke by hiding him in the oven where her bread was supposed to be baking.

The Young Poet of Great Promise

BLOXWICH. A busy mining and manufacturing centre not far from Walsall, it has a patch of brilliant green round its peace memorial cross, and nature is still beautiful in its God's Acre close by. It is proud to have the first King George Playing Field in the county (the fourth in the country), 40 acres of recreation ground for Walsall, approached through memorial gates bearing the king's heraldic panels.

Two things there are to see in Bloxwich churchyard, one the base of a medieval cross and the other the tombstone of a man who has been called a village Hampden. He was Samuel Wilks, who died in 1764, a locksmith and overseer who stood out bravely and successfully against an unfair distribution of the local taxes. Inside the church is the roll of honour, a book beautifully decorated and written with the names of 316 men who fell in the Great War.

One of these heroes was Harold Parry, a soldier poet whose life was cut off at 21 in Flanders. He said of a man who fell that "England has lost another who would have been an even greater credit to her in life than in this most glorious death," and we may say it of him too.

This young lieutenant from Bloxwich, who fell in Flanders six months before his 21st birthday, left writings and memories which tell us that he might have been a fine poet and certainly was a fine man. The poets he loved were Swinburne, Wordsworth, Keats, and Francis Thompson, and their influence on what he wrote is evident. Again and again in his letters comes something of his sensitiveness to natural beauty. We see it in this:

> *The simplest things in life are loveliest:*
> *The smile of little children whose sweet eyes*
> *Have not yet ceased from wistful wondering,*
> *And innocent, as though the melodies*
> *Of Life were all they knew, and cleanly things*
> *Were all they saw and all they cared to see.*
> *Would, would to God that I were such as these,*
> *Taintless and clean as once I used to be.*
> *This other thing is lovely too: a lonely flower*
> *Set in the fields; a single tinted head*
> *Above the growing grass; an opened bud,*
> *A daisy white; wide petals touched with red.*

In this little poem on the North Wind we have an insight into the faith that saw beyond the misery of war:

> *When Winter drags her chariot wheel*
> *Through the deep snow,*
> *And skies are blue as hard cold steel,*
> *And North Winds blow,*
> *Keep Faith—some day the world will mend*
> *Your broken mind;*
> *Keep Faith—for maybe grief will end*
> *With the North Wind.*

He was intensely loyal to Queen Mary's Grammar School at Walsall, where he was School Captain, Cricket Captain, Football Captain, and Cadet Officer. He won the Open History Scholarship at Oxford, but by the end of his first term at Exeter College he felt he must join up. He felt that nothing worth while could be done till the war was over, and he left for France. At the front or behind the lines he could not overcome his horror of it all:

How long will it be (he wrote) *before I can dream the old splendid dreams, build up the shattered castle of hope, and set my face resolutely towards the achievement of the beautiful and good things I desire to do? Let it be soon, I pray.*

He cheered his men when he felt far from cheerful himself; he carried their rifles when he was dead tired.

He hoped to be a teacher; he wanted to teach children love and beauty, but he wrote home that he feared he must go out into the unknown with all his hopes unrealised. He was killed by a shell in 1917, and among his belongings they found poems written on the backs of envelopes and scraps of paper, with some on neatly-written pages, all now in a book, with a niche of their own in Staffordshire's contribution to our literature.

The Parson Botanist

BLYMHILL. Agriculture is still its parent industry, and the countryside has much of the charm that must have marked it when its famous botanist rector was exploring it last century.

A pretty road bordered by holly brings us to the church, which has been partly refashioned since the botanist parson knew it, but here is the fine tower which has been an impressive landmark for 500 years. In the churchyard is a grand yew which can be little younger, and the dial on a stone pillar has recorded centuries of sunshine.

In an outer wall is a recessed tomb, believed to be that of the builder of the chancel, which comes unspoiled from the 14th century. The oldest part of the interior is the 13th-century arcade, with fine arches on octagonal pillars.

The chancel screen, a charming effort of modern craftsmanship, is crowned by a Crucifixion, beneath which are birds eating fruit. The ten modern choir-stalls have carved miserere seats.

The botanist parson was Samuel Dickenson, of a family long conspicuous here. When his last sermon was preached in 1823 he had been 46 years rector, happy years for himself and the village, for he botanised with such success that his fame and skill are still a subject of local pride. Very pleasant were these fields and hedgerows to him.

The Good Lawyer

BOBBINGTON. A small place on the Shropshire border, its oldest living inhabitant is the great yew behind the church. About 21 feet round, he is showing his age, but is able to do without the crutches that support his younger brother not far away.

A Norman sculptured figure greets us in the porch, and we pass inside the church to a Norman arcade. There is a 13th-century font, and a crooked old chest hewn out of solid oak with two compartments and lids, covered with bands of wrought iron.

The tablet to Edward Corbett tells how he practised as a lawyer for 30 years in the historic court of Westminster Hall, more than a century before English justice moved to the present Law Courts in 1882. We read these good words of him:

> *Many he assisted in the Law,*
> *More he preserved from it.*

Browne

BRADLEY. High farming has kept its hillside acres fertile through the centuries, and high fortune has kept safe for it one of the noblest of Staffordshire's treasures.

The church, its gate shaded by a magnificent chestnut, has gifts of beauty from the ages. The tower is 500 years old; the arcades in the nave and chancel rose splendid in the 13th century. The font is Norman, with a beautifully moulded bowl.

A 17th-century alabaster wall tomb has the painted kneeling

figures of Browne of Shredecote, a bearded man in a long cloak, and his wife in a tight-waisted dress, with a ruff and flowing head-dress. Those who saw him to his last rest found time to write a rhyming inscription for his tomb, but not to mention his Christian name; he is merely "oraculous Browne."

There is the head of a queen among the fragments of ancient glass in the nave; and the chancel screen, a fine example of carving, beautiful with grapes and roses, is worthy of the company it keeps. We noticed that Walter Collins was rector here for 54 years of the 18th century.

Anne Snape's Love-Knot

BRADLEY-IN-THE-MOORS. Nearly 200 years ago it remade its little church, when the four vigorous yews in the church-yard, which were growing in Cromwell's England, were just getting into their stride for their journey down the centuries. There is a sundial on the tower, but only one thing here is older than the yews, a coffin lid which was already ancient before the old church came down and the yews were planted.

At first sight the tombstone to Anne Snape seems to be the patriarch of the churchyard, for the date 1307 accompanies the inscription:

> Thus Death between us two has got
> And so hath broke a true love-knot.

But there is a slip even in love, for the mason was 500 years out in his figures. His 3 should be an 8, and the year 1807.

BRAMSHALL. Here is a gracious lady of the past, but the sur-roundings with which she was familiar are gone, and a 19th-century church rises in the place of the old shrine she knew. We found in the churchyard a glory of rhododendrons, but all that remains of Bramshall's past are fragments of old glass with the heads and shoulders of a boy and girl, and the charming figure of Alice Tame in a white flowered dress and ruff. She was Lady Verney.

BRANSTON. Its red cottages look into Derbyshire, but here, among the trees crowning a hill, is more of Burton Abbey property than Burton itself can show. The town has but a vestige of its wonderful old building, but Branston has the ancient summer home of the monks who made the abbey famous.

It is Sinai Park, a moated and timbered 15th-century house, now a farm, forming three sides of a square, and still very striking in its splendid situation. The modern church has a charming stone reredos with three delicate niches in which is the Good Shepherd, with vines, flowers, and ears of wheat.

Dr Johnson Turned Away

BREWOOD. It has material for a dozen Scott novels, for it has been the setting of centuries of romantic history. It has in its story the thrill of Saxon forest life, the coming of the Normans, and the perfect love-story leading to the founding of the famous Giffard family, with figures shining in war and scholarship, suffering because they could not abandon their old religion, and suddenly producing one of the most astonishing villains in our annals.

We have visions of King John in purring pleasantry and in typical rascality; and we see our first Edward terrible in wrath. We move on through the ages and find a man who was prepared to die for Charles the Second; and we see Dr Johnson turning poor and sorrowful from the school that feared his scarred face.

Brewood was a royal forest until King John declared it disafforested and all its people free of the penalties attending the frightful forest laws. Then, repenting of his unwonted generosity, he made the town pay for the privilege he had already granted, a fact which was afterwards to count in saving the heir of the Giffards.

Where the gabled house called Blackladies now stands with its tall chimneys was a Norman convent of Black Nuns. Here in 1276 a stag started by Edward the First in Cannock Chase was shot by John Giffard's arrow, and died in the fishpond. Charged before the Forest Court, Giffard was able to plead that the area had twice been disafforested by John, and so escaped the terrible punishment. He was fined, and the nuns, who had received some of the venison, were pardoned because they were poor, and "for the good of the king's soul."

Chillington Castle, where a young Norman Giffard wooed and won the heiress in the 12th century, stands in a wooded park graced by magnificent avenues nearly two miles long. For 800 years the family has been here and in the park is a rough old wooden cross about four feet high marking the site of a famous life-saving feat of archery which figures in its story.

The house, made new by Sir John Soane, has in the hall a 16th century fireplace by which Queen Elizabeth may have sat.

Among other charming houses, some Queen Anne and many of them timbered, Brewood Hall was built in Tudor days as the home of the Fowkes.

The grammar school founded by Edward the Sixth is still here with its little bell turret, interesting because it was here that in 1736, the year of his marriage to his adored Tetty, Samuel Johnson came, a gaunt, towering figure with scarred features, his head and limbs agitated by uncontrollable movements. He sought the humble post of usher, but the master denied him, fearing lest he should become the butt of the school's derision.

A fine medieval tower and spire beckon us to the church, mainly 700 years old. Somewhere in its churchyard lies Colonel William Carlos, who shared the perils of Charles the Second after Worcester and, during the night of hiding in the Boscobel Oak, supported the head of the fugitive king as he slept. Here also is the tomb of the famous teacher Jeremiah Smith, who returned to the village in which he learned his A B C, after years as headmaster of Manchester Grammar School.

The church, which is a gallery of monuments, has its 13th-century chancel, a 14th-century aisle, a nave along which 15 generations of Giffards have walked, and a little 16th-century font. The modern reredos, with beautifully carved canopies, has a central picture of the Last Supper, and at the sides carved figures of John Baptist and nine saints and archangels. A curious feature of the clerestoried south aisle (19th century) is the group of five gabled windows, an effect gained by continuing the woodwork down from above.

The oldest of the monuments is the alabaster tablet engraved with the figures of a 16th-century family, Richard Lane, his wife, and their 11 children. In the same aisle is the storied brass tablet to Joan Leveson, who died in 1572, after having married three husbands. By an extraordinary mischance the brass wandered from the church and was built into the house of the stationmaster at Four Ashes three miles away. In the same aisle are the beautifully coloured kneeling figures of the families of Edward Moreton, who died under Charles Stuart, and Matthew Moreton, who saw the Restoration.

But the most important monuments are the painted alabaster

44

tombs of the Giffards. First is the hero of the great archery feat at the place where the old cross stands—Sir John Giffard, who lies with black hair and pointed beard in armour such as he wore at the Field of the Cloth of Gold, when Henry the Eighth rewarded him with a gift of Blackladies. With Sir John lie his two wives in close-fitting hats, necklaces, and long tight-waisted dresses. Round the tomb are ranged their 18 children, 13 of them as babies. Sir John died at 90, only four years before his son Thomas, who is here in armour like his father's, with black hair and pointed beard and with two wives, but with only 17 children.

Next there is another John, who, dying in 1613 after long imprisonment as a Roman Catholic, is shown short and stout, with black hair and beard, in fine armour inlaid with steel. By him is his wife, in the usual tight-waisted dress with necklace and ruff. Their 14 children are round the tomb, so that on these three monuments there are 49 young Giffards. Among John's children is Gilbert Giffard, the Iago of the family, who sold Jesuit secrets to Protestant statesmen and Protestant secrets to Jesuits.

On the fourth tomb are Walter Giffard and his wife; he was the son of John, stout and tall, with black hair and a pointed beard, and wearing armour.

A Stirring Chronicle of Adventure

THE GIFFARDS of Chillington Castle were already Counts of Longueville before three of them came to England with the Conqueror and were rewarded with English lands and titles.

In the 12th century Peter Giffard fought valiantly under Strongbow in Ireland. Rewarded with grants of land, he returned to England, and became possessor of Chillington and other Staffordshire properties. From that day to our own the Giffard line has not failed here. We can trace them down the centuries at peace with their tenants and neighbours, at war with the king's enemies, serving in Parliament, sheriffs of the county; warlike Normans thoroughly anglicised, always lovers of the chase in the adjoining forest, and often of learning.

It was not until the time of Sir John Giffard, who lies resplendent in the chancel of the church, that the family resumed a foremost position in national affairs. Warrior and member of Parliament, standard-bearer to Henry the Eighth, he received the gift of the Black Nuns convent here.

The great thing in Sir John's life is the adventure with the leopard commemorated by the old cross in the park. In common with other lords he received gifts of wild animals brought back from Africa and the East, and in 1513 had captive a splendid leopard, which one morning escaped from its cage and bounded across the park.

Sir John set out in pursuit, armed with his cross-bow and accompanied by his son. He followed hot-foot in the wake of the animal, which had by this time approached a woman with a baby in her arms. Fitting an arrow, he was about to shoot when his son checked him, saying to him in French, "Take breath, pull strong." The elder man did both, and as the leopard made its leap his arrow pierced it. The old cross is said to mark the scene of the adventure. News of the exploit became noised abroad, and Henry granted Sir John a coat-of-arms showing the leopard's head, the bearded archer, his cross-bow and arrows, and, as a motto, the warning words uttered by the son. They are borne by the family to this day.

The Giffards were Roman Catholics who, although they profited by the Dissolution, did not conform to the reformed religion, and, themselves guiltless, suffered in common with other Roman Catholics in the days when members of their church were constantly planning assassination and invasion.

One who did not so suffer was Gilbert Giffard, figured as a child on a tomb in the church. His father, John Giffard, had endured imprisonment for his faith, but Gilbert, born about 1561, and educated in safety by Jesuits abroad, consciously vowed himself to villainy. "Evil, be thou my good!" he might have said. Admitted to the most secret councils of the Jesuits, he sold his information to Elizabeth's ministers, and calmly betrayed his Protestant paymasters to Spain.

Gilbert Giffard insinuated himself into the Babington Plot; it was he who devised the scheme of the beer barrels with false bottoms which contained letters sent to Mary at Chartley, and came back empty with her replies concealed in the same way. A more complete villain has rarely been produced in real life. When all was over he wandered away to France unharmed, and his death there in 1590 was not connected with his treachery.

He was the one moral and intellectual freak of the family. The Giffards never wavered in their loyalty to the Stuarts. Peter Giffard was 61 when Charles raised his standard at Nottingham, but he garrisoned the castle here, and himself took the field with all his sons and nephews old enough to fight.

The Giffards owned Boscobel, and the Penderels were in their service; it was the Giffards who made possible the escape of Charles the Second after Worcester.

The King in the Oak Tree

THE story of William Carlos, who lies in Brewood churchyard, is told to every boy and girl at school; it is the story of the oak tree in which Charles the Second hid.

Carlos was a member of a family which seems originally to have spelled its name Careless. He was a colonel in the Royalist army, and, on the advance of Charles the Second from Scotland into England in 1651, he fought on his side at the battle of Worcester.

When the field was lost, Carlos fled to Boscobel woods. Here stood the memorable oak, grown thick and bushy, and in it Carlos hid. Two days and nights passed, and then there came stealing through the woods a tall man dressed as a peasant. It was Charles, fleeing from Whiteladies, with a troop of horse hot on his track.

Carlos invited him into his oak, and they hid together while pursuers beat the woods about them. So they remained for more than 24 hours, during which time Carlos made hazardous forays in search of food. A price of £1000 was set on the King's head, but his companion was one of the many faithful to him during his terrifying six weeks of hiding.

At length the fugitives parted, for Carlos was a known man, and his presence would have endangered the King. Five days after the battle he succeeded in escaping to France, where, after the arrival of Charles, he shared the pangs and privations of the exile until the Restoration. On returning to England he was rewarded with a coat-of-arms, a third share of a tax on all the hay and straw brought into London and Westminster, and the office of inspector of livery stables.

BRIERLEY HILL. On a hill indeed, it is a busy industrial town, with big iron and glass works. Crowning all is the church, among its stained windows being one of the Crucifixion given by

John Corbett, the Salt King of Droitwich. One of its 18th-centur
vicars was Thomas Moss, the poet who wrote the lines beginning

> Pity the sorrows of a poor old man,
> Whose trembling limbs have borne him to your door.

There are wide views from the tower; Shropshire hills and th
Malverns can be seen, as well as a dozen other churches and
melancholy multitude of factory chimneys.

Izaak Walton and the King's Jewel

BROUGHTON. With a story of a thrilling adventure of Izaa
Walton, a church containing fine old glass, and a hall ric
with Tudor beauty, it has a quiet fascination which fixes it in th
traveller's memory.

The church, its porch in the shadow of three veteran yews, wa
built by Thomas Broughton, who lived at the hall when Charle
Stuart was still at peace with his people. His crest is in the church

The font is curiously placed, built into a niche in a wall under th
tower. The first parson to use it, William Ingram, dying when th
church was new, has a quaintly worded brass inscription with thes
lines:

> Here lies the first whom Death translated
> After this church was consecrated.
> True fight he fought, true race he ran,
> He was, he is, a blessed man.

Splendid glass of the 15th and 16th centuries fills two windows
One in the sanctuary shows rich figures of David and three saints
with shields of the Delves and Broughtons; another has two saint
and the kneeling figures of Ellen Delves and her husband Sir John
who fought and fell in 1471 at Tewkesbury, one of the last battle
of the Wars of the Roses. A third window has old heraldic glass
The church still has the high oak pews of Stuart days.

The home of the Broughtons, facing the church, is a fine gable
and timbered Elizabethan house with a central balustrade. Among
its fine carving are Tudor roses and grotesques as corbels, and som
of the windows have 17th-century Flemish glass with Bible scenes
It was from this charming house that Thomas Broughton watche
his church rise, and saw that it was good.

Relics of Blore Forest survive in Burnt Wood and Bishop's Wood

The Peace Memorial Garden

St Paul's Church and the Town Hall

BURTON-ON-TRENT

Ilam   Norman Font **Gnosall**   Norman Wall

Brewood   Moreton Family **Blore**   William Basset

whose 5000 acres make a glorious picture. We see the woods from a storied farm which was the Blore Pipe House of Izaak Walton's perilous adventure.

After the Battle of Worcester there came for hiding at the house a Royalist refugee, Colonel Blagg, who had been entrusted by Charles the Second with one of the Crown Jewels. On stealthily quitting the house he left the jewel with his host, George Barlow, and he himself was captured soon afterwards and imprisoned in the Tower.

Izaak Walton, who was then 58 and had been living for a generation in London, never forgot that he was a Stafford man, and at this time he was on one of his periodical visits to his old home. Trusted in an unobtrusive way by the Royalist party, he came out from Stafford to Blore Pipe House while the incriminating jewel was in his friend Barlow's possession. Izaak took on himself the risk of carrying the dangerous gem away with him. To have been detected would have meant the Tower for him, but he passed on his way unsuspected. Blagg escaped from the Tower, and Izaak contrived to meet him and restore the jewel, enabling him at last to discharge his trust by carrying it to Charles in France.

Izaak Walton's part in this dangerous transaction was the one astonishing hazard in his long tranquil life, and the memory of it adds a zest and piquancy to the reading of his placid pages.

The Failure That Led to Success

BURNTWOOD. It has illustrious names in its story, names such as Darwin, Johnson, and Peel. It may be that Literature owes it thanks for an ingratitude, for it permitted one of the greatest of Englishmen to languish in neglect where he might have prospered in inglorious obscurity; it let him fail and wander in poverty to build for himself a temple of immortal fame.

The church was built soon after Waterloo, on ground given by the father of Sir Robert Peel. Two miles away, behind a belt of lofty trees, stands Maple Hayes, a fine house with the famous Botanic Garden laid out by Erasmus Darwin, and celebrated by him in verses famous for their prediction of steam locomotion and mechanical flight.

It is a more enduring place in literature that Burntwood owes to its neighbour Edial, where still stands the 18th-century hall regarding which the Gentleman's Magazine published the famous advertisement in 1736:

> At Edial, near Lichfield, in Staffordshire,
> young gentlemen are boarded and taught the
> Latin and Greek Languages by Samuel Johnson.

Here he came, a bridegroom of 27, with Tetty as his bride, a widow of 47. He was "lean and lank, so that his immense structure of bones was hideously striking to the eye," deeply scarred, his hair "straight and stiff and separated behind," and given to convulsive starts and gesticulations that excited surprise and ridicule; she was stout, florid, and painted, flaring and fantastic in dress, and affected in speech and in behaviour.

Only three pupils answered the advertisement, David Garrick, his brother George, and a boy named Offley, but for 18 months Johnson kept the school going for them, little dreaming that his Davy would one day tell the story of his "tumultuous and awkward fondness" for the wonderful Tetty, and mimic the gait and gestures of the weird genius who was to make him a great master of elocution and enable him to restore Shakespeare unmutilated to the stage.

Convinced that schoolmastering was his great chance, Johnson formulated a system of teaching the classics which he thought must eclipse all its predecessors, yet he found time to write here nearly the whole of his tragedy Irene. It was with this as his sole literary asset that in March 1737 he closed the door of the house behind him, and, with Garrick for his companion, set out for London, "when I came with twopence-halfpenny in my pocket, and thou, Davy, with three-halfpence in thine," as he used fondly to recall.

Who shall say that if Staffordshire had sent her sons here to be educated by him Dr Johnson might not have missed his immortality? She neglected him and drove him to the pitiless capital to live on eightpence a day when he had it and to starve for 48 hours at a time when he had not, but in spite of all to write and talk his way to fame.

The Mother of the Potteries

BURSLEM. Standing by the Trent, and served by a canal, it is a little kingdom of industry surrounded by coal, ironstone, and the precious clay and marls which for more than two centuries it has been converting into crockery.

The Mother of the Potteries, it is the Bursley of Arnold Bennett's Five Towns, and with Tunstall, Hanley, and Longton forms part of the federated borough of Stoke-on-Trent; but as the birthplace of Josiah Wedgwood it will always remain to the world an individual town, made famous by his labours.

No town and no industry has ever owed more to one man than Burslem and pottery owe to Wedgwood. When he was born in 1730 Burslem was a poverty-stricken little place, making the crudest earthenware. Dragging a maimed limb after him for most of his life, he effected such a revolution that Burslem wares attained almost world-wide celebrity.

The town grew rapidly, without beauty or symmetry, and it bears the ill-favoured impress of its infancy; but behind the grim walls of these works, like pearls in the rough shell of the oyster, are realms of enchantment where mounds of clay and marl are blended, shaped and moulded, baked and fired, painted and glazed, and given abiding beauty. In these works we forget the dull streets of Burslem and lose ourselves in wonder.

Fittingly the town's noblest building is the Wedgwood Institute, the first stone of which was laid by Mr Gladstone. On the front are 12 stone panels showing various processes in the making of pottery; above are the figures of the months, with mosaics and signs of the Zodiac, each month in its own arch. Over the porch, with one of his vases in his hand, stands the Father of English Pottery, looking serenely down on the Mother of the Potteries. In the porch are portraits in relief of Flaxman, whose genius developed in making exquisite designs for Wedgwood's famous ware; and of Bentley and Priestley, names highly honoured in Staffordshire. The Institute has a library, picture-gallery, and a museum with a magnificent collection of pottery.

The parish church is not a comely building, but it has its 15th-century tower, and in the chancel are two fine examples of Wedgwood, a beautiful figure of Christ in black, and a Wedgwood plate reproducing the Descent from the Cross by Rubens. It is here in memory of Enoch Wood, who made both the plate and the statue.

St Paul's Church, with a tower 115 feet high, was built last century, and has an oak pulpit with seven canopied figures of Apostles, and an east window with 12 scenes from Bible story.

St Joseph's Church has a romantic story of the glass in its 22 windows. Among the congregation were past and present students at the Art School, whose director suggested that they should design and make the lights. Twelve gifted volunteers gave their leisure to the task, designed and cut the glass, assembled and leaded it, and completed a work of beauty which, apart from saving the young church thousands of pounds, is in the opinion of some experts equal to medieval craftsmanship.

The undertaking, highly creditable to all concerned, was quite in the spirit of Wedgwood, who held that art and craftsmanship form a natural partnership. One of the men who grew up under his influence was Noah Heath, Burslem's potter poet.

The Evangelist of the Fields

IT was here in those days that another potter gave up the ambition of being a champion dancer and became the founder of Primitive Methodism. He was William Clowes, one of the most successful evangelists in religious history. Born at Burslem in 1780, he was a potter by trade. And as a dancer he was widely known before his conversion at the age of 25. He joined the Wesleyan Methodists, became a local preacher, and took part in open-air evangelist services called Camp Meetings, with Hugh Bourne and others.

The Camp Meeting form of service, usually held in a field, was officially forbidden by the Wesleyan Methodist authorities, but Clowes continued his connection with Bourne and his associates and was expelled. Between 1807 and 1811 the Camp gatherings were so successful that the nucleus of a new denomination was formed at Tunstall, where a chapel had been built. So rapidly the movement spread that both Bourne and Clowes lived to see the Primitive Methodists numbering more than 100,000 members.

Bourne was the organiser of the denomination and Clowes its orator. Clowes was a man of fine presence, with a magnificent voice, and a natural eloquence that kept thousands spellbound. He and his comrades took over the early open-air preaching of the Wesleyan Methodists and carried it on until the Salvation Army annexed it. He continued his work almost to the end of his 71 years, and the last nine years he had a pension of £25.

The Town of a Thousand Years

BURTON-ON-TRENT. For a thousand years it has watched the river flowing by, and for long has played its part in history, with a 7th-century saint to bless it, an 11th-century abbey to shield and foster it, and a 16th-century grammar school to teach it.

It has been destroyed by fire, shaken by earthquake, and swamped by the bursting river; it saw the Barons' War and the Civil War, and it raised a million-pound building for making machine guns in the Great War.

Once a centre of the clothing world, war destroyed that great industry, but for two centuries Burton has been the home of brewing. It is said that even in the 13th century an abbot of Burton was using water from the wells here for brewing, and it is this clear water which has led to the saying that Nature meant Burton to brew. We may prefer the clear water, but we are bound to be impressed by the wonderful growth of this industry.

It was in the 18th century that Burton brew started to become world famous. One firm quickly found customers overseas, Peter the Great and the Empress Catherine of Russia among them, and Burton beer was drunk in Danzig to celebrate the departure of Napoleon. William Bass founded a business, producing 2000 barrels a year at first, which now has 750 acres of works and sends out barrels by the hundred thousand.

Altogether there are nearly 20 breweries, employing 6000 people and producing 2,000,000 barrels a year. Some of them are established in factories like great arsenals, and there are kindred firms dealing in malt, yeast, and food extracts.

The immense establishments of the maltsters, the coopers, the makers of machinery, and all the apparatus of the industry depend on the brewing, and to serve these many firms there is an unparalleled number of level crossings in the public streets, where we feel like a trespasser in a vast dock siding, for trains pop in and out and cross the roads like trams.

Burton's 4000 allotments are connected with the breweries, for they are mainly cultivated by the labourers. But there is more than industrial Burton to see. The town has fine wide thoroughfares with pretty peeps of the river, which is a joyous summer picture.

Opposite the town hall is the bronze statue of Michael Bass whom his old friend Mr Gladstone made Lord Burton. He left the town rarely enriched, in part aided by his father, but mainly by his own gifts.

To him Burton owes its ferry bridge, its town hall, the magnificent St Paul's Church, St Margaret's Church, the drill hall, the clubs, and other social centres. He died at 72, and his fellow townsmen raised this monument in front of the handsome town hall.

One of the proudest of the town's modern possessions is the three-storeyed museum and art gallery, the repository of an interesting collection of British, Roman, and Saxon relics, including urns, shields, bosses, buckles, and brooches, and a wonderful group of birds and animals. The most interesting medieval original in the museum is one of Burton's 15th-century knights, an alabaster figure in chain mail who once slept where the monks chanted mass at the abbey here.

Of the abbey itself, founded before the Norman Conquest and endowed with over 70 manors, we could find only part of a grey wall, with three forlorn pointed arches, a few mouldering stones, and the sadly worn busts of a man and woman. The pathetic remainder rests behind the town's great market, which has six entrances and 1100 square yards of selling space. We could not but recall in imagination a different scene of 700 years ago, when Nicholas of Tusculum was here as papal legate at the abbey, with King John cringing for the return of his crown, securing by his servility the lifting of the Papal Interdict and the support of the Pope in defying Stephen Langton. From the abbey, and the scene between these three, it was but a short journey in time and space to Runnymede and Magna Carta.

The grammar school, founded by a 16th-century abbot and made new last century, is a bold brick building. Lovers of the past lament the loss of the medieval bridge, which made a beautiful picture, as we may see from the model of it preserved at the manor house. The new stone bridge, 470 yards long and carried on 32 arches, is a splendid structure, erected last century in place of the bridge which had served the town from medieval times.

But the original was rich in history. Generations of monks wore its surface smooth. During the Barons' War it rang with the clamour of battle, when Edward of Lancaster held it for three days against the forces of Edward the Second; then, outflanked by a crossing at Walton, he reduced the unhappy town to ashes, and went his way. The bridge survived, and over it in 1586 passed one of the saddest figures history ever saw. Mary Queen of Scots, detected at Chartley in the act of plotting the assassination of Elizabeth, rode across the bridge on her way to her trial and execution at Fotheringhay.

The parish church, St Modwen's, an 18th-century structure on the site of the abbey church, stands on a gentle slope by the Trent, where we picture the monks diligently fishing on Thursday for Friday's dinner. The only probable relic from the ancient church is the 15th-century font. An elaborate 19th-century wall monument to Thomas Salt has three seated women and two children.

St Paul's, like a cathedral in miniature, with a central tower, is a magnificent building rich with beauty. The chancel screen is of delicate ironwork; that of the lady chapel is gilded oak with linenfold panels and charming grapes and roses. The chancel floor is of red and white marble, and its roof, like that of the tower, is beautiful with gold and colour. The fine sanctuary window has the Madonna and Child, John Baptist, St George, David, Moses, and Gideon, with six Saints.

In the vestry is a portrait tablet to a faithful musician, Arthur Plant, who was organist here for 40 years.

All is nobly rich and beautiful in this wonderful church, but we pause long in the 19th-century Holy Trinity, with its tower and spire, for here is lovely ancient glass from the earlier church, with sunshine setting on fire its reds and golds, and bringing back to its greens, purples, and blues the colours its makers created long ago when they lovingly made up these pictures of Peter, Paul, and the Four Evangelists. The window affords a satisfying conclusion to the exciting round of wonders we have seen, for it is the town's supreme Old Master.

Remote as may have been its century, it is still too modern to have been seen by the founder of the first church here, for the earliest Christian settlement at Burton was two centuries before Alfred. St Modwen, the founder, was the daughter of an Irish prince when Ireland was keeping alight the torch of learning in the Dark Age of Europe. After thrilling adventures she established a little convent here 1300 years ago. Many religious houses sprang from the convent, but Modwen passed on to aid her brother in Scotland, and there in 700 she died. Three centuries later her body was brought here and laid to rest, with a Latin inscription meaning:

> *By Ireland life, by Scotland death was given,*
> *A tomb in England, endless joy in Heaven.*

The translation of her remains to the scene of her fruitful labours must have been effected by Wulfric, the Mercian earl who founded the abbey. His great building succeeded hers, which the Danes had destroyed; they were to destroy him too, for he fell in battle with them near Ipswich in 1010. Somewhere here he still sleeps.

Around the great abbey the town grew to become a seat of learning and the birthplace of an important historical work written by the monks, the Burton Chronicle. All this was a long while ago, but it is pleasant to find an industrial town of rapid modern expansion treasuring the story of its past as Burton proudly does.

One of its sons, Isaac Hawkins Browne, literature would remember even if Burton forgot. Son of a rich vicar of Burton as father, he went from Cambridge University to the Bar but did not practise, devoting his time to literature and Parliament. Perhaps nobody outside Staffordshire now reads his serious poems on Design and Beauty and on Immortality, but his witty parodies of the six leading poets of his age, published as A Pipe of Tobacco, greatly admired in their day, were the ancestor of a numerous progeny. He was declared by Dr Johnson to be of all conversationalists the most delightful with whom he was ever in company, and that from the prince of talkers is a very trumpet tribute of fame. Johnson, talking to Boswell and Bennet Langton, paid his friend this further compliment: "We must not estimate a man's powers by his being able to deliver sentiments in public; Isaac Hawkins Browne, one of the first wits of this country, got into Parliament and never opened his mouth."

A thousand speeches of his own could hardly have assured him greater fame than these two judgments of our English Socrates.

The Old Hall

BUSHBURY. The houses of Wolverhampton are creeping out towards it. They had nearly reached the village church, when we called, but fortunately the growth of the town will never affect the historic building in this neighbourhood—Moseley Old Hall. It is a treasure, a vital link in one of the most exciting episodes of English history and it is now in the keeping of the National Trust.

Here, after dusk on the evening of Sunday September 7, 1651, came Charles the Second, his cause lost at Worcester and he himself unable to escape across the Severn into Wales. Across these fields he came with six men to the back of the house, entering by this door still on its hinges. Thomas Whitgreave the squire did not recognise him, with his hair cut short and his face stained with walnut juice.

Thrilling it is to walk about this old house (if we are fortunate enough to do so), to see the panelled bedroom where the king slept, the attic windows where the squire's three sons kept watch for the Roundheads, and the hiding hole where Charles was hidden when the soldiers actually came to make enquiries. All these are much as they were, but the outside of the hall is different, its timbers now encased in brick. The king got safely away from Moseley, and after the Restoration he showed his gratitude by granting a pension to the squire and his son.

In the 14th-century church of Bushbury is a memorial to Thomas Whitgreave, who lived on until 1702, and there are other things to see: the carved beams of the chancel roof, the old font, and the much-worn figure of a priest believed to be Hugh de Byshbury, founder of the church. There is a silver plate 600 years old, and a fine Elizabethan chalice.

George Borrow came with his gipsy friends to a service here in 1825 and described it in a chapter of Romany Rye. The beech trees in the churchyard, the benches for the poor, and the little chancel door were all remembered by him.

BUTTERTON. It lies at the heart of a noble moorland picture, and builds itself up of stone hewn from the hills near the River Manifold.

The modern village occupies the site of a settlement of remote antiquity. Just to the east lie ancient barrows, which they call lows here; and from these have come spearheads and articles of adornment buried with those who wielded and wore them in prehistoric times.

The church, made new last century, has a fine spire crowning an imposing tower, and has saved the old font from the old church.

The Two Henrys

CANNOCK. Who has not heard of its famous Chase, 25 square miles of moorland with deep valleys, masses of bracken, brown streams, birch woods, and hills crowned with pines? Once the hunting-ground of kings, it has been in olden days a wild and desolate country where wolves were heard and outlaws sought refuge.

An old town and once a fashionable spa, Cannock has a charming corner by its handsome peace memorial, with figures of a soldier and sailor holding a flag. Close by is a quaint old prison and behind the memorial are noble limes sheltering a green, a haven of peace in a busy little world.

A boy who played here lies in Westminster Abbey. Henry Cary, famous for his fine translation of Dante, lived in a house near by, born in Gibraltar in 1772 but spending much of his childhood here.

An ancient cross keeps company with the modern church, the tower of which has watched Cannock growing bigger for 400 years or so. The quaint 18th-century gallery is still here. Among the windows is a fine modern one from the workshops of Christopher Whall, showing Adam, St Michael, and Hope.

Here it was, before the church was made new, that Henry Sacheverell, the much-hated and despised champion of the High Church and Toryism, preached many of his violent sermons, the kind of sermon that was afterwards to bring about his trial for sedition and libel, to cause tumult and riots, and finally the burning of his sermons by the hangman.

On the old Watling Street here is a quaint inn, half brick and half timber, for three centuries known as the Four Crosses. On a beam over the window is a Latin inscription meaning

> *You would weep if you knew you had*
> *but a month to live. You laugh*
> *when perhaps you have not a day.*

It is said that Jonathan Swift often slept here on his journeys from London to Ireland, and there is a story that, liking the inn more than the landlord's wife, he scratched on a window pane the unfriendly rhyme,

> *Thou fool, to hang four crosses at the door!*
> *Hang up thy wife! There needs not any more.*

Ruin Upon Ruin

CASTLECHURCH. It has a little company of houses near its church and castle. A mile or two from Stafford, its church is modern except for a tower built 500 years ago with a 17th-century sundial engraved in its stone. A lovely avenue of old yews shades the pathway to the porch.

Inside are four windows with figures of the Evangelists in beautiful glass, and outside is the oldest thing Castlechurch has to show, an oak 25 feet round, keeping watch over the grave of Thomas Mulock, whose daughter wrote John Halifax, Gentleman.

Long before we come to the village we see what is known as Stafford Castle standing proudly above the trees on a hill. It is Staffordshire's young ruin, a house begun about the time of Waterloo and never finished. It is a ruin on a ruin, for it stands on the foundations of a castle destroyed in Cromwell's day, a pathetic pile, slowly crumbling. We should climb one of the towers for the marvellous view stretching beyond Staffordshire and Shropshire into the mountains of Wales.

Seven Times Seven

CAULDON. It is all stone, its houses built of stone quarried for centuries at Cauldon Low, while weapons of the Stone Age have been found in what is called Big Low. In the churchyard of the 18th-century church is a gravestone with an inscription saying, Here lieth Margaret Manifold, aged seven times seven years old.

The Flag Riddled with Bullets

CAVERSWALL. It has memories of a man who defied a king, of an immortal admiral, a company of invincible seamen, and a famous writer.

The writer was Robert Buchanan, son of a journeyman tailor. Gifted and versatile, he wrote dramas, novels among the best of our prose romances, and poems in all moods, some of great tenderness and beauty.

Here he must often have looked with wondering eyes at the noble towers of Caverswall Castle, with its red stone walls glowing among the trees. The first castle was built 700 years ago; the present house, almost like a fortress in its massive strength, corner turrets, fine windows, and a Roman Catholic chapel notable for 14 carvings of the Road to Calvary, was raised by a man who might have foreseen that he must build for defence as well as for beauty.

He was Matthew Cradock, who, about the time the Mayflower sailed, saw the walls of his new home rising on what had degenerated into a farm. One of the founders of Massachusetts (where Winthrop was elected governor because Cradock did not arrive to fill the post) he helped the colony with money and provisions, but was kept occupied at home by events leading to the Civil War. It was he who stood up in the Long Parliament and declared that if Charles fortified the Tower he would see to it that London paid no taxes. Matters were nearing a crisis when he died suddenly in 1641, leaving his new home to serve as a fortress for the Parliamentary forces.

The church has still its 14th-century tower, its 13th-century chancel, and 17th-century arches borne on pillars set up when the old castle was new. The pulpit and two finely carved pews may be the work of the craftsmen who made the Jacobean altar table. There is an alabaster tablet with the arms of Matthew Cradock but there is a sculpture much more lovely—Chantrey's exquisite figure of Lady St Vincent, who has knelt here since 1816, veiled, with clasped hands, her coronet beside her.

She was the wife of Admiral John Jervis, Lord St Vincent, who saved us from invasion, quelled an alarming mutiny in the fleet, and purged the Admiralty of the hordes of knaves who were robbing the Navy and the nation. A stern, relentless man, he sleeps a few miles away at Stone.

Here over the chancel arch is something on which he would have smiled a grim approval, the proudest treasure of its kind that any Staffordshire church has. It is the tattered and shot-riddled flag which flew in a desperate hour at the mast-head of the steamship Clarissa Radcliffe. She was torpedoed in the Great War by a German submarine, whose commander ordered her crew to abandon ship. The men refusing, the enemy poured their fire into her, but, badly as she was damaged, they kept her afloat, defeated the enemy, and staggered proudly into port. At her mast-head flew this flag, riddled by 17 bullets.

The Bitter Life of Robert Buchanan

ROBERT BUCHANAN, born here in 1841, was one of the vigorous spirits of last century. His father, also named Robert Buchanan, was a newspaper writer who had started life as a tailor at Ayr, and he took his son back to Scotland, where he was educated at Glasgow University. At 19 Robert came to London with his friend David Gray, a weaver poet who lived just long enough to see one of his poems set up in type. Poverty oppressed them both. Robert became a journalist, writing for the Athenaeum and for All the Year Round, edited by Charles Dickens. He thus made many illustrious friends, keeping some all his life, but losing more by his very independence of character, which at times became perversity.

He established himself as a poet with his Undertones, followed by a volume of London Poems, revealing a deep and tender sympathy with the unhappy and unfortunate. In these, as in all his best poems (notably a beautiful love story, White Rose and Red), he showed fine narrative power, and a rare mastery of melody.

The perversity of his nature showed itself in a satirical poem, signed Caliban, in which he attacked Swinburne and other poets, who replied with vigour. He then wrote a famous article on The Fleshly School of Poetry, in which he hotly assailed the Pre-Raphaelites. Rossetti answered this with The Stealthy School of Criticism, and a long battle of words followed, ending in a libellous letter by Swinburne for which Buchanan recovered £150 damages. Five years later, however, he admitted that his criticisms had been exaggerated and he dedicated his novel God and the Man to Rossetti, "the old enemy."

He wrote a great deal of poetry, some of it with deep feeling and power; in a lighter vein he wrote of Love, sweeter than hearing or seeing, sadder than sorrow or death:

> The love that comes to the palace,
>   That comes to the cottage door:
> The ever-abundant chalice
>   Brimming for rich and poor.

In 1876 he began his career as a novelist, producing year by year work of power and imagination. He had worked in the grip of a bitter personal tragedy, his beautiful wife dying after a long and

painful illness. She had shared with him from the age of 20 all th
hardships as well as the successes of his life. Her sister Harriet Ja
was an actress, and with her help Buchanan now turned his novel
into plays and wrote many other dramas which met with success bot
here and in America. In spite of boundless generosity to friends les
fortunate than himself, he seemed on the way to fortune, whe
suddenly he lost all his savings in an unlucky investment and wa
made bankrupt. In the same year he was attacked by paralysis an
a few months later, in 1901, he died at Streatham, a poor man afte
all his labours.

A Page of History

CHARTLEY HOLME. It has been a stage for drama among th
most thrilling in our history, the parts played by queens
nobles, and high-born desperadoes, with the Spanish king in th
background; and with plot and counter-plot as astonishing as th
wildest fancies of fiction.

Old houses with grand timbers look out on the glories of a par
of nearly 1000 acres, but there is no church; the interest centres o
the manor house and the hilltop ruins of the 13th-century castle
With ancient yews about them, here are two round ivy-clad ston
towers, their walls 12 feet thick, pierced by narrow openings fo
the discharge of arrows, and bearing an engraved cross proclaimin
that the builder bore his part as a Crusader.

He was Ranulph, sixth Earl of Chester, who, while this castle wa
rising in 1220, was also building Beeston Castle in Cheshire. Wit
Ranulph in Palestine, as everywhere, was his brother-in-law Willia
de Ferrers, Earl of Derby. They were together at the deathbed o
King John, and witnessed his will. At Ranulph's death the castl
passed to the earl and remained in his family until 1461, when Si
Walter Devereux married the heiress of Chartley, leaving her her
when he went to fight for Richard the Third and to die by his side a
Bosworth Field.

His son brought here as bride the heiress of the great house o
Bohun, which had given Thomas of Woodstock a wife and Henry
the Fourth a queen. Devereux was father of the man from whom
descends our oldest viscounty, and grandfather of the first Earl o
Essex, who, married to Lettice Knollys, cousin of Queen Elizabeth,

as called by the queen the rare jewel of her realm, and the bright ornament of her nobility.

By this time the castle was replaced by a manor house which in the 18th century was again replaced by the grey stone house we still see peeping through the trees. Here, while Essex was breaking his heart in Ireland, Elizabeth came on a visit to her cousin Lettice, liking her entertainment so well that she stayed ten days. Essex dying the following year, the royal favourite Leicester married the widowed countess, and was responsible for the introduction to Court of the young earl then growing up as a model of grace, learning, and valour, though not of wisdom, he who was hero for a time of the queen and the nation alike.

When the earl was 18 his home was chosen, against his will, as the prison of Mary Queen of Scots, who was brought here during the Christmas season of 1585. Within a month Gilbert Giffard appeared on the scene, a plausible villain of 24, educated abroad, and secretly in the service of the Roman Catholics as well as of Elizabeth's watchful ministers, betraying each to the other.

He came here to Mary with French credentials, declaring his will and ability to convey letters to her, and to transmit her replies in turn. Unaware that Walsingham knew and approved of his coming, Mary trusted him fully, and he carried out his bargain to the extent of smuggling letters to her and from her; but before they left his hands all were copied, and duplicates forwarded to Walsingham.

Giffard was the intermediary between Mary and the conspirators in the Babington Plot. His method was to secrete letters for her in a box hidden in the false bottom of a barrel in which beer was supplied to her. On delivery the beer was drawn off, the box secured, and its contents read by Mary, whose replies were placed in the box, which was then carried out in the empty cask. As soon as the letters reached his hands Giffard translated them from their French cipher. But he not only gave Walsingham copies, he also contrived to let the Spanish Ambassador in Paris know the contents, and through him Philip of Spain, who pronounced the plot a holy enterprise and promised that it should have his support in men and money.

In the barrel came Babington's letter informing Mary of his scheme to murder Queen Elizabeth, to release and crown Mary, and to rouse all Roman Catholic England on her behalf, a task in which he was to have the assistance of a Spanish army of invasion. Mary replied approving the plan, and urging immediate action. As she had been an accessory in Scotland to the murder of her husband Darnley and had married his assassin, so here at Chartley she was accessor to the plot against her cousin, and was reported to be willing, i case he killed Elizabeth, to marry Babington.

In August 1586 Walsingham struck; Babington and his 13 fellow conspirators were arrested and executed. Mary was seized and imprisoned while her apartments here were searched, her cabinet forced, and all her correspondence impounded. Within a few day of the terrible penalties on the conspirators Mary left Chartley, an in September 1586 began the journey to Fotheringhay which was t end at the place of execution five months later.

Twenty years afterwards James the First came here and mad merry in the scene of his mother's imprisonment. After Mary' departure the house reverted to the young second earl, but he wa little here; his wonderful career, which kept him mainly in cour and camp, ended in his execution when he was only 34. He left widow, who had been the wife of Sir Philip Sidney, and an heir Robert Devereux, the third earl, destined to become the first Genera of Cromwell's Army. He died in 1646, and the estate passed to Si Robert Shirley, whose son Charles the Second created Lord Chartley Queen Anne added the earldom of Ferrers to the title, and it was th fourth Earl Ferrers who brought disgrace to the Chartley home b murdering his steward. Dressed like a bridegroom, he drove t Tyburn in 1760 in his own landau, drawn by his own horses, an driven by his own coachman, and there, in the presence of 200,00 people, he was hanged.

Some 20 years later the house was destroyed by fire, and the presen structure took its place, so that the crusader's castle has, in its ruins outlasted the hall which succeeded it as the setting of so much history. The Shirleys, a family of great antiquity, continued in possession until the opening of this century, when, for the firs time since the Conquest, the estate was sold.

There are still here mighty trees Queen Elizabeth saw, but of the famous herd of Chartley cattle there is no sign. Among the mos famous herds in existence, the Chartley cattle were white, with black ears and long branching horns, descendants of the great British

Castlechurch   **Stafford Castle**

Stafford   **High House**

Cheadle   Old house in High Street **Mow Cop**   18th Century Castle

Dudley   **The Castle**

urochs domesticated by the Romans. For a thousand years they ranged the great Needwood Forest. Soon after Ranulph had built the castle the present park was enclosed and the cattle fenced within its boundaries; and here for 700 years they remained, never wholly tamed, one of the wonders of the countryside. Then, while the estate was still in the hands of its last Shirley owner, tuberculosis attacked the herd, and only a few escaped. These passed into the safe keeping of the Duke of Bedford at Woburn; and there, with specimens at the London Zoo, we must seek the remnants of one of the most ancient and famous of all our cattle herds.

CHASETOWN. It is a town that lives on coal, but its outlook is not black. Chasetown has a justifiable pride in the lovely country at its doors, in the Mining Institute where its young men learn the higher branches of their industry, and in the park given by the Marquis of Anglesey and the Cannock Colliery Company. It has also a very proper regard for its modern church, which we believe has the distinction of being the first in England to be lighted by electricity.

Old and Rich

CHEADLE. With 100 million tons of coal below and miles of magnificent moorland above, old Cheadle is rich. It goes back to Roman times, and its market cross, raised on six steps, is a link with the Middle Ages.

There is a beautiful group of timbered and gabled Tudor houses and a 19th-century church at the end of an avenue of small firs. Its most notable possessions are an old oak chest with two locks and the 17th-century altar rails.

The splendid Roman Catholic church is not yet a century old. Built of red stone, it is one of Pugin's masterpieces. Its spire, rising 200 feet, is seen far off, and its west door is guarded by rampant lions heavily moulded in brass. Inside is a wealth of colour and ornament. The roof is sprinkled with stars on a blue background; there is a Doom over the chancel arch; and in a chapel is a brass screen of fine workmanship. A Jesse tree shines in one of the windows, and the gilded altar screen, a 15th-century triptych of the Last Days of Our Lord by a Flemish craftsman, is exquisite.

A mile away stands Hales Hall, built by the granddaughter of Sir Matthew Hales. It has noble trees and an avenue of old yews.

From Cheadle we come up the wooded valley of the Churnet t
the lonely spaces of Hawksmoor Nature Reserve, saved for th
nation by John Beech Masefield, to whose memory a gateway ha
been opened by his famous kinsman, John Masefield, our Poe
Laureate. The Reserve of 250 acres of woods, moors, and marshe
is the home of many birds and animals, a rare spot for wild flower
ferns, and rhododendrons.

CHEBSEY. In this little spot are fragments of Saxon Englan
one in a sunken Garden of Remembrance in the churchyar
the shaft of a cross decorated with knotwork, others in the church
thought to be bits of a cross the Normans may have saved when the
began building a church here.

Some of their work is still standing, a simple doorway now buil
up, and one where folk come in and out today. The chancel arc
and massive arcades are 13th century. The tower is 500 years old
it has an outside stair turret and a bell that was ringing befor
the Reformation.

Saxon and Dane and Norman are Here

CHECKLEY. The little river Tean flows murmuring to the Dove
the smiling fields, the splendid trees, and the snug hedge
rows carry the eye to the hills swelling on the horizon. Little ca
have changed in this beautiful country since the Normans buil
their church, a wonderful picture as we look down on it from
Checkley Bank.

It is the venerable mother church of a wide area, with a churchyar
as impressive as anything of the kind Staffordshire has to show
Here are three magnificent shafts of Saxon crosses about five feet high
an astonishing heritage for a village churchyard. On one are thre
figures believed to be bishops slain in a battle between Saxon an
Danes at the hamlet half a mile away, still called Deadman's Green

Above these Saxon relics rises a grand 15th-century tower from a
massive Norman base. On an outer wall is an old stone sundial
A prettily vaulted Jacobean porch guards a fine 14th-century doorway with ballflower ornament. The high and beautiful interior, with
a 17th-century clerestory, has a Norman arcade with its arches
pointed, a second arcade which has been here 700 years, and a fine
Norman font.

To this font may have been brought for christening the 13th-century knight who lies in armour in an aisle. A Tudor alabaster tomb shows Godfrey Foljambe in armour and ruff, and his wife in close-fitting hat, ruff, and belted gown.

In the lofty 14th-century chancel, one of the finest we have seen in village church, are traceried windows which have rose-decked tone bosses, and are filled with Flemish glass 600 years old. The olouring is sober, the drawing of the figures primitive yet imaginative and impressive. In the sanctuary window are four saints and a 3th-century bishop, and below, with the Crucifixion, are St Margaret nd her dragon, Abraham and Isaac, the scene of the murder of Becket, and Henry the Second doing penance for the crime.

Other chancel windows have the Madonna and Child and two aints; Moses with the tables of the law, and Saints John and Simon. n yet another, with much heraldic glass, are delightful roundels vith the occupations of the months: February for netting, March or pruning, April for plantings, May with its flowers, July for the ay-cutting, another month for the harvest, and finally, for October, he fattening of the swine. With a reaping machine in place of the cythe, the pictures might characterise the march of the months over hese fertile fields today.

In a chapel is a fine old screen, its linenfold enriched by heraldry. Three 16th-century choir-stalls have richly carved poppyheads with oses, animals, and figures wearing headdresses suggestive of Red ndians, whose habits and attire could hardly have been known y the carvers.

There can be no mistaking the significance of the initials A.D. on he poppyheads; they stand for Anthony Draycott, rector here and hancellor of Lichfield, a sore scourge of Protestants in the red reign f Mary Tudor.

Windows by Great Artists

CHEDDLETON. It lies on a hillside amid charming scenery near the River Churnet. A red stone lychgate with a figure of Christ in a canopied niche brings us to the church with a tower of Queen Elizabeth's day, a chancel 600 years old, and an arcade a century older. One of its glories is a group of fine windows, two with the touch of great artists in them—a lovely St Cecilia by Rossetti and

three trumpeting angels by Burne-Jones. Other windows have glow
ing pictures of Peter and Paul, Moses and Elijah, and Our Lord an
the Evangelists. The 14th-century chancel has two rare treasures,
medieval brass eagle on the lectern and an oak panel in the rered
with painted figures carved by a craftsman 400 years ago. The pan
shows the burial of Christ. In one of the choir stalls a brass tabl
tells us that Fred Wilshaw sat there as a chorister for 56 years.

In the churchyard are the stone stocks, and the clustered shafts o
an ancient cross set on three steps.

CHURCH EATON. The old builders and our modern craftsme
have given this attractive village its greatest possession, a churc
in memory of St Editha, whose well is at High Onn, about a mile away

Norman masons built the tower and 15th-century builders adde
the spire. An arcade and a beautifully moulded font are also Norman
A fine window with tracery nearly five centuries old fills the eas
wall of the chancel. Its modern glass has nine scenes from the lif
of Christ, portraits of bishops, and St Michael, all from the hands o
the artists who filled the old windows of the tower with new portrait
of the patron saint.

In the churchyard is the marble tomb of Arthur Talbot, wh
preached in this place for 54 years last century.

Three Counties Meet

CLIFTON CAMPVILLE. Its treasures are gathered in th
remarkably fine church standing proudly near the spot wher
three counties meet.

Much of the church was built in that fine period of English archi
tecture, the 14th century, and it was then that the tower and spir
were raised to a height of 189 feet, both lovely and slender, the spir
set off with flying buttresses. The north transept, a century older
has a chapel with a vaulted roof under a priest's chamber, the
fireplace and the 13th-century windows still here.

The church is rich in screens, with three of the 14th century, on
of the 15th, and one of the 17th. The gates of the 15th-century
screen were fixed 200 years later, and on them is the name of the
rector who saw them brought into the church. The eight stalls
nearly 500 years old, have finely carved misereres adorned with leaves
and grotesques.

Blithfield
Sir Lewis Bagot and three wives, 1534

Marchington
Walter and Mary Vernon, 1593

Hanbury
Ralph Adderley and his two wives, 1595

Blithfield
Francis and Mary Aston with their son, 1593

STAFFORDSHIRE PEOPLE ENGRAVED IN STONE

Fading away on the wall of a recess are portraits of a medieval knight and his lady receiving a blessing from Our Lord; and on a brass is a lady, thought to have been the wife of Sir Richard Stafford, shown in the height of fashion 600 years ago. On a marble wall monument is a beautiful woman weeping for John Watkins, who was rector here last century; and among other monuments is one by Rysbrack, with a casket between two pillars in memory of Sir Charles Pye of 1721, and one with an urn in memory of Sir Richard Pye of 1724.

More striking is an alabaster table tomb with figures of Sir John Vernon, a lawyer of Henry the Eighth's day. He wears a long bonnet and gown, and lies by his wife who is in a square hood and flowing dress, a knife, a purse, and beads at her side. Round the tomb sit seven monks, some with books and others with rosaries, and at the head are a son and daughter kneeling at prayer. In a recess in the nave, in a stone coffin with an engraved cross, it is thought that the founder of all the beauty round about may lie at rest.

CODSALL. There are old giants in this village of red cottages a few miles from Wolverhampton. Two of them, in the ground of Oaken House, are among the highest wych elms we have seen, one 22 feet round and one 24. Two other giants are yews in the churchyard, one 15 feet round; both have weathered centuries of storm, and with them on a pillar and three steps is a sundial which has marked years of sunny hours.

The church, refashioned last century, has a tower 600 years old and a doorway 200 years older, its zigzag moulding and carved capitals finely preserved.

Inside is an attractive modern screen and an old knight's tomb. The screen has beautifully carved roses; the brightly painted and golded tomb has a figure of Walter Wrottesley, Sheriff of Staffordshire in Charles Stuart's day. We see him with his head on his helmet and a gauntlet at his feet, his five children gathered round him, one of the sons in armour and two in red tunics. The daughters wear black dresses with golden collars and cuffs.

A Company of the Mighty Dead

COLWICH. It lies in beauty by the Trent, with the lofty hills of Cannock Chase splendid in the distance. It thrills us with

memories of one of our most ancient families, and recalls the fame
of a shining soldier-hero of the Empire.

Just south of the village, in a spacious timbered park, is Wolseley
Hall, the home of the Wolseleys since the days before the Conquest.
It has much fine woodwork, including a staircase said to have been
carved by Grinling Gibbons. Here, say the Wolseley records, the
line was already established when, in the 10th century, King Edgar
gave the family its present lands as a reward for destroying wolves,
with which the county was overrun.

Many of the Wolseleys rest in this ancient church, whose churchyard gives us a superb picture of the river winding through the fields
and of the distant glory of the forest heights. With a handsome 17th-
century tower, the church has a 13th-century arcade and much work
of the following century, but the 28 canopied choir stalls are modern.

The great possessions of the church are the Wolseley and Anson
monuments, but there are others of interest, among them a tablet to
James Trubshaw, who sleeps here. The son of a Colwich builder,
he worked for William Beckford in building Fonthill Abbey, built
three fine halls, bridged the Derwent at Derby, set upright a church
tower in Cheshire which was five feet out of plumb, and, crowning
achievement (said by the great Telford to be impossible) crossed the
Dee at Chester with a bridge of a single span 200 feet wide, which
was then the widest arch in Europe.

Under a beautiful arch is a wall monument with engraved figures
of Christ, an angel, and two wounded soldiers, to Lady Chetwynd,
who ended a life of good works in 1860. The glass includes a
memorial window to Major Hodson, hero of Hodson's Horse, whose
astounding feats in India included the capture of the King of Delhi.
He was killed in 1858 by a shot from an unseen enemy hidden
in a house at Lucknow. His father was vicar here for 22 years of
last century.

The Wolseley memorials represent only a few of the members of
this ancient family sleeping here. The first with a monument is Sir
Robert, who lies on a 17th-century tomb in long breeches, tunic, and
cloak, with two angels and two girls holding skulls above him. Born
a subject of Queen Elizabeth, he suffered confiscation of his estates
during the Civil War, and died poor in 1646.

His heir Sir Charles made his peace with the Commonwealth while still a youth, and became deeply attached to Cromwell, sat in two of his Parliaments, was called to his House of Lords, and was one of the committee which urged him to accept the Crown. A scholar and a gardener, Sir Charles was the father of 15 children. There is a tablet to his son Sir William, who was drowned during a thunderstorm by the bursting of a mill-dam while driving in his carriage. His coachman escaped, " being carried by the torrent into an orchard, where he remained fast until the flood abated," but Sir William and his four horses were overwhelmed.

Sir Charles's youngest son Richard fought in Ireland, where he acquired property and founded the Irish branch of the family which in 1833 produced one of the bravest soldiers of the century, Field-Marshal Wolseley, whose arms are on a wall of the church here, though he sleeps in St Paul's.

Few men have had a more remarkable career than he. Joining the Army at 19 he fought through the Burmese and Crimean Wars, and in the Indian Mutiny and the Chinese War of 1860, while still in his twenties. In Canada he commanded the Red River Expedition, adding the province of Manitoba to the Dominion.

He met Gordon in the Crimean trenches, and remained his devoted friend up to their last parting, which was when Gordon left Charing Cross in a tall hat and frockcoat, with nothing in his purse but the odd money Wolseley gave him. It was not his fault that he arrived with his relief expedition too late to prevent the death of Gordon at Khartoum.

As Commander-in-Chief Wolseley reorganised the British army, completed 48 years of service, and died after 13 years of happy retirement, enlivened by the writing of an appealing autobiography. He invented the name of Thomas Atkins for the private soldier.

Wolseley lies in St Paul's with Nelson; with the Wolseleys here at Colwich sleeps Lord Anson, forerunner of Nelson. There is a fine monument by Westmacott showing an angel reaping corn in memory of Thomas Lord Anson, who died in 1818, and a wall monument with a graceful figure of a weeping woman to Lady Anson, who died in 1843, though to the greatest of the line, the immortal voyager, who was brought to his last rest here in 1762, there is but a modest tablet.

The Ansons had been long in Staffordshire before establishing hemselves at Shugborough at the beginning of the 17th century. It was here, where never sea wind sang, that young George Anson conceived his passion for an ocean life, and from here that he went to join his first ship. His immortal expedition, described by his own pen in one of our sea classics, brought out the magnificent character of the man, his wisdom and courage, his discipline and humanity. It was Anson's account of the loss of one of his sailors in a storm which inspired Cowper's poem on a Castaway, in which are the lines:

> *No poet wept him; but the page*
> *Of narrative sincere,*
> *That tells his name, his worth, his age,*
> *Is wet with Anson's tear.*

Anson left no family and his barony became extinct, but he was succeeded in his estate by a nephew, and from him descend the Earls of Lichfield.

For Anson's grave Colwich is a place of pilgrimage; his achievements give him a place apart in our imperial story.

Forerunner of Nelson

GEORGE ANSON, born here in 1697, developed early the romantic passion for the sea that had animated Drake and Hawkins and Raleigh; and from 14 onwards he served as a volunteer, at one time, as acting lieutenant in the Hampshire frigate, being under Peter the Great, who had been given command of the English ships sent to the Baltic.

Service against the Spaniards took Anson in 1723 to South Carolina, and his popularity in America is attested to this day by the fact that Anson County is named after him. He had his first holiday for 19 years when peace brought him home in 1735.

In 1739 there occurred the war fomented by the story that an English captain named Robert Jenkins had had his ear cut off by a Spanish captain at Havana. Into this war plunged Anson, sent in the Centurion, with five other ships to round Cape Horn and harass the Spanish shipping along the coast of Peru.

His ships were in a deplorable condition. The food was scanty and unwholesome, and his 2000 men included invalids from hospitals, infirm pensioners, and men who had never hauled a rope or handled a gun. Such was the little fleet that staggered out to cross the world. At the mercy of wind and waves, Anson lost himself unable to find the longitude of Selkirk's island, Juan Fernandez where he wished to recruit his men and save his sick. His ship had been used in 1736 for the successful demonstration of John Harrison' marine timepiece for finding the longitude, but that instrument lay rusting in London while Anson, steering east and west in search of the island, lost eighty precious lives!

Yet Anson continued, till his ships were reduced to the Centurion and his men to 200; capturing Paita and various prizes, and anchoring at the island of Tinian to recoup. There a storm carried the Centurion away, and Anson was a thousand miles from civilisation with only a little 15-ton prize to save him. For three weeks he laboured to lengthen this craft, and one day the Centurion came sailing back to the island, and in her he sailed to China.

He stayed at Macao, repairing for five months, then set sail for Manila, where a Spanish ship hove in sight, a galleon heavy with treasure, which was captured, with five hundred prisoners. Anson finally reached England, by way of the Cape of Good Hope, in June 1744, slipping through a French fleet in the fog to do so. His log laconically records the sequel:

July 2. Fresh gales and cloudy; sent away treasure in 32 wagons to London, with 139 Officers and Seamen to guard it.

It was a treasure indeed, "1,413,843 pieces of eight, and 35,682 ounces of virgin silver"; over two millions sterling in our currency.

Anson's voyage round the world is the classic of the 18th century, a tremendous feat ranking with Drake's, and to the same end. Honours crowded upon him, the only sad note being his selection of Byng for the expedition that brought disgrace and death to that unfortunate officer. Anson was guiltless of his fate.

He died a rich man at Moor Park, Hertfordshire, and was brought back to his birthplace to sleep in the tomb of his kindred.

CRESWELL. It had a small church long ago, but all that is left of it is a pathetic ruin in a field. There is part of a chancel wall with big buttresses which have nothing to support, though once they helped to hold up a 15th-century roof; and of the north wall there are a few stones and two lancets 700 years old.

Great Names and Great Memories

CROXALL. With a mound to remind us of its Saxon days, it is a little place of great names and great memories, the resting-home of a woman celebrated in song by Byron, and of a man who helped to decide one of the puzzling problems of the literary life of last century.

To the south of the village is Oakley, a three-storeyed farmhouse behind a wall, which 500 years ago was the manor of Sir John Stanley, whose family was to produce the first Earl of Derby. Sir John was often the host of Edward the Fourth.

Croxall Hall, a gabled brick house with spacious windows and tall chimneys, was for generations the home of the Curzons, who sleep in the church, and after them of the Earls of Dorset. Two miles away is Catton Hall, a fine modern house in a park. It has in its grounds fragments of tracery from windows and an old shallow font, believed to be Saxon, which are the last remains of a 16th-century chapel, and now form part of a rockery.

Near the hall a little red chapel with a bell turret occupies the site of a Norman building. In it is a round Norman font, restored to honour after having long been drowned in the Trent.

The church, standing near the River Mease, and overlooking a wooded dell, has a 15th-century tower on a base as old as Magna Carta. In the floor of the 14th-century chancel is a remarkable series of tombstones to the Curzons. The oldest shows Thomas and his wife, he in the plate armour and pointed helmet of the Wars of the Roses, she in a long dress and a high-crowned hat.

John Horton lies in armour such as was worn by the men who fought at Agincourt; his wife, a Curzon, has a long belted gown, and with them are their six children. George Curzon wears plate armour; his wife has a ruff and a richly brocaded dress.

The figures of William and Elena Shepherd, engraved in 1500, have suffered sadly, and little John Howes, lonely under the tower, wearing his christening robe, has been as harshly treated by time since they laid him here in 1554.

The most beautiful thing in the church is the lovely Chantrey monument to Eusebius Horton of Catton Hall, showing her two daughters standing by the grave of their parents, each seeking to soothe the other's grief.

But the monument for which this church is famous is the wall monument with two little angels above an inscription to Sir Robert Wilmot-Horton and his wife Anne, who survived him 30 years.

He is the man who had a leading part in the burning of Byron's Journals, and she it is who "Walks in Beauty like the Night."

She Walks in Beauty Like the Night

BORN at Osmaston in Derbyshire, he was a cousin of the poet, his mother being a daughter of the famous Admiral Byron. Byron first saw Lady Wilmot-Horton at a ball wearing a black robe starred with spangles, and her beauty so stirred his imagination that that very night he wrote the famous stanzas *She Walks in Beauty*, which open his series of Hebrew Melodies:

> She walks in beauty, like the night
> Of cloudless climes and starry skies;
> And all that's best of dark and bright
> Meet in her aspect and her eyes:
> Thus mellowed to that tender light
> Which heaven to gaudy day denies.
>
> One shade the more, one ray the less,
> Had half impaired the nameless grace
> Which waves in every raven tress,
> Or softly lightens o'er her face;
> Where thoughts serenely sweet express
> How pure, how dear their dwelling-place.
>
> And on that cheek, and o'er that brow,
> So soft, so calm, yet eloquent,
> The smiles that win, the tints that glow,
> But tell of days in goodness spent,
> A mind at peace with all below,
> A heart whose love is innocent!

Byron's brief domestic happiness and its tragic sequel centred about the time this poem was written. In that year he married; 12 months later he parted from his wife and infant daughter, never to see them again. In the protracted negotiations which followed Wilmot-Horton had a conspicuous private share. His rôle was delicate, for he was a friend of the unhappy wife and the champion of his cousin, Byron's stepsister, Augusta, to whom the injured wife ascribed much of her unhappiness.

Byron gave Tom Moore the manuscript of his Memoirs, to be published after the poet's death. Moore sold them to John Murray for 2000 guineas, on the understanding that they could be redeemed, unpublished, on the repayment of that sum, during Byron's lifetime or within three months of his death. Read by various people of discretion and understanding, the Memoirs were declared gross and scandalous, and ruinous to the reputation of persons then living. Wilmot-Horton, acting in the interest of Augusta, was among the most active in staying publication, and was present in Murray's drawing-room when, after a stormy debate, the manuscript was solemnly burnt and Moore refunded the money.

The Heart of the Worst King of England

CROXDEN. It is possible that here, amid the finest monastic ruins in Staffordshire, lies the heart of the worst king England ever had, whose body lies in all the glory of Worcester Cathedral.

Croxden, in a charming valley with a stream flowing to meet the River Dove, has a modern church of red stone seen among the dark foliage of six cedars; but it is the abbey we come to see. Its founder was a 12th-century Crusader, Bertram de Verdun, who built Alton Castle and is believed to have been buried in one of three stone coffins here. Most of the ruins are 13th century.

Lovely in decay, the abbey is in a fair setting. Of the fine old church there is still standing the west front, the walls perhaps 40 feet high. Here are three exceeding tall lancets above a magnificent doorway with clustered pillars, and a much-worn figure of a cross-legged knight. The walls of the south transept, and the west front of the chapter house, with a fine arch between windows once overlooking the cloisters, are still defying wind and rain. There is still something to see of the sacristy, the kitchen, the common room, the abbot's house, and the 14th-century guest house; and in a field near by are the lonely stone coffins of the monks. One of the monks was old William de Shepesheved, whose 14th-century Chronicle of the Abbey is now in the British Museum.

Perhaps all who come to this peaceful spot, where we found peacocks strutting on the lawns, think of King John, who died in his misery not far off. It has long been said that he was ministered to on his deathbed by the monks of Croxden, though the claim has also

been made for the monks of Croxton Abbey in Leicestershire. Is i
in the shadow of these venerable stones, we may wonder, that th
heart of England's worst king lies humbled in the dust?

New and Beautiful

DENSTONE. There is nothing old here, but everything new i
beautiful. Oliver's Mound can be seen from the road, an
the church built by Sir Thomas Heywood has an elaborate fon
adorned with angels and splendid windows with a series of 20 scene
from the life of Christ. Denstone College has one of the mos
magnificent views from any school. Its handsome buildings, with
company of firs on a hilltop, look over the glory of the Churne
Valley to the Weaver Hills. There is a fine bronze statue of St Georg
by Alfred Drury, a memorial to the Old Boys of the school who die
for peace; and in the great hall is a portrait of Sir Thomas Heywood
whose gifts to the school will long be remembered. The chapel ha
a Mother's Window from the workshops of Christopher Whall, th
source of some of the best modern windows we have seen.

A Hundred Thousand Tributes

DILHORNE. Here are a hundred thousand tributes to a ma
unknown beyond his county, a mighty host of trees plante
by John Holliday where he found only barren moors. That was i
Nelson's day, when the tree-lover was at Dilhorne Hall, now gone.
As delightful as anything for miles around is the village, below
steep hill a mile or two from Cheadle; and very pleasing is its church
with stones bridging the centuries from the 12th to the 19th. Th
aisles and nave are modern, but the chancel is 15th century, th
arcades are 13th, and the base of the tower is Norman, the only
tower in Staffordshire with eight sides. The altar table and rails ar
from Charles Stuart's day, and the font has been here since th
Normans were building the tower.

The Draycotts of Draycott

DRAYCOTT-IN-THE-MOORS. Generations of Draycotts
lived here at Paynsley Hall, a fine old house reached by a
stony road. It was a Draycott who shut the door of the house in the
face of the Roundheads, so that they broke in and held it for the
Parliament; it was a Draycott who opened the door to the con-

pirator Anthony Babington. Also it was an Anthony Draycott who
was rector here in Mary Tudor's day, and became notorious for his
cruelty to Protestants. He suffered persecution in his turn when
Elizabeth came to the throne, spending his last years in prison. Here
he is said to sleep.

For 700 years Draycotts were worshipping here, one of them
probably the founder who may have seen the tower built in the 13th
century) lying carved in stone, his cross-legged figure in armour, his
sword ready.

Engraved in alabaster in the chapel of the hillside church is the
worn portrait of Sir William Draycott, who left money for the poor
housekeepers of the village in 1512. On an alabaster tomb is a 17th-
century figure of Richard Draycott with his son and two daughters,
all under arches, and finely preserved are the painted figures of John
Draycott of 1600, a knight ready for battle, and his wife, she wearing
a closely fitting hat and a ruff. There is a handsome painted monument to John Fitzherbert, wearing armour and two necklaces, his
wife with him in the fashionable dress of Mary Tudor's day, and their
12 children in a row.

In the churchyard is a yew with a hollow trunk 18 feet round.

The Garden Sir Robert Peel Loved

DRAYTON BASSETT. Few people know it, but everyone has
heard of its famous son, who has been sleeping here since the
dramatic ending of his great career in the middle of last century.
Honoured for all time, and one of the most remarkable of our
modern statesmen, the nation mourned him as a father. He stands
in London facing the Parliament in which he served the people nobly
by giving them cheap bread, but it is here he sleeps.

By the river Tame and next door to Shakespeare's county, Drayton
Bassett has a curious peace memorial at the boundary between
Warwickshire and Staffordshire. A stone signpost with the names of
the village heroes, it is said to stand on the site of a boundary stone
set up by Lord Bassett of Drayton before Magna Carta.

A big yew and a fine beech are old friends of the modern church
Sir Robert Peel built. The 15th-century tower is all that is left of the
building where for centuries the Bassetts used to come; a powerful
Staffordshire family 500 years ago, their lands passed to the Countess

of Essex who is said to have been visited here by Elizabeth. The ol
house was rebuilt by Sir Robert Peel's father.

The church was built a hundred years ago in the days of grea
prosperity for the Peels, the father being the founder of a cotto
factory and a pioneer of modern business methods. He was an abl
politician too, and the author of a book on the National Debt an
national prosperity. An advocate of reforms which brought abou
great changes in factory life, he is remembered for giving Londo
workhouse children a chance to be useful citizens. He died at h
house here and has a stone monument in the church. His funera
sermon was preached by a rector who had been here 30 years the
and was to preach for nearly another 30 years before his long da
was done.

With the founder of the church lie his father and his son. The so
was of no importance and did little to bring credit to the honoure
name he bore; but the great Sir Robert has a marble tablet under
beautiful canopy; and Drayton Bassett is proud to be the shrine o
so great a man, statesman, reformer, repealer of the Corn Laws, an
great English gentleman. He used to come to this church, and
was on going home from here one Sunday that his father told hi
the strange story of the child at Fazeley close by, who fell from a
attic window of the inn without hurting itself.

Sir Robert Peel's house has gone, pulled down a year or two afte
the war, but we found a crowd of children enjoying the beautifu
gardens Lady Peel loved so well. The house which stood in thi
garden was the house Lady Peel loved best of all, and here Sir Robe
longed to be with her. In the midst of a busy life which produced
hundred thousand public documents in our archives, he would leav
his desk in Downing Street to shop for her or to find her seed
and plants.

He wrote to her one day that he had been all the morning occupie
about her cloak, and had had a long consultation about it with th
tailor; and he wrote again: "You shall have the packet of seeds; th
violet has been watered." At another time, just returned fron
executing her botanical commission, he wrote: "I found a Stephanoti
and a plant which bears a yellow flower and grows over the house
The blue campanula was not so easy to find."

"Home, sweet, home," he wrote again, "I long to be back. I tur

Caverswall   The Stuart Castle

Lichfield   St John's Hospital

William Smythe and Wives　　　**Sir Thomas Arderne's Tomb**

Sir Thomas and Matilda Arderne　　**John Stanley**

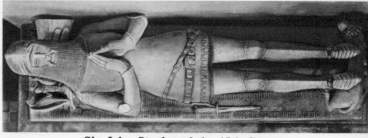

Sir John Stanley of the 15th Century

THE OLD FOLK OF ELFORD

way from the fifteen little black teapots I see on the table before me and think of our little round table, my Julia opposite to me, and little Julia and Bobby dividing the biscuits."

He had lived at Drayton since he was ten, and once as he was going to Parliament from his London house he wrote home to his wife, "I cannot mention Drayton without bitterly lamenting that I am away from all I hold dear. I am just going to that wretched place I left last night heartily wishing I might never enter it again." If he could love her more he said, the sight of others and their odious ways would make him do so.

A Prime Minister of Great Courage

SIR ROBERT PEEL was born near Bury in Lancashire in 1788. His father, a wealthy cotton manufacturer, sent him to Harrow, where Byron was one of his form-fellows, and to Oxford, where he acquitted himself with distinction. Handsome, eloquent, and witty, he was withal incurably shy except with intimates, and Wellington, complaining later of difficulties at Court, lamented, "Peel has no manners and I have no small talk."

Entering Parliament at 21, he was Chief Secretary for Ireland for six years and Home Secretary for five, bringing into existence our Metropolitan Police Force, whose members were called Peelers and Bobbies after him. His new force was received with fierce opposition in some quarters and was actually declared a preliminary to a stroke by which Peel was to set Wellington on the throne!

After long resisting Roman Catholic Emancipation, Sir Robert Peel supported it, so alienating the Old Tories without conciliating the Whigs, and during his first Premiership he was equally opposed to Reform. Prime Minister again from 1841 to 1846, he faced his task with a broad and open mind. "Work," Dean Jackson had urged him, "work like a tiger or like a dragon (if dragons work more and harder than tigers)"; and work he did, 17 hours a day, his family almost strangers to him. He loved his home but saw too little of it. Although he had an able Chancellor of the Exchequer, he himself as Prime Minister introduced two Budgets.

Upon him rested the responsibility for a great reversal of policy in the national interest, the repeal of the Corn Laws, of which he had consistently approved. He saw famine in Ireland, and want and discontent in England, and, holding that his duty to the nation was greater than his duty to his party, he dared to propose repeal and himself introduced the measure abolishing the duties. His party was split asunder, but as he left the House on the night of his resignation in 1846 a silent multitude awaited him, and, with bared heads escorted him home as the saviour of the country.

During the last year of his administration he was bitterly attacked by Disraeli, in a speech as dishonourable as any ever delivered in Parliament. Peel listened, *with a letter in his pocket from Disraeli begging for office*, and, great gentleman that he was, he kept the secret. But that night he entered his secretary's bedroom and said "Never destroy a letter; no public man who respects himself should ever destroy a letter." That was all.

His last four years were spent as a private member in support of Liberal Free Trade policy, and his life ended tragically in July 1850 He went out riding on his horse and was thrown, being taken home to die on the day after a speech which John Bright declared to be the speech of peace, "that beautiful, that most solemn speech."

The Proud Castle of the Pennines

By a strange freak of boundaries Dudley is an island of Worcester shire entirely surrounded by Staffordshire, but by a still stranger freak Dudley Castle remains in Staffordshire. Here we give both, for they belong essentially to the Staffordshire the traveller will expect to find in any book on the county.

DUDLEY. It stands with its proud castle on the Pennine slopes a town which has thrived for centuries on the riches of the earth. Around it are found all the materials necessary for the great industry of smelting iron—ironstone, limestone, fireclay for lining furnaces, and the thickest seam of coal in the kingdom. For many generations the furnaces of the smelters consumed the forests near by until in Stuart times a young man found that coal could be used instead. He was Dud Dudley, summoned from an Oxford college to manage his father's ironworks at Pensnett. Today the town of Dudley gives us not only raw iron, but iron and steel manufacture of every kind and size from a nail to a railway bridge.

We cannot wonder at any place losing its beauty amid slagheaps and the waste mounds from mine and furnace; and in winning its ndustrial reputation Dudley has lost much. But it has not lost its chief treasure and its greatest interest, the ruined castle on a hilltop far above the chimneys. No one can travel hereabouts without being drawn to it, for it is seen all over the Black Country and beyond.

Perhaps there was a fortification here in Saxon times. Certainly it was one of the Conqueror's men who raised these earthworks which have been the foundation of the castle ever since, for they come into Domesday Book. What buildings the Normans had here we do not know, but the inner walls of the great gatehouse are theirs, and a Norman arch is still visible in one of the walls of the buttery.

The castle has a great courtyard bounded by a 14th-century curtain wall sometimes eight feet thick, with a long line of ruined buildings running about halfway round the wall. Starting from the massive battlemented keep, we pass in succession the 17th-century stables, the impressive gatehouse, the 14th-century chapel with its big yawning window and its vaulted cellar, the remains of the Great Chamber, just as old, the Tudor hall with its gaunt mullioned windows, the buttery with a beautiful two-storeyed bow window, and the shell of a building with two great gables which once included the kitchen and some of the bedrooms. Bringing this long line to an end are two more buildings which would be chiefly used by the servants, the first with a tall staircase turret, and the second a gatehouse that has lost its gables.

The keep is chiefly 14th century, and is not only a fine stronghold, but a wonderful viewpoint from which we can look into seven English counties and even into Wales. Close to the toposcope are two Russian guns captured at Sebastopol. The great gatehouse was also raised upon its Norman core by 14th-century hands; and so immensely strong had it become a few decades later that the enemy who sought entrance here was confronted once by a drawbridge, twice by a portcullis, and three times by great doors.

During its 800 years the castle has seen more than one great family come and go. From the end of the 12th century to the beginning of the 14th it belonged to the De Somerys, one of whom, Sir John de Somery, built the curtain wall, finished the gatehouse, and began the keep. He seems to have ruled the neighbourhood in what we may call gangster fashion, extorting money and labour from everyone in exchange for the protection he could give. After the De Somerys came the De Suttons, who built the chapel and added the barbican to the gatehouse; and then, generations later, came their descendant John Dudley, son of that Dudley who with Empson appears unpleasantly in our history books among the unscrupulous agents of Henry the Seventh.

To this John Dudley, who became Duke of Northumberland, we owe much of the charm the castle has, for it was he who refashioned all the domestic buildings in the Tudor style, employing as architect Sir William Sharington who had made himself a fine house out of Lacock Abbey in Wiltshire. They are very remarkable buildings for their time, simply and finely made, the forerunners of the splendid country houses of the Elizabethan Age. How many of his days the Duke spent here we do not know, for he was prominent in the country's affairs in those short years of Edward the Sixth. He strove to set on the throne Lady Jane Grey, his daughter-in-law, and the reign of Mary Tudor saw him executed at the Tower, where he lies with Anne Boleyn and Catherine Howard.

It is possible that the ruined outer buildings on the way up the castle hill were built in his time, and not many years after his death Queen Elizabeth came this way in all her majesty, a special withdrawing-room being set aside in her honour. The Civil War saw the end of the castle as a fortress, but the beautiful domestic buildings were hardly touched until they were brought to ruin in the 18th century by a terrible fire which raged for three days. It is said that red-hot lead from the roof streamed down the hillside, setting fire to the long grass and terrifying the town.

Far down beneath the castle are the strange limestone caves where for many years the solid rock was quarried and carried away by water. A strange experience it must have been for the members of the British Association in 1849 when they met in one of these caverns by the light of thousands of candles.

By the castle entrance stands the white stone figure of a 19th-century Earl of Dudley, and in the marketplace is a fountain he set up in Renaissance style with figures of Mining and Agriculture, Industry and Commerce. The town museum is celebrated for its collection of fossils and coral, and the town hall is a fine building of brick and stone opened by Stanley Baldwin in 1928. Its entrance hall is consecrated as a peace memorial to 718 men who fell in the war.

The churches have not the attraction which great age brings, yet here are things to see in four of them. St Edmund's, built a few years after Queen Anne died, has on its walls marble portraits of a magistrate and of a surgeon who was 65 years in the town. The Roman Catholic church has a fine brass portrait of a 19th-century priest in his robes. St John's has a peace memorial lychgate, a wonderful view of the castle, a most attractive glass picture-gallery of scenes showing Christ and the Disciples, and a marble font in memory of one who was vicar 62 years. And St Thomas's, with a fine spire rising 175 ft., has a reredos sculptured with the scene of Doubting Thomas, up above being a remarkable painted window of the Ascension, illuminated from behind by electric lights. It has, too, one of the most elaborate fonts we have seen, a mass of fine carving with little Bible scenes, rich canopies, and angel figures. The beautiful cover is fashioned as a tower and spire, and has eight tiny figures under canopies.

But if Dudley has lost all its ancient churches it has still the remains of one of them, the ruins of what was perhaps the most important of all. We must look in the grounds of the Priory Hall, where after six or seven hundred years are still standing some walls of the church belonging to a priory founded in the 12th century. The walls have seen strange sights since the monks left them, for 150 years ago a tanner was living and working in what had been a sacred place. He was followed by a thread manufacturer, and later by people who ground glass, polished fire-irons, and made fenders.

The priory had its connections with the men who were lords of Dudley. Here in 1273 they laid Roger de Somery who owned the castle and obtained the king's permission to fortify it. And here about 200 years later they laid one of the greatest of the long line of Suttons, the 6th Lord Dudley, who was celebrated as a statesman and who saw, at the end of his long life, the opening years of the Tudor Age. He was the grandson of Sir Walter Blount, who comes into Shakespeare with Falstaff and Hotspur, and before he was 28 they had made him Lord Lieutenant of Ireland.

Through all the troubled Wars of the Roses he lived, and in his will we get an interesting glimpse of the funeral ceremony of a rich man in those days. Here at the priory 24 new torches were to be lighted during the service. Every priest was to have fourpence and every singing-man threepence, and as soon as he was buried a thousand masses were to be said for his soul at a cost of £16 13s 4d. His "goodly monument," which was to cost £20, was eventually taken away from the priory and lay for many years in an older St Edmund's church.

On the very backbone of England stands Dudley, on our great central watershed. It is said that from one side of High Street the rain-water flows into the North Sea, while from the other it finds its way into St George's Channel. It is one of a small group of streets we have come upon where this remarkable division of the water takes place.

Dud Dudley and Abraham Darby

THIS great town of iron has every reason to remember those two 17th-century ironmasters, Dud Dudley and Abraham Darby. Their lives overlap, their work was related, but each toiled independently of the other and took his secret to the grave. Dudley was one of the 11 illegitimate children of the fifth Earl of Dudley, who sent him to Oxford and in 1619, when he was 20, recalled him to take charge of his ironworks here.

In the midst of abundant coal Dudley, in common with the rest of the industry, was using charcoal to smelt iron. Our forests were vanishing so quickly that the bulk of our iron was imported from Spain and Sweden. Dud Dudley succeeded in using coal for smelting, first coking his fuel, it is believed. At Pensnett, at Cradley, and elsewhere he met with great success; but floods destroyed some of his works, rioters ruined others, charcoal-using rivals persecuted him with lawsuits, slanders, and injuries, and then came the Civil War.

Dudley followed the fortunes of Charles, fought in many battles, fortified cities, cast iron artillery, was captured, sentenced to death, escaped on crutches, and then, penniless and broken, secured support and cautiously resumed his work as an ironmaster. With the Restoration he failed to regain the patents granted earlier to him, but, poor and slighted, went to his grave with the knowledge that he alone possessed the secret which could make his country supreme in iron-producing. He died in 1684.

Abraham Darby was born in 1677 at Wrensnest, a Quaker farmer's son, and was put to kiln-building. With Dudley dead and

is secret lost, the country was still burning wood for iron-smelting
and importing its ore from abroad, together with the iron pots and
pans used for cooking in palace and hovel. Darby made fruitless
experiments in iron pot-casting, then went to Holland, source of our
supplies, and learned the Dutch method.

Returning, accompanied by skilled Dutch workmen, he established
a flourishing foundry, first at Bristol and later at Coalbrookdale in
Shropshire. At first he used only charcoal, but later he coked the best
available coal, improved the draught of his furnaces, and succeeded
beyond all hope in producing pig-iron in unprecedented quantities,
and converting it into excellent pots, pans, kettles, door-frames,
weights, pestles and mortars, and a wide range of implements for
farm and industry.

He died in 1717 at Madeley Court, leaving a great business to the
care of the ignorant guardians of his two little sons. Disaster followed
and the founder's son, the second Abraham Darby, had practically
to re-discover his father's methods. His son, the third Abraham
Darby, carried the work to triumphs unimaginable to the originator,
for, taking control in 1758, when only 18, within a year he constructed
the first iron bridge ever erected, spanning the Severn at Broseley,
near Colebrookdale. He died in 1791, leaving an England that no
more burnt her forests for the smelting of iron.

Here Five Bishops Sleep

ECCLESHALL. For centuries the home of the Bishops of Lichfield, five of whom sleep in its midst, it is surprisingly behind
the times, a town with an ancient market but three miles from a
station. The bishop's fortress-palace is only a remnant, but its church
remains one of the glories of the county, with Saxon and Norman
speaking from its stones, but with nothing to show that during the
Civil War it was a Commonwealth stronghold.

The Romans were the first to build here; Saxons came as
fierce pagans and stayed to raise a church, which the Danes
burned down. The Normans built another church, and civic life
was renewed.

The town has seen a sad day in the life of one of our queens. Here
in 1459 came Margaret of Anjou, consort of the hapless Henry the
Sixth, fleeing from the stricken field at Blore Heath, where the second

battle of the Wars of the Roses had resulted in the capture of the king. With her here was their only child, the little Prince of Wales who was to live to be murdered by Richard of Gloucester after the battle of Tewkesbury.

The Bishops of Lichfield, who are said to have lived here from the time of the early Saxons, had their manor house on the site where Bishop Walter Langton built the castle, a mighty structure whose wide moat, now a garden, is still crossed after 700 years by his beautiful two-arched bridges.

Round the castle and the church centred the life of the town until the Civil War came. Bishop Wright garrisoned the castle for Charles and died after having withstood a siege; the Parliamentary forces made the church their fort, without damaging it. Towards the end of 1643 the Cavaliers gained the town and shut up the Commonwealth men in the church, but hot on their heels came Parliament men from Stafford who captured the Stuart reinforcements and ultimately the castle itself. The old episcopal fortress was dismantled, and late in the 17th century was replaced by a fine house which continued to be the home of the bishops until last century. It is now a private house.

The magnificent clerestoried church, with a fine lychgate carved with roses in 1829, stands as a record of the ages. In the flower-bordered churchyard, under a granite cross, sleeps John Lonsdale, a much-loved Bishop of Lichfield for more than a quarter of the 19th century. The stones of the south wall are grooved by the metal tips of arrows sharpened on them by men who helped to make the bowmen of England the military lords of medieval Europe.

The great medieval tower, nearly 100 feet high and continued into the nave, where it is supported by three beautifully moulded arches on clustered pillars, rises from a 12th-century base. At the foot of the belfry steps is some Norman moulding, but the oldest treasures are the carved Saxon stones in the tower, in the south arcade, and, finest of all, in the 13th-century vestry, where a stone shows carvings of two men, one thought to be an archbishop and the other St Chad, shown in the act of mounting the horse on which he rode 1300 years ago.

Much 13th-century work remains, including a chapel and nave arcades with floral capitals. The modern marble reredos has a Crucifixion, five scenes from the life of Christ, and 12 Bible figures.

The chapel reredos has beautiful oak carving of our own day. There is a fine modern screen, and on the organ-case are two splendid angels with trumpets. Richly coloured modern glass fills 17 windows with Bible pictures.

The monuments include those of five Bishops of Lichfield; the battered figure brought in from the churchyard may be a sixth. The earliest is the 16th-century tomb with the engraved figure of Richard Sampson. Chaplain to Wolsey, friend of Erasmus, lawyer, ambassador, he earned the dubious distinction of standing high in the favour of Henry the Eighth by assisting him in the divorce from Catherine, and in the proceedings which sent Anne Boleyn to execution.

A finer character is recalled by the engraved figure on the tomb of Thomas Bentham, lying in his robes as he was known in the years just before the Armada. His figure is repeated on the side of the tomb, with his wife and four children. A great scholar, ejected by Mary Tudor from his fellowship at Oxford, he fled to Switzerland, but returned and bravely sustained London Protestants throughout the days of their persecution. With his two wives in tight hats and long robes, kneeling under arches in the wall above him, lies William Overston, in his bishop's robes, his head on a Bible. He was bishop during the Armada, and at the death of Queen Elizabeth had to encounter stubborn opposition to the reformed doctrine.

The next bishop, after the battered stone figure who may be Bishop Wright, was laid here after two centuries; he was James Bowerstead, who died in 1843, and lies under a beautiful canopy wearing his mitre, and his crozier in his hand. The last of the group, John Lonsdale, whose monument is in the churchyard, was one of the noblest of the line, a model of learning, humility, and tolerant commonsense. He ordained in this church 646 clergy and 567 deacons, and ended his long life dramatically in the midst of his work. As an old man of 78 he presided at a diocesan gathering and died in his chair immediately after.

At Slindon, two miles away, is a delightful little red stone church, with a stone figure of St Chad in an outer niche, a charming vaulted stone roof over the chancel, and an alabaster reredos with a carving of the Last Supper.

A Chapter of Tragic History

ELFORD. It is a little casket of wonder, splendour, and history. Not far away, without leaf or life but still upright when we saw it, is the famous Slang Oak, which the village believes to have been already a century old at the Conquest.

Elford Hall, a fine old building with tall chimneys, mirrored in the shining water before it, stands on the site of the house in which Henry the Seventh slept the night before Bosworth Field. In the church lies a brother of the man who crowned him on that snowy upland.

The village, a storied gem of the beautiful Tame valley, has charming old cottages with roses rioting over quaint porches and a splendid avenue of limes, a living aisle, leading to the church door.

The church, which we found still lit by candles, has its ancient tower, but the rest of the building was made new last century. Within it is a gallery of medieval glory, superb sculptures wonderful in beauty and eloquent with history. Magnificent examples of medieval carving, they were faithfully preserved in the 19th century by the skilled hand of Edward Richardson, who restored the figures of the Knights Templars in the Temple, London.

The modern work forms a worthy setting for this rich heritage. Under a beautiful oak canopy the font has eight angel heads. The new pulpit has panels showing the Crucifixion, Christ walking on the sea, and Christ entering the Temple. A delightful feature is the carving on a chancel capital. During the restoration the architect found that a swallow had realised the words of the Psalmist and near the altar had " made her nest where she might lay her young"; and in this charming picture in stone a mason has perpetuated the incident, showing the bird alighting on the nest, where with open beaks the young ones await her.

There are two brasses to rectors, one a portrait of John Hill, wearing the long cloak he wore in 1621 and a tablet to Francis Paget's 47 years last century.

Ancient Flemish glass in an aisle window has Joseph with his staff and a beautiful Madonna kneeling before a bishop. In a modern window kneel Matilda Camville, Matilda Vernon, Matilda de Arderne, Cicely de Arderne, and, in their tabards and cloaks, Sir R. Stafford and Sir Thomas Stanley, names linking us with the past.

The famous monuments are themselves milestones, in whose presence
we feel that

> *Meditation here*
> *May think down hours to moments.*

The earliest monument is the alabaster tomb on which lie Sir
Thomas Arderne, who fought at Poitiers, and his wife Matilda. He
wears plate armour and has on the front of his helmet the words
Jesu Maria. The sword in his hand is richly chased, and his gauntlet
has a diamond pattern. Like his wife he wears the SS collar. She has
a Plantagenet bonnet, a cloak, and a flowing robe, and her little
hand is clasped in his. At the sides of the tomb are 22 statues, 12
shield-bearing angels and 10 mourning kindred.

On a restored tomb lies the magnificent alabaster figure of Sir
John Stanley, builder of the north chantry. The statue, 15th-century
sculpture at its best, shows him in armour, his head resting on a helmet
with the crest embodying the Stanley legend of a child saved by an
eagle; every link of his sword-chain perfect, a tiny face clear and
winsome on its buckle, and the border of his tunic richly adorned.
It was his brother who was gaoler of Good Duke Humphrey's wife,
accused of attempting the life of Henry the Sixth by witchcraft; it
was he who at Bosworth with a diadem picked from a thorn bush
crowned Henry the Seventh on the battlefield; it was the beginning of
the dazzling Tudor dynasty, *The day was done, the dog was dead.*

Near his tomb is the most appealing of all these splendid works,
Sir John's little grandson, a curly-headed boy in a long robe, holding
a ball in one hand and pointing with the other to his temple, where he
was fatally struck by the ball when playing tennis.

A curious feature among this lavish beauty is a painting under an
arch in the chancel wall showing William Staunton between two
wives, one of whom was Margery Stanley, sister of the little boy
killed at play. The two women are small yet complete, but of their
husband only part of his body is seen.

Latest of the monuments is the alabaster tomb of Sir William
Smythe, who lies in armour between two wives, in flowing gowns, the
first wearing a three-cornered hat, the second in her coronet, for she
was niece of Warwick the Kingmaker.

It was a tremendous chapter of history that closed in the grave with her. Reared in the home of one of our proudest nobles, she shared the wildest vicissitudes of fortune; her father and the King-maker fell at Barnet, and their bodies were exposed for two days at St Paul's, to convince the country that the formidable brothers were really dead.

Then the proud beauty we see here was beggared by the confiscation of her father's estates, and her eldest brother, the heir, because of the poverty to which the family was thus reduced, was degraded from his rank, being declared incapable of supporting his title. Few women have known such crushing sorrows and reverses as she who rests here serene in her coronet.

A Village Which Knew Adam Bede

ELLASTONE. Immortalised in literature, it is a delightful village with houses looking into Derbyshire across the River Dove, and the Weaver Hills rising behind them to over 1000 feet.

It is of George Eliot that we think here, for she loved this place and made it the scene of some of the incidents in Adam Bede. This village was her Hayslope, Loamshire was Staffordshire, and what she called Eagledale was the romantic Dovedale with all its charm of cliff and wood. The village inn she wrote about is here still, and Donnithorne Chase was perhaps Calwich Abbey or Wootton Lodge, a mile away.

Her father, Robert Evans, who spent his early life here, was the Adam she portrayed so vividly; her uncle Samuel was the original of Seth Bede, and Samuel's wife gave George Eliot the idea of the story when recounting an incident in her career as an Evangelical preacher. Her grandfather's house remains, and though the famous workshop where her father was a carpenter has suffered an unhappy change there is something to recall the early chapters of Adam Bede. Samuel Evans's house has been much rebuilt, but Ellastone is a place for George Eliot's readers to wander in, its folk still much as she portrayed them, and a score of its houses the very picture of the one in which Mrs Poyser lived. In the churchyard we find her grand-father's tombstone.

The church in company with four fine yews has a tower of 1586 and a chancel finished two years later in Armada year; the rest has been rebuilt. Among its monuments are a medallion portrait of

Walter Davenport Bromley, a friend of the poor last century, whose ancestor let Wootton Hall to Rousseau for a year; there is a stone in the chancel to Bernard Granville of Calwich Abbey, the only neighbour Rousseau made friends with, and a tomb with the broken figures of John Fleetwood and his wife, who first turned the abbey into a home 400 years ago. Both have lost their hands and faces, and the knight's feet have gone, but he still has his armour and a weapon each side of him, and round his tomb are the family coats-of-arms. John died in 1590 and is not buried here, but his son Thomas built this memorial tomb and was himself buried under it.

Here Passed Many Famous Folk

THE story of Calwich Abbey begins in Norman England when a monastery was founded here beside the River Dove. We can trace the old fishponds, and here is a yew they may have planted, but the monks themselves were driven out in 1530, and John Fleetwood converted their abbey into a home and set an antiquarian writing:

> Calwich being a cell or house of religion,
> now a Lancashire gentleman is owner thereof,
> who, as I have heard, hath made a parlour
> of the chancel, a hall of the church, and a
> kitchen of the steeple.

In 1603 Richard Fleetwood was reigning at Calwich, and in the Ellastone church register we read of his marriage to a girl of six, whose first child was born and buried here before she was 13. A few years later James Stuart sold Richard a baronetcy in return for money for soldiers in Ulster, and Sir Richard, now turned Roman Catholic, decided that Calwich was too small, and had built for him the stately Wootton Lodge, still one of the finest houses in the county.

His son Thomas remained quietly at Calwich through the Civil War, though the rest of the family got into trouble by fighting for the king, and thus he was allowed to keep the third of his estate which had not already been forfeited because of his religion. But the early 18th century saw the last of the Fleetwoods of Calwich, and Bernard Granville arrived, pulled down the old monastery house, and built himself a new one by the stream, which he broadened into a lake.

A morose bachelor, he planted trees and added to his house and garden till Calwich was known as the prettiest place in Staffordshire and Derbyshire, and in spite of his taciturn temper, which became more extreme the older he grew, many were the famous guests who visited him here. Handel came often, and played on the organ he designed for his friend, to whom he gave a manuscript copy of his works in 38 volumes.

Then, in 1766, came Rousseau, to spend a haunted year at Wootton Hall near by, and to make friends with the only neighbour who could speak French with him. When Mr Granville closed his country house for the winter Rousseau so missed his friend that he filled the time by writing his immortal Confessions. As for the grumpy old bachelor, he missed the Frenchman equally when, crazed with fear of imaginary persecution and treachery, Rousseau fled back to France.

But there was one woman who was glad to see the last of Rousseau, and she was Mr Granville's sister, the matchless Mrs Delany, for she eyed with alarm Rousseau's gallantry to her favourite niece Mary Dewes, and the girl's obvious pride in the attentions of the great man, and certainly Rousseau's letters addressing her as the beautiful shepherdess of Calwich were a change from her Uncle Bernard's, which began *Dear Madam* and ended *Your most faithful humble servant*!

Mrs Delany loved Calwich, where she spent whole summers even after her marriage to the Irish don which so offended her brother. She chats about the house in letters which we may read today, as we may also see in the British Museum the wonderful collection of paper flowers which this great dame of the 18th century started to cut out when she was 74.

More glowing accounts of the house were written by Anna Seward, who came here when the bachelor's nephew had inherited Calwich. But in the 19th century it passed out of the hands of the Granvilles, and down came the house which had known the inimitable Mrs Delany and her devoted Irish husband, the immortal Handel (his gruffness softened here), and Rousseau with his furtive, restless eyes.

The Dancing Man

ENDON. It is the village of a man who danced more days and slept more nights than most of us, a scene of loveliness famous for its ceremony of dressing the well on the 29th of May, when Endon's oldfashioned holiday begins with a service in the church

STAFFORDSHIRE

and ends with dancing on the green. Another thing of which the villagers are proud is their own bit of the Cauldon Canal, said to be at this point the highest of any canal in England.

The church, high up with miles of beautiful country to see from its churchyard, has a fine east window by Burne-Jones, glowing with colour showing Mary Magdalene, Christ holding the world, and St John. The churchyard is the resting-place of old Will Willett. His more famous namesake of our own day saved the world hours of daylight, but Will Willett of long ago believed in darkness as well as in light, and enjoyed his hour of fame for having (as he said) danced for 12 days and nights in 1752. The truth was that his dancing began on the evening of September 2, when England altered the calendar and dropped 11 days, and ended on the morning of the next day, September 14.

Old Roger is Seen Again

ENVILLE. Looking out over village roofs the modern tower of Enville is built in the style of Somerset's famous towers, attracting us up the hill to the old and beautiful things in the church.

Oldest of all are two fragments of Saxon work in the wall, a bishop in a niche and a figure standing on a grotesque head. This figure is holding a type of fan used in the Eastern Church.

The bold arcades of the nave are Norman, and the rest of the church was rebuilt in the 14th century. Some fine carving is seen on the four old misereres in the chancel. One has musicians, another a scene of bear-baiting, another a horseman caught in a falling portcullis, and a man and woman praying with beads and a book. The armrests are carved with faces and animals. Oak panels in the modern reredos are inlaid with woods mentioned in the Bible.

Still sleeping here after nearly four centuries are the figures of Thomas and Anne Grey and 13 children, he with his long pointed beard and she with her pet dog pulling at her skirt. In a window above them are some figures in old glass, a Madonna, St John the Baptist, St Michael with the Dragon, and St James.

The carved figure of Roger de Birmingham, a 14th-century priest who rebuilt this chancel, has a thrill all its own, for when the church was restored last century and his tomb was opened they found his skeleton with some traces of his vestments and a cup and paten.

95

Two other memorials will interest the traveller in Enville. One is to Thomas Amphlett of 1763, a young merchant in the East India Company, who was barbarously massacred in " the confusion of the times"; the other is a tablet to William Wrighte, who died two years later, the youngest son of that Sir Nathan Wrighte who was Lord Keeper of the Great Seal of England.

Three stone coffin lids are lying in the churchyard, and part of the medieval cross still stands, with the flat, raised tomb of Peter Lafargue, a Huguenot refugee of 1711, close to it.

Not far from the church is Enville Hall, with a fine collection of paintings, and lovely grounds designed by the poet Shenstone whose brother was married before the altar at Enville. A mile or two away is Highgate Common, the largest unenclosed stretch of land in Staffordshire after Cannock Chase, and a splendid vista of heather and bracken in summer. By the roadside at Highgate Farm is a superb giant of old England, a spanish chestnut about 26 feet round.

The Wedgwood Village

ETRURIA. It is in the heart of the Potteries, a gloomy and somewhat sinister world of chimneys and kilns, but it is the birthplace of much that is beautiful, and the King of England is lord of the manor.

Here in 1769 Josiah Wedgwood founded the famous pottery works still carried on by his descendants. Here England's master potter built a village for his workmen and gave it its Italian name under a mistaken impression that a famous classical vase he admired and imitated was Etruscan. Here Wedgwood built up his business and made his name a byword for excellence throughout the world. Here he made his wonderful reproductions of the Portland Vase, one of the great Roman treasures of the British Museum. Here he perfected the processes which, combined with his excellent taste and technical skill, were to make his pottery the finest in the land.

Etruria Hall, where Wedgwood lived nearly a quarter of a century, happy in his work and in his friends, is still standing, although it is a house no more. It saw the passing of the great Josiah in 1795 and the birth of his famous son Thomas, who has been called the first photographer, chiefly remembered for his discovery of the use of light for making pictures. But he is also remembered as a generous

Great Barr   Barr Beacon

Croxden   The Medieval Abbey

Gentleshaw   Beaudesert Hall

The Straight Yew Walk

The Pleached Walk

THE BEAUTIFUL GROUNDS OF HOAR CROSS HALL

riend of genius, and generous were the tributes which genius paid to im. Sydney Smith knew of no man who appeared to make such an npression on his friends, and to Wordsworth he gave "an impression f sublimity." Thomas Campbell spoke of him as "a strange and vonderful being full of goodness." He died a few months before Trafalgar, and we come upon him at his grave in the ancient church f Tarrant Gunville in Dorset.

Hail and Farewell

FAREWELL. We greet it with delight and bid it farewell with a sigh. Its people walk in beauty. An enchanting scene it is, vith haystacks by a sparkling stream hurrying to the green meadows past the little church among the elms. The church, descendant of a priory founded by a 12th-century Bishop of Lichfield, was transformed in the 18th century, but has kept its 700-year-old chancel, the old altar rails, and four 13th-century oak stalls. The reredos has a painting of the Crucifixion in memory of a daughter of Henry Binfield, vicar of this fair farming village for 40 years. The neighbouring Hall is 18th century and has an oak staircase and grand oak panelling.

Sir Robert Peel Hears a Story

FAZELEY. A busy village on Watling Street, it has a church built by Sir Robert Peel, the great industrial pioneer who, in dedicating his famous son to the service of his country, gave his own name immortality. The church has an unusual clerestory with ten small windows shaped like clover leaves, and an east window of three lancets with figures of Paul and the Evangelists shining in memory of Cyprian Thompson, vicar for half of last century.

It was here one winter's day in 1825 that a child of three, leaning from the attic window of the village inn, fell to the pavement but was hardly hurt. On hearing of it Sir Robert Peel was greatly interested and related the story in a letter to his wife.

A Soldier of Garibaldi

FENTON. Stoke has swallowed up its streets, but not its fame. One of the busy Pottery centres, it is also noted as the birthplace of Whieldon ware, the beautifully coloured and glazed pottery fashioned here in the 18th century by Thomas Whieldon, master of Josiah Spode.

This home of skilled craftsmen was also the birthplace of an artist who has been called the greatest of the idyllic painters of England, George Heming Mason, son of a master potter, was born here in 1818. At 25 he set out on a Continental tour with his brother Miles, eventually settling in Rome and taking a studio. A change in the family fortunes forced him to seek a career with his brush and he managed to eke out a frugal existence at portraits.

When the Italian war broke out his brother Miles joined Garibaldi's army and he himself helped to nurse the wounded, narrowly escaping being shot as a spy during the siege of Rome. However, better times were in store and Mason rapidly became a successful artist. In 1858 he came back to England, married, and went to live at Wetley Abbey. His first painting after his return was the Wind on the Wold, once in the possession of his great friend Lord Leighton and now in the Tate Gallery. Henceforth the Staffordshire countryside was to be his inspiration, and the genius that had blossomed under blue Italian skies was to flower in the grey but softer air of his native land.

The County's Biggest Lake

FORTON. It is near the Shropshire border, nestling below a hill crowned by an ancient cone-shaped building called the Monument (nobody knows why).

The church, suffering at the hands of 18th-century builders, has an aisle 600 years old and a grand 15th-century tower with Norman stones in it. There is a fragment of a Norman font, and a fine tomb with figures of Sir Thomas Skrymsher, a 17th-century lord of the manor, and his lady. The knight is in armour, his head on a helmet, she is in a loose gown, and their nine children are with them. He is said to be descended from one of the Magna Carta barons.

There is a brass inscription to Mark Whitmore, who sang in the choir for 68 years. All through the Crimean War, the South African War, and the Great War he was singing here. A window with the Adoration of the Kings pays tribute to Sir George Boughey, who preached here 45 years in Mark Whitmore's time.

The churchyard has an ancient yew 17 feet round, and a glorious view with a stream winding its way through the fields toward Aqualate Mere and the deer park of Aqualate Hall. The Mere, with a Roman well close by, is over a mile long and 700 yards wide, the county's

ggest lake, a jewel of shining silver with an emerald setting where
e herons nest.

Two Friends of Dr Johnson

AILEY. It has given its name to three reservoirs alongside
Watling Street, the Gailey Pools, which serve the Stafford-
ire and Worcestershire canal. As lovely as natural lakes with their
inge of rushes and trees, they are the haunt of many water-birds,
nd at the last heron census 12 nests were counted.

There is a modern church with a carved oak pulpit, windows with
rightly coloured figures, and a brass tablet to Mary Elcock, a nurse
or 50 years.

But it is a doctor we remember here, for at Kinvaston close
y Robert James, a famous 18th-century physician, was born. At
ichfield he was a schoolfellow of Dr Johnson, who was to praise
is skill in ungrudging terms. "I enjoyed many cheerful and instruc-
ve hours (he said) with companions such as are not often found—
ith one who has lengthened and one who has gladdened life: with
Dr James whose skill in physick will be remembered, and with
David Garrick."

Dr James is best known as the inventor of a powder famous in
s day for the treatment of fevers. Oliver Goldsmith took some
uring the attack of fever from which he died, a fever which Dr
ohnson thought was really increased by financial worry. Poor
Goldsmith's apothecary believed the powder aggravated his con-
ition and a bitter controversy ensued. It did not, however, dim
he popularity of Dr James, and the powder was given to George
he Third in his pathetic mental collapses long afterwards.

AYTON. It is a tranquil village with a fine old church rather
badly treated by the 18th-century builders, who gave it a brick
ower and built a wall into the north arcade. It has kept its fine
Norman chancel arch and a 13th-century arcade; the plain font is
lso Norman. In the nave are some ancient tiles and in the chancel
s a battered figure of a 600-year-old knight.

In the churchyard is a tall yew perhaps 300 years old.

ENTLESHAW. It stands high up on Cannock Chase with
a brick church and a fine old hall.

The church has an oak reredos with stone panels of the Crucifixion,

the Annunciation, and the Resurrection, and a tablet to Elle
Woolley, a good and faithful servant for 54 years.

Beaudesert Hall, which once proudly looked through the trees i
a hollow of its great park, was once a palace of the bishops of Licl
field, but had been for many centuries the home of the Pagets.
few parts of the 14th-century walls remained, but the rest of the hou:
was Elizabethan with additions made by Henry Paget, who lost
leg at Waterloo. The hall is now dismantled.

Near one of the park entrances is a hill of 800 feet crowned by a grea
earthwork called Castle Ring, with a glorious view of eleven countie.

John Till Goes On Preaching

GNOSALL. It has a church which after 800 years of change
still one of the finest in Staffordshire, a stately building wit
much that is massive and a little that is delicately beautiful, all th
grandeur given it by the Normans, and grace added in the 15th cen
tury. Norman masons built its oldest walls and the four arches of th
central tower. There is Norman work in the south transept, with
fine triforium and two arches. The nave arcades are 13th century,
transept door is 14th, and the clerestory is 15th. The flowing tracen
of the east window is thought to be about as old, though the fir
portraits of Christ and the Madonna, with saints, prophets, an
angels, a soldier, a sailor, and a nurse, are a memorial to the heroe
of our own time.

The central tower is 15th century above its Norman arch, and wa
perhaps built by the men who raised the south chapel, now enriche
with a modern arcade. The roof timbers of the north aisle are ove
400 years old, and there is an ancient dug-out chest with three lock.

In this noble place lie a child and a soldier in stone, the child lyin
in a recess of the chancel, the knight dressed in crusading mail, h
head on a pillow, his feet on a lion.

A grand old servant of the church was John Till, whose name is i
enduring brass. He preached here for the first time in 1845, and wa
still preaching here when the 20th century came.

GREAT BARR. It has in its church, which has been rebuil
a painting of the Madonna and Child, sombre yet appealing
by Alessio Baldovinetti, an Italian artist of the 15th century who wa
skilful also at mosaic work. He invented a new way of mixing colour

but it was not a success, and some of his pictures have come down to us in bad preservation.

A mile or two from the church is Barr Beacon, perhaps the proudest possession of this little place, for it is the Staffordshire and Warwickshire peace memorial and belongs to the public. Rising to 700 feet, it is a glorious stretch of windy ridge, capped by beeches and a lookout platform with a toposcope. Here we can stand while our eyes range over England from Lichfield Cathedral to Dudley Castle and from Birmingham Town Hall to the Wrekin in Shropshire.

GREAT HAYWOOD. The two sights of Great Haywood are a bridge and an arch. What is known as Essex Bridge, built over the Trent by the Elizabethan Earls of Essex as a short cut to Cannock Chase, is low and narrow, with grey walls and recesses over the buttresses, safety-zones for humble folk who might be crossing when the noble lords came riding by. Years ago the bridge had 40 arches; today there are only 14.

There is little to keep us in the village, with its winding main street, but Shugborough Hall, a fine house said to stand on the site of a bishop's palace, has memories of one of our admirals. There is a Chinese temple in the grounds, but more notable is the impressive triumphal arch of stone and marble, a brother's tribute to George Anson, who was born here in 1697, sailed round the world, and came home to lie in the neighbouring church of Colwich. The arch has busts of Anson and his wife.

GRINDON. It is high up on the moors, among the everlasting hills and friendly valleys; much of the lovely countryside is in the keeping of the National Trust. Its modern church, with a bold spire soaring far above the sycamores bordering the churchyard, has a font adorned with roses and tracery, angels bearing up on the chancel roof, and a lovely iron screen. All these are modern; relics of the ancient church are two coffins and a battered Norman font.

The Victorious Little Army

HALES. High among the hills near the Shropshire border is Hales, so old that it is thought to be on the site of a Roman camp. Here a Roman certainly lived, for his house has been found in our time.

The Normans are said to have built Tyrley Castle hereabouts, though little remains of it; but still standing in pleasant grounds with a fine yew hedge is Hales Hall.

By a noble beech on a hillside stands the modern church, with a big chancel arch decorated with roses and leaves, its capitals finely carved; but it is a rough stone cross in a field a little way off that we come to see. Known as Audley's Cross, after Lord Audley who was in command of the Lancastrian Army, it was set up on a big pedestal in the 18th century, and stands on the site of the battle of Blore Heath, the second great fight of the Wars of the Roses. Here in September 1459 Richard Neville, Earl of Salisbury and father of the Kingmaker, came to blows with the Lancastrians. Neville had 5000 men and the Lancastrians twice as many, but the little army defeated the big one, victory going to the men of the White Rose.

Servant to Dr Johnson

HAMMERWICH. It remembers a man who gave us our Hospital Sunday, and the servant of our greatest talker. In memory of Thomas Barber Wright, originator of Hospital Sunday, is a cottage hospital; and in the church registers is the name of Charles Bird of Burntwood, who was proud to the end, we think, to tell that he was servant to Samuel Johnson in those hard days spent at Edial Hall in 1736.

The modern church has a beautiful west doorway in Norman style and an attractive chancel with a vaulted roof. From the churchyard with the stump of an old yew 12 feet round, we look over miles of fine country in the neighbourhood of Lichfield and Cannock Chase, on to the Peak, and into Warwickshire.

Small Village of Great Treasure

HAMSTALL-RIDWARE. Great treasures we found in this small village among the meadows near the River Blythe, one of the three villages named Ridware from an old word for river-folk. Its ancient cross on three steps has been restored as a peace memorial, and its Elizabethan manor house, now a farm, has a fine old gateway with two towers, the holes still in them for pigeons to come in and out.

Near by is the church on a gentle slope above the river. It has 15th-century aisles and a tower begun 600 years ago, its spire half as old. In the tower hang four bells, one with a Madonna and Child;

and over the tower arch is a deeply-splayed window in a Norman wall. The walls of the nave and chancel have stood 600 years, and have quaint medieval paintings on wood.

Much old glass shines in the windows. There are nine apostles in 16th-century glass, and three belonging to modern times. In the south chapel are two 14th-century women, one a queen; and more precious still are a few fragments in the north chapel, for they are thought to be 13th century. Both chapels are enriched with screens two or three centuries old, one showing two boys stealing apples.

We noticed an inscription to one who must have been descended from a race of mighty men, Thomas Strongintharme, who died in 1778; the curious name is still found in the west end of London. We were charmed with the fascinating tomb of Richard and Joan Cotton, of 1502. Painted on its shields are their eight sons and six daughters, each shield having an eagle and a portrait. Time was when the tomb had also little histories of the children, but only one can be read today, the brief story of the brief life of William, who was clerk to the King's auditor and died in London when he was 20.

One other treasure here is a 14th-century chalice dug up in 1823, and so beautiful that it has been on show at South Kensington. Close by is Pipe Ridware with two old yews by the new church, and in the church a splendid Norman font with interlacing bands.

The Great Families

HANBURY. It has in its church a veritable sculpture gallery of members of the aristocracy of Staffordshire, Hanburys, Agardes, Adderleys, and Egertons.

Under a richly decorated arch is Sir John Egerton in tunic and breeches. He died in 1662, and was a staunch Royalist, a worthy son of his father Sir Charles, lying here curly-haired since 1624. Sir Charles was axe-bearer in Needwood Forest, and his fine monument shows him in armour with a round shield.

Ralph Adderley wrapped the drapery of his couch about him and lay down to pleasant dreams as long ago as 1595. With him on his alabaster tomb are his two wives in Stuart dress, and his 15 children. The Agardes here are of the 17th century, their painted monuments with busts of a husband and wife and daughter, the man in a cloak and frills, his wife and daughter with broad black hats.

Perhaps the monument Hanbury treasures most is the tomb of Sir John Hanbury, a cross-legged knight in armour with his sword and shield. Sir John finished his fighting days in 1303, and his admirably sculptured form is thought to be the oldest alabaster figure in England.

The church in which these proud folk lie is 19th century, but has arcades 600 years older, and a font at which Sir John Hanbury may have been baptised. It has a modern alabaster case with a cross on each side. Scenes from the life of Christ adorn the chancel walls. In a niche outside the tower is a fine statue of St Werburgh holding a staff and book, a copy of a carving at Lichfield Cathedral. St Werburgh, a niece of Ethelred, King of Mercia, was prioress of a Saxon nunnery here of which no stone remains. Chester owes its Cathedral to her, for after sleeping here her body was removed to Chester and the cathedral begun as her shrine.

From the churchyard, with its old yew, we look out over the valleys of the Trent and the River Dove to the borders of Derbyshire, Leicestershire, and Notts. It is said that somewhere in this pleasant spot lies Leicestershire's earliest historian, William Burton.

From Cromwell to the Great War

HANLEY. It gave us Arnold Bennett, who has immortalised it in his story of the Five Towns. One of the busiest of the Potteries, it has little beauty of its own though it is for ever sending fine things to the ends of the earth.

Thrilling it seems to come to Hanley and turn from the street thronged with the potters of our own day to a priceless masterpiece made by a potter 40 centuries ago. In the Museum and Art Gallery here are many treasures, but the rarest of all is a great vase found at Ur of the Chaldees, perfect after over 4000 years. Among many wonderful things here is a collection of pottery, and a statue of Josiah Wedgwood holding a vase.

Hanley's church comes from the 18th century, its east window with a beautiful portrait of Christ in a rich purple robe. There is an inscription to Ino Middleton, its first rector, who died just before Trafalgar after being here for the astonishing period of 64 years, followed by Robert Ellis Atkins for 46 years. It would have been possible for the first of these rectors to have known a man who saw

Cromwell and for the second to have known a child living on into the Great War.

Shelton, once a little village, is now part of Hanley. It has a 19th-century church where the two things to see are a fine oak reredos with stone carvings of the Wise Men, and the east window with rich old glass showing scenes from the life of Christ.

It was at Shelton Hall that Elijah Fenton, one of the laziest of all Englishmen, was born in 1683. The youngest of 11 children of an attorney, he went to Newcastle Grammar School, published a volume of poems when he was 26, became a friend of Pope (for whom he translated four books of the Odyssey) and wrote a life of Milton. Dr Johnson said he would lie in bed and be fed with a spoon, and even Pope who wrote the epitaph for him in East Hampstead church declared that he died of indolence.

A Misfit in Vanity Fair

ENOCH ARNOLD BENNETT, novelist, playwright, and miscellaneous writer on life and books, was born at Hanley on March 27, 1867, and his best books picture the ordinary life of his early surroundings. After some years experience in a lawyer's office he went to London and, joining the staff of a weekly paper for women, brightened it by natural writing which showed a wide range of shrewd observation.

It was a short step from miscellaneous journalism to the writing of stories, short and long, and before he was thirty he had attracted many readers by his types of character representative of his native district. His Old Wives' Tale gave him a standing in fiction that seemed to promise lasting renown. It was true to life in a remarkable degree. Clayhanger kept the promise open, but its successors did not sustain it.

Heroically industrious, and determined to take the world by storm, Bennett launched out into fiction covering a wide range of subjects and style, into drama in which he gained considerable success, and he also wrote a number of small books giving hints for personal management of life, until he was one of the best known of living writers, wealthy and outwardly successful in a high degree. But his career was somewhat of a tragedy from the point of view of admirers of the Old Wives' Tale.

The life of no man is more open to the whole world than that o
Arnold Bennett. He kept a Diary which has been published, and i
conjunction with his books it shows him clearly as he saw himsel
He gained what he sought to gain, but his gains were those of a rathe
vain materialism. In essence he was a son of the Potteries and fron
them inherited a sense of humanity suggesting a noble use of hi
sensibility in literature. He was a marvellously acute observer an
a clever writer in a vein that every reader could understand. Bu
while he, with his keen observation of life, was telling people hov
to manage their lives he had no ideal for his own life worthy of hi
abilities. His aim was to be an artist in fiction, and he becam
Frenchified in spirit by study of French models. The vain shows o
wealth consummated his ambition. He found his paradises in th
best hotels and the proud possession of a luxurious yacht. He was
clever man but not a great man, and he lost his way because h
never realised what constitutes human greatness, though he hac
gleams of a true humanity. He lived for his work, and laboured i
making himself a misfit in Vanity Fair.

HARLASTON. Here is Haselour Hall, a charming picture witl
five gables and transomed windows and old timbers, all in
lovely setting. Inside is a priest's hiding-place and a wonderful oal
chimneypiece. On it are muzzled bears that have been climbing pole
since 1610, and panels showing the battle of Hastings and a boa
hunt. In the private chapel, which has stood since the 14th century
are grand old oak beams and an east window with three saints.

The attractive little church of this small village by the Rive
Meece has been mostly rebuilt except for part of the 13th-century
tower, which still keeps its timbered bell-turret.

The Royds Carry On

HAUGHTON. It has quaint cottages, old hall with timber
that have weathered all the storms since Tudor days, and a
church refashioned in the 18th and 19th centuries, but with a 14th-
century doorway and windows 400 years old. And Nicholas Graviner's
tower is still standing, while, lying in the church where he preached
till about 1520, is Nicholas himself, his portrait engraved in alabaster,
two angels supporting the cushion at his head.

In the church is a beautifully panelled old oak chest, and an altar table made from a cedar which fell in the rectory garden. One of the windows has the striking figure of a fighter pilot—Clement Fletcher Royds, RAFVR, who was killed in action in 1945.

For over a hundred years the rectory has been the home of the Roydses. Edward, who came in 1822, was followed in 1831 by Charles, who was laid to rest in the churchyard in 1879. Gilbert followed him as rector till 1922, a century after the first Royds preached his first sermon here; and after him came the fourth Royds, who was still caring for his church when we called.

The oldest of all old things hereabouts is on the way to Castlechurch—Berry Ring, a prehistoric earthwork of about seven acres.

HIGH OFFLEY. Three viaducts carry its only link with the modern world, which seems to be the Shropshire Union Canal. We come uphill to a church with stones that have weathered 700 winters. The east window of the south aisle is 13th century, the deeply-splayed west window a few years older. There is a Norman arcade with round arches on massive round pillars; and the tower, 17th century above and Norman below, has a pointed arch into the nave. Of four bells in the tower one is 15th century, and another has the prayer: *God save the church, our Queen and realm,*
And send us peace in Christ. Amen.

It came with its prayer in 1601; in 1603 it tolled for Elizabeth.

Crooked House

HIMLEY. Close to the park gates of Himley Hall stands the little 18th-century church, ugly with plaster outside but with an attractive interior. Its oak screen and panelling are excellent Georgian work; and it has a graceful lectern of brass given in memory of Edward Davies, rector here for 41 years. The font was given by village children.

About two miles away, among the coalpits and brick works of the Dudley road, is a remarkable inn. The Crooked House it is called; and crooked it is, for the mining operations underground have caused one end of it to sink several feet into the ground. How it stands up we do not know, but it is certainly one of the most astonishing sensations in the world to walk about this house. Astonishing things they will show you, too. One of the grandfather clocks is leaning

absurdly sideways, and another touches the wall at the bottom and
has to be more than a foot away at the top if it is to go. Most wonder
ful of all, they will start a ball rolling down an inclined table and
watch you gape as it turns back and rolls up again!

Holbeach House, on the Stourbridge road, is the modern successor
of a famous house in which the Gunpowder Plotters had their last
refuge, and the home of one of them, Stephen Littleton. The 13
conspirators arrived here tired and dispirited two days after the
capture of Guy Fawkes. Sir Everard Digby saw that they were in a
hopeless plight and went to hide in the woods, followed by Stephen
Littleton and two others. The rest stayed and were besieged by the
Sheriff of Worcestershire, who ordered the house to be set on fire.
Catesby and three others were shot dead as they dashed from the
building; four were captured, Digby and his followers were soon
found, and, with the remainder of the gang, executed in London.
Part of the old house remains, with two secret hiding places the
plotters doubtless knew and intended to use, one behind a fireplace,
the other next to the kitchen chimney.

Doctor's Advice

HINTS. It is a village on Watling Street, where a strange relic
was dug up one day in the 18th century—a lead pig weighing
150 pounds, with a Roman inscription. The loveliest corner is the
churchyard, superbly kept with a lawn like velvet and superbly
situated on a slope down to thick woods in the steep little valley of
Bourne Brook. It is a marvellous place to be at on a summer's day.

The peace memorial stands on the base of the medieval churchyard
cross, a fine linking-up of the centuries; but the inscription to our
heroes in the church takes us back far beyond medieval times, for it
comes from Thucydides, and was put here at the suggestion of a
farmer. These are the words:

> *These men dared beyond their strength;*
> *they hazarded beyond their judgment;*
> *and in the utmost extremity they were of*
> *an unquenchable hope.*

It is remembered that it was a boy of this village who grew up to
be the famous doctor Sir John Floyer. He was one of the cleverest
doctors of his time, the first to make regular observations of the rate

of the pulse, a great advocate of the benefit of cold baths, and he is remembered especially because it was he who advised Dr Johnson's parents to send their son to be touched by Queen Anne to cure him of disease.

The Wonder Our Own Age Has Given to Time

HOAR CROSS. Majestic oaks, survivors of Needwood Forest, crown the hill above it, and a stately tower seen from afar beckons us to a picture of surprising beauty.

Snug among its meadows and woodlands, the village has pleasant black-and-white cottages, and in place of the old moated manor is a fine modern hall with domed towers and tall chimneys, set in grounds beautiful with flower borders, shrubberies, luxuriant hedges, and charming walks, home of the Meynell Ingrams.

Yet the supreme glory here is the wonderful 19th-century church, which has been called the most beautiful modern church in England. In 1863 Hugo Meynell Ingram brought to the Hall as his bride Emily Wood, daughter of the first Viscount Halifax, and, dying eight years later, left her his estates here and in Yorkshire. The young widow gave the rest of her life to building to him a shrine which was to be as lovely as art and wealth and devotion could make it.

Designed by George Frederick Bodley, one of the architects of Liverpool Cathedral, the church is the work of a generation of building and the result is a very masterpiece, renowned for its architecture and sculpture, its craftsmanship in glass, metal, and wood. It is a building in rich red stone which, as the sun begins to set, glows with a dreamlike rosy loveliness. The deeply buttressed central tower, its embattled parapet 110 feet above the lawn, is a model of simple and massive dignity.

The exterior has three portrait statues. On a buttress, from which he appears to bless those who pass, St Chad has the head and features of the beloved George Selwyn, Bishop of Lichfield, who conducted the first service here. By the south porch, which has over it a Madonna and Child in a canopied niche, is a figure of Athanasius reading a book, the head a portrait of the founder's brother, second Viscount Halifax. On a column at the other side of the doorway is Bodley the architect, carved as St Basil. In the west chapel is a tablet to Bodley and his assistant Thomas Garner, and another, carved with a mallet, chisel, and other tools, to Robert Bridgeman, one of the workmen who helped to build this place.

In the churchyard, with its stone lychgate, its cross, its six dwarf yews, and one towering ash, is the tomb of the founder's brother, Frederick Lindley Meynell, who, having helped to build the church, raised his sister's monument and adopted her name. He lies under a floral cross with four lovely angels to guard him, a lifelike figure in his robes as High Sheriff of the county.

The outer aspect of the church arrests us by the dignity and restrained beauty of its lines, by its fine buttresses, and its great windows in tower, clerestory, and nave. The interior is a picture of old in new, of splendour and richness in which a little cathedral seems incredibly to have come straight from the 14th century. It needs but the mellowing of time to rank it with our supreme Gothic treasures. No slavish copy of a style, it reveals that joy in solemn loveliness, in exquisite form and colour which made medieval England so wonderful.

Arcades of beautiful aerial arches rise from lofty clustered pillars; the black-and-white marble floor catches a thousand hues from the sunlit windows. The font has an oak canopy whose carving challenges comparison with the finest old craftsmanship. Exquisitely chiselled, it rises like a delicate spire almost to the full height of the arch beside it, with three tiers of what look like belfries with flying buttresses, ending in a lovely pinnacle crowned by a pelican on its nest. Doors open into this fine canopy, the interior of which is richly decorated.

The beautiful stone pulpit, its canopy like a crown, is entered through the thickness of a great pier, which has been pierced for the purpose. The stone reredos, splendid with carving, has a Crucifixion, about which are grouped 16 canopied angels holding the chalice, crown, and emblems of the Passion. On one side are our patron saints, George being a copy of Donatello; on the other side are the British Saints Augustine, Columba, Anselm, and Paulinus, all wonderfully sculptured.

The beautiful chancel, its vaulted stone roof rich with bosses, is one great company of angels, saints, and martyrs. Sixteen angels seem to trumpet music from their niches on the wall; others carry sacred emblems, some sing, some swing censers, others appear to e sustaining the walls in place. Some serve by the tower arch, and they are on pillars and arches and in the windows, everywhere. The church is named after them, the Church of Holy Angels.

On either side of the magnificent altar are three carved seats under delicately chiselled arcades; and here is the bishop's carved oak chair. In the floor at the foot of the altar steps are the Meynell Ingram arms, lighted by the superb east window, with a central mullion in which, niche above niche, are delicately sculptured angels, the whole window framed in magnificent tracery under a deeply moulded arch. In the window is a host of saints.

The beautiful glass, all designed by Bodley and filling every window in the nave, the chancel, and the five chapels with colour, is a veritable gallery of loveliness. The windows show the Almighty giving blessing, scenes from the Passion, a Madonna with the Infant Christ standing on her knee to bestow a benediction, the Wise Men, the Kings offering their crowns, an Annunciation, St Elizabeth blessing the Madonna, Christ in the Temple and disputing with the doctors, Apostles, prophets, martyrs, and saints.

The woodwork is everywhere beautiful. Round the walls are 14 magnificently carved Stations of the Cross, almost the last work of two old master craftsmen in Antwerp. The screen, divided by the pillars of the tower, and extending in three sections across the church, with splendid iron gates in the centre, is a brilliant example of English craftsmanship. The organ, part of which came from Bangor Cathedral, is placed level with a chancel wall so as not to obscure the beauties of its setting, and is lavishly gilded and coloured, the pipes engraved.

In the vestry is a beautiful cross, the base of which is made of wood from Holy Land; the Chantry Chapel has a lovely ivory Crucifix which Fra Angelico may have handled, for it came from the scene of his life and artistic triumphs, the convent of San Marco at Florence. With the peace memorial, a bronze tablet framed by crowns and laurels, is an illuminated volume in which is entered not only the name but the personal history of each man who served, a proud possession for the village in days to come.

All this beauty and splendour is the common property of the village, which has here its own parish church, as free as if the villagers themselves had built and given all. Yet it is still a shrine, the crown and consummation of a woman's tribute to a man, and her thank-offering for her happiness in life. He himself lies in the Chantr Chapel, under a richly carved stone canopy, with angels guarding A splendid alabaster figure, he wears the uniform of the Stafford shire Yeomanry, over which is draped a military cloak, and at hi feet lies one of his hounds.

By him is the lovely alabaster figure of his wife, who survived hir 33 years, spending all this time in building this place. She lies unde a massive carved oak canopy, on a superbly sculptured altar tomb with the Madonna and Child, angels, rich heraldry, and the famil motto of One God, One King. The figure shows her serene an tranquil, as though conscious of a great task achieved. The head carved by Chevailleur and said to be a perfect likeness, rests easi on a cushion, with a drapery of lace falling over the shoulders the hands are raised in prayer. The dog at her feet was modelle from the little animal which was long her cherished companion.

Such is something of the wonder and beauty raised by a woman' love in this quiet remote Elysium. In very few of our ten thousan villages have we seen so worthy a memorial of our time.

The Meynells were Meynells for centuries before adding Ingra to their name. They were in all the wars. They had a heroic repre sentative at Crecy and Poitiers. Here they have an echo of the day in which they were at their doughtiest, and we may feel that nothin more beautiful than this was done by those craftsmen of old who ha the generations and centuries in which to build, to better, and t make perfect. Time has given us many wonders; here is a wonde which our own age has given to Time.

A Soldier of the King

HOPTON. It is on a hill three miles from Stafford, with a littl church fashioned out of a barn, and a great history, for Hopto Heath was the scene of the only big battle fought in Staffordshir in the Civil War.

On March 19, 1643, a Royalist force led by the Earl of Northamp ton repulsed the Parliamentarians. Many of the slain, both Cavalie and Roundhead, were buried in the neighbouring churchyards o Sandon and Weston. Among the Royalist casualties was the Earl o Northampton, who was surrounded when his horse was shot bu refused to surrender, and fought bravely to the end. The earl's sor

Hoar Cross   The Hall and Gardens

Hoar Cross   The Grave of Frederick Meynell

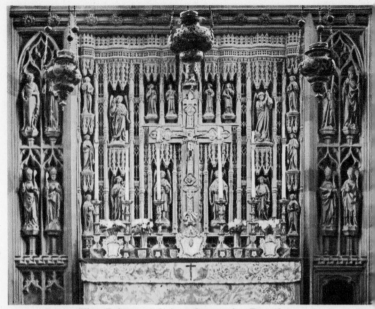

The Saints and Angels on the Reredos

The Chancel Screen   Font and Cover   The Founder's Tomb

THE LOVELY MODERN CHURCH AT HOAR CROSS

oung Lord Compton, who was also wounded, wrote to his mother wo days later, mentioning nothing of his own wounds but telling of is father's death. " Our loss is not to be expressed," he wrote, " for hough it be a general loss to the kingdom, yet it toucheth us nearest. 'ray, Madam, let this be your comfort, that it was impossible for anyone to have done braver than he did. Think that no man could nore honourably have ended his life to be partaker of heavenly oys. We must certainly follow him, but can hardly hope for so orave a death."

The Sad Little Poet of Spring

HORTON. It is near the lovely Rudyard Lake after which Kipling was named, and it is the last resting-place of Staffordhire's own poet of the moorlands.

The church, mostly 16th century, although its north aisle is a century older, has a plain medieval font, a simple 15th-century screen in the tower arch, and a 400-year-old brass of John Wedgwood with his wife and eight children. The churchyard has an ancient yew over 20 feet round and a timbered lychgate. Here is a grey stone elling us (we need not believe it) that Mary Brooks was 119 when she was laid to rest in 1787, and near by is the grave of George Heath, the poet they brought here nearly a century later, when he was only 25. He was born in the spring, and in the spring he died. As a boy he worked on his father's farm, but later he became a builder's apprentice, and it was while he was helping to restore this very church that he caught the chill which led to his death from tuberculosis. He was writing poetry when he was 20, and published a book of Simple Poems when he was 21, but his story is one of tragic unfulfilment, and sadness was the keynote of his work.

In his diary one day in May 1864 he wrote " Praise God for one more day," and on the following day his spirit fled. The grey stone cross above his grave has these few lines found among his papers, among the best lines he wrote :

> His life is a fragment—a broken clue.
> His harp had a musical string or two;
> The tension was great, and they sprang and flew,
> And a few brief strains, a scattered few,
> Are all that remain to mortal view
> Of the marvellous song the young man knew.

I 113

The Happy Valley of Rasselas

ILAM. With a rich heritage of natural beauty it is a little wonder land of charms and interests. It has Saxon relics and a master piece of 19th-century art; it was the birthplace of a famous play and the inspiration of an immortal book; it was the last home of a saint it knew William Congreve the dramatist and the poet Charles Cotton and it saw Boswell and Dr Johnson arm in arm, with the doctor disbelieving the evidence of his own eyes.

Spread out before it is the glory of Dovedale, and, adding mystery to beauty, here the Rivers Manifold and Hamps, after an underground journey of several miles from Darfus Crags, rise from the earth unite, and tinkle away to join the Dove at Ashbourne. So lovely i this scene of the rebirth of the lost rivers that it bears the name o Paradise.

It was Jesse Watts-Russell who last century remade the splendid Tudor hall, with its lofty tower and turret and high twisted chimneys Standing in fine timbered grounds above the meeting of the waters it looks out across the river to the grandeur of the hillside woods beyond, itself a stately landmark in a picture of rare beauty, with a spring named after the saint in the church, and a heronry which had 13 nests at the last census. The hall and its 50 acres of grounds now belong to the nation, the gift of Mr Robert McDougall, who has given us so much of Dovedale.

The village was rebuilt by Jesse Watts-Russell while he was remaking the hall. At the heart of things, near the tree-shaded bridge spanning the Manifold, he raised in memory of his wife a fine Eleanor cross, 30 feet high, with four figures of women in its four niches. He added a fountain, with the inscription:

> *Free for all these crystal waters flow.*
> *Her gentle eyes would weep for others' woe.*
> *Dried is that fount; but long may this endure*
> *To be a well of comfort to the poor.*

The fine church is in the grounds of the hall, a veteran cedar growing by it, 15 feet round; the churchyard itself is as a garden, fair with yews, hawthorns, and a thriving monkey puzzle.

Here are treasures rich and rare; side by side stand two lichened Saxon crosses. One, 7 feet high, has figures on two sides and two birds beak to beak.

Restored last century by Sir Gilbert Scott, the church, with three chapels, has still the 13th-century base of its tower, and a wall of the same age. Its most ancient jewel is the wonderful font, so old that it is Saxon or Norman, the round bowl carved with humans and dragons.

A famous 13th-century monument, guarded by railings, is the shrine and tomb of St Bertram, whose fame was so great that for long pilgrims from afar came here to lie stretched on his tomb, in hope of cure or consolation.

On a 17th-century tomb in another chapel lie Robert Meverell, in breeches and tunic with ruff and cloak; and his wife in a long flowing dress and a ruff.

Kneeling on a wall monument with her four children is their daughter, who was married to a descendant of Thomas Cromwell and related to a greater Cromwell, for her brother was the husband of Dorothy Cromwell of Hinchingbroke, aunt of the great Oliver.

One who was born early enough to know Lady Cromwell and her children, Robert Port, sleeps in the chancel with a generous inscription by Charles Cotton, one of Charles Lamb's poet heroes, friend and collaborator of Izaak Walton. In it are these lines:

> Here, reader, here a Port's sad relics lie
> To teach the careless world mortality;
> Who while he mortal was unrivalled stood,
> The crown and glory of his ancient blood;
> Fit for his prince's and his country's trust,
> Pious to God, and to his neighbours just;
> A loyal husband to his latest end,
> A gracious father and a faithful friend;
> Beloved he lived, and died o'ercharged with years,
> Fuller of honours than of silver hairs;
> And to sum up his virtues, this was he,
> Who was what all we would but cannot be.

The most beautiful picture in the church is in the octagonal chapel designed by Chantrey, with a charming vaulted stone roof supported by eight praying angels. Here is the great sculptor's lovely white monument of David Watts, raising himself from his deathbed to murmur a last blessing on his daughter, the woman in whose memory the village cross and the fountain were raised.

She kneels, a graceful figure of wistful solicitude, looking up at her father as he lays his hand on her head. With her are her three delightful children. A little boy cranes his neck in order to see round the Bible, which, slipping from the pillow, obstructs his view of his grandfather; the youngest, overcome with grief, buries its head on the sorrowing mother's knee.

A moving tribute of affection hangs in a chapel arch—two old paper wreaths and two pairs of white gloves, which, with rustic piety and poetry, it was customary to leave in church after they had been used at the funeral of a young girl. It was such a wreath as this that was allowed Ophelia in Hamlet, and comes into the scene in which Laertes denounces the churlish priest.

When the 17th-century chapel was built round the 13th-century shrine of the saint the hall and the park belonged to the Congreves, and here came William Congreve, a youth of 18, to recuperate after an illness. In a grotto in these grounds he wrote his brilliant but reprehensible comedy, The Old Bachelor, which established him as the first wit of the age.

This comedy was among those singled out for censure when a little outlawed parson, Jeremy Collier, in his tremendous Short View of the Stage, scourged the Restoration dramatists in general and Congreve in particular. Congreve's defence that the play was written " to amuse myself in a slow recovery from a fit of sick ness " brough Collier's retort, " What his disease was I am not to enquire, but it must have been a very ill one to be worse than the remedy." The gallant little parson cleansed the stage at a blast.

Congreve passed majestic to his grave in the Abbey while Samuel Johnson was a threadbare starveling at Oxford, 50 years before he sat down to write the dramatist's life, and to pooh-pooh the story of The Old Bachelor as the composition of an invalid. Johnson was himself strangely linked with this spot. When he was 68 he made Boswell accompany him here from Ashbourne, astonishing him in advance with his minute description of the history, romance, and grandeur of the scene.

They explored the grounds, they were shown the place where Congreve wrote the play, and they saw the two rivers rising from the rocks. Johnson would not believe that they changed their course from the open air to passage underground, though, as Boswell wrote, they " had the attestation of the gardener, who said he had put in corks where the Manifold sinks into the ground, and had caught them in a net placed before one of the openings where the water bursts out."

Yet Johnson knew Ilam so well that the grounds of the hall had already inspired him to one of his most heroic achievements. When he was 50 and poor, and his mother lay dead, he wrote his only novel, Rasselas, in order to earn money for her burial and the payment of her debts, 45,000 words in the evenings of a single week. Here is his golden valley, which he transports to Abyssinia; without it there would have been no Rasselas.

It is interesting to remember that when Lord and Lady Cromwell lived at Throwley Hall they lent books from their library to Thomas Tomkinson, son of one of their farmer tenants here. He was a Puritan, but hearing of the teaching in London of Lodowicke Muggleton, who had founded a strange new religion, he joined them in denouncing Puritanism and all other creeds and became a Muggletonian.

Such was the name of the little community that came into being to preach, among other dogmas, that God left man to look after himself, and had made His last revelation to Tomkinson's cousin Reeve. A man of real ability, this farmer's son was the chief pillar of the Muggletonians, and among his writings was a poem of 26 stanzas entitled " Joyful News from Heaven, for the Jews are Called."

A Village Church by Wren?

INGESTRE. Bounded by the Trent, the beautiful park embraces the cottages, the stately hall, and the fine church.

Long the home of the Chetwynds, the hall passed to the Earls of Shrewsbury. Fire destroyed the Tudor house last century, but the new one, charming with its domed turrets and handsome bays, is like its predecessor. In this house with its famous gardens King Edward the Seventh spent pleasant holidays, at times driving over to Alton Towers, the still more famous home then belonging to his host.

Among precious documents destroyed in the fire were those relating the story of the church, which is believed to have had Sir Christopher Wren as its architect. The style of the building, its mastery of proportion and subordination of decorative to constructive detail, satisfy the experts that the church is either Wren's or that of an unknown contemporary who left only this one masterpiece. Village

tradition assigns the plan of the church to the architect of St Paul's
though the church was actually built by Walter Chetwynd.

Beginning his work in 1673 and seeing it completed three year
later, Chetwynd contrived that on the day of its consecration all th
sacred rites, baptism, marriage, and burial, should be solemnised
He sleeps amid his work, with an alabaster tablet to his memory.

There are many Chetwynd and Talbot memorials, among th
most notable the marble tomb on which lies the fine bronze figur
of Viscount Ingestre, who died in 1915 and is shown in the uniform
of the Royal Horse Guards, with his streaming red-plumed helme
below. Lord Talbot, who died in 1849, lies on an altar tomb i
his robes as lord-lieutenant; the 18th Earl of Shrewsbury lies in a
ermined robe, and another fine monument is to Lady Victori
Talbot, who died in 1856. The sanctuary window, with fine glas
showing the Nativity and the two St Johns, is in memory of th
19th earl.

A charming plasterwork ceiling with fruit and flowers spans th
roof of the nave; a fine old oak chancel screen is carved with flower
and angels; the old canopied oak pulpit has fruit, flowers, and angels
and cherubs, flowers, and fruit adorn the chancel's rich oak panelling

John Sneyd's Ten Thousand Larches

IPSTONES. A gem of the moors, it lies among grand scenery or
the breezy slopes of Ipstones Edge. It has many lovely old grey
houses: Whitehough, a farmhouse built the year before the May
flower sailed; Sharpcliff, long hidden in the trees; and Moss Lee
with a grand oak staircase made in Cromwell's day.

The church, made new in the 18th century, has a Norman tympanum with two fighting dragons. The finely carved oak pulpit with
a lectern, and a grand screen completely filling the chancel arch, are
all modern, and the lovely 20th-century chancel has some fine fres-
coes painted during the Great War. Over the arch is Christ in Glory,
the throne surrounded by a great concourse of angels and disciples,
saints and prophets, while on the east wall is a charming Annunciation. The east window has more saints in memory of John Sneyd, a
19th-century vicar.

Many generations of his family lie in this church, among them the
John Sneyd who planted thousands of trees and beautified the rugged

moorland hereabouts. Many of the larches, veterans of the noble army of ten thousand he planted here, are still thriving.

At the foot of a steep hill close by stands Chapel House, which, with its traceried windows and its low tower, looks strangely like a church.

Elijah Cope, one of Staffordshire's poets, was born in this village, the son of a gardener who gave him the Bible as his only book of lessons. He grew up to teach woodcarving in the neighbouring villages, and became an authority on the folklore of the moorlands. He wrote many poems, and his Elegy on George Heath, another Staffordshire poet, was praised in a kindly letter from Tennyson. He died in 1917, but his simple charm and kindly character will long be remembered in these parts.

The Wonderful Hedge

KEELE. It was for centuries the home of the Sneyds, a fine old Staffordshire family. Their grand old hall (destined to be the University College of North Staffordshire) hides its Dutch gables in a park graced by an avenue of deodars and a wonderful holly hedge, 500 feet long and over 20 feet high. The church, where many generations of Sneyds have been baptised and buried, was made new in the 18th and 19th centuries. It has a slender tower with a spire soaring 130 feet, and a fine iron screen to the memory of Henry Sutcliffe, rector here for nearly half of last century. The figures of the Elizabethan William Sneyd and his wife, which the 18th-century builders had left under the church floor, were rescued after many years of oblivion and are now back on their altar tomb, battered but serene.

Here Died the Lord of Godiva

KING'S BROMLEY. An enchanting village near the Trent, it has borne its proud name since Saxon days. Here the husband of Godiva had a house, and here he died a few years before the Conquest, his body being taken to his church at Coventry.

The Normans built here worthily, and although their church was reshaped in the 14th century and again in the 15th, when it was given a new tower and a clerestory, their south wall and one of their windows can still be seen. The church has a 17th-century font and pulpit, some plain old stalls, and a fine modern reredos. There is a lovely screen with fruit and flowers and heads of monks, some of its carving being 16th century and some of it new. In an aisle window are lovely fragments of ancient glass showing a man and a boy with golden hair, a monk and a nun, and St Giles stroking a hart. On the chancel wall is a wooden cross from Flanders fields. The churchyard has a cross on a medieval base, and an archway of ancient yews.

The Bad Old Days

KINGSLEY. It is on a hill with collieries below it and the glory of the Churnet valley spread before it like a panorama. It has a hall two centuries old hiding among the trees of its great park, and an ivied rectory which is now a farmhouse.

The refashioned church has kept the tower set up 600 years ago. Here is a tablet to the memory of brave Rowland Beech, who was killed while leading men to the rescue of others stranded in mine-shattered trenches near Ypres. There is an ancient wooden sundial on the tower wall, and by the churchyard gate are grim relics of the bad old days: a stone pillar with a ring to hold any village malefactor who needed a whipping, and blocks of stone to which the hapless beasts were fastened in bull-baiting days.

The Norman Dragon

KINGSWINFORD. It has some pleasant corners and an old house or two to keep company with the ancient possessions in the church. Several treasures this modern building has, the oldest a Norman tympanum carved with a quaint St Michael thrusting his sword into the dragon's mouth. The saint has enormous wings and the dragon looks only too ready to receive the sword. There is an old chest with exceptionally fine carving, and a Breeches Bible with the famous verse telling how Adam and Eve "sewed fig tree leaves together and made themselves breeches." A brass plate tells of William Thomas Abbot, who was parish clerk for 56 years and head-master for 33; and on these walls we come across the name of Addenbrooke. One of this family, John Addenbrooke, was born here in 1680 and grew up to found the great hospital bearing his name at Cambridge.

The steps and shaft of a medieval cross are in the churchyard, and on an outside wall of the church is a simple memorial to Jim Horton, a seaman of HMS Hood, who was drowned in an ice-bound pool while saving the lives of four choirboys.

In the new church along the road at Wordsley is a fine piece of craftsmanship made of alabaster and Caen stone. It is in the reredos, a sculptured group of the Wise Men and the Shepherds round the cradle, with saints and little angels under canopies at the sides. Altogether there are 29 figures, as well as a delightful little lamb fast asleep in the foreground.

The Prehistoric Hill

KINVER. A little town of hills and views, it is beloved by those who come here from the Black Country. The church is perched high above the streets, and from it we get a magnificent outlook across the Stour, the houses winding far below and Dudley Castle on the skyline eight miles away.

The bold hill jutting out is Kinver Edge, the property of the nation today and once the property of prehistoric men who lived in the camp of seven acres on the summit. Very ancient, though perhaps not prehistoric, are the inhabited dwellings in Holy Austin Rock, rooms hewn out of the solid sandstone and made with the help of a few bricks into homes for several families. Uncanny they look with the smoke curling up out of the hill.

The church is mostly a 14th- and 15th-century building, though the great brick arches in a chapel are ugly relics of the 18th. The roodloft staircase, cut open and exposed to view, is thought to be Norman. The pulpit was carved in 1625. Hanging on the wall is a charter granted by Charles Stuart in 1629, freeing the people of Kinver from certain taxes.

The fine group of brass portraits shows us Sir Edward Grey of 1528 with his two wives, seven sons, and ten daughters; and the damaged figure lying in the Foley chapel is John Hampton, who died in 1472. A staunch Lancastrian, he was squire to Henry the Sixth, ranger of Kinver Forest, constable of Chester Castle, and one of the trustees for the building of Eton College. He built the chapel in which he lies, and it is thought he was also the original builder of Stourton Castle two miles away. Now much modernised, it was the birthplace in 1500 of Reginald Pole, the man who was a cardinal in Italy while

England was Protestant and came home to be Archbishop of Canterbury in Mary Tudor's fearful reign.

The Cardinal Extraordinary

REGINALD POLE was born at Stourton Castle in 1500, a younger son of Sir Richard Pole, who had links with the Tudors and married Margaret Plantagenet, the last of unblemished descent of the royal house. She was a niece of Edward the Fourth.

Henry the Seventh having removed her brother from his path, Henry the Eighth gave her great estates, made her godmother and governess of the future Queen Mary, created her Countess of Salisbury, and helped with money and supervision the education of Reginald. From the outset Reginald was destined for the Church, and while still a youth was presented with various livings by the King; yet he became only a deacon, although Henry had marked him out for the archbishopric of York after Wolsey.

At first Pole seemed to favour the King's divorce, but, living abroad without fear, and realising that the divorce could not be attained without the separation of England from Rome, he sacrificed his prospects by writing a treatise vehemently condemning the proposal. Retiring to Italy, he was made a cardinal and sent to stir up Spain and France to invade England. His missions were fruitless except that they brought disaster to his family at home, where Henry beheaded his two brothers and then his mother for complicity in the plots he had set on foot. Meanwhile Pole was dogged about Europe by would-be assassins in the pay of Henry. Sir Thomas Wyatt, the English ambassador in Spain, poet and gentle wit though he was, was long busy in Madrid for the murder of the hated cardinal.

The Pope gave him a pension and a bodyguard, and sent him as mediator between the warring kings of Spain and France. The years passed on and Pole was still a refugee from his native land, though so great a figure in Europe.

Twenty years passed; Henry and Edward the Sixth were dead and Mary was married to Philip of Spain before the cardinal again set foot in England. He had twice been proposed as the husband of Mary; he had twice narrowly missed being elected Pope, once by his own choice. Now he returned as the Pope's representative to preside

Haughton : Nicholas
Gravinar, 1520

Sandon
Hugh and Elizabeth Erdeswicke, 1500

Uttoxeter : Thomas
Kynnersley, 1510

Mavesyn Ridware : John and
Elizabeth Cawarden, 1485

Sandon
Hugh and Cecile Erdeswicke, 1473

Mavesyn Ridware : David
and Maud Cawarden, 1557

OLD STAFFORDSHIRE FOLK ENGRAVED IN STONE

over that almost incredible scene at which Protestant England, through its Parliament, implored forgiveness of its sins and entreated him to readmit her into the Roman Church.

In the same week that Cranmer was burnt at the stake the Cardinal of England was made a priest, and in the choir of Bow church was consecrated Archbishop of Canterbury in the martyr's stead. When Philip finally left England he left Pole virtually in charge of the nation's affairs.

What part the new Primate actually had in the martyrdoms of Mary's reign is not definitely known, but from the time of his becoming Mary's supreme adviser the persecutions increased in violence and horror. Towards the end he was superseded as legate and ordered to appear before the Inquisition on a charge of heresy, but the issue was left undecided. Mary Tudor died at seven o'clock on the morning of November 18, 1558, and he died at seven in the evening of the same day. England was well rid of both.

It was Protestant England under Elizabeth that laid his body in state for a month at Lambeth Palace, and then bore it with regal pomp for burial in Canterbury Cathedral.

The Old Dutch Font

L APLEY. It has something of a Saxon priory and something of a Norman church, and is a picture of rural beauty. It has also three fine houses, Lapley Hall, Lapley House, and Lapley Castle. It is the hall that has the remains of the priory, one traceried window still surviving from Saxon days.

The castle is a fine turreted and battlemented building, but it is Lapley House to which the romance of history clings. Although modernised, it has much that was here when the Commonwealth managed to gain possession of the house and to possess the church. In 1643 the commander of the Royalist garrison at Chillington Hall, three miles away, guided by an old servant, came marching at dead of night with his musketeers. Seven men scaled the walls, dropped in the midst of a company of startled defenders, overpowered them, threw open the gates, and stormed the house. They took captive also the Parliament men who were holding the church.

In the lime-shaded churchyard is part of an ancient cross 15 feet high, but it is the magnificent central tower by which our attention

riveted. The church, built by the Normans for the priory they
found here, has still the base of the tower placed in position by these
old masters; it was the 17th century which completed it as we see it,
with its quatrefoil windows and a band of ornament below the
stately parapet.

One Norman window is perfect in the chancel, which has a notable
13th-century window of five lancets, an interesting study in the progress from plain masonry to elaborate tracery. The old Dutch font,
sculptured with scenes from the life of Christ, including an admirable
Nativity and Wise Men, is the mystery of the church, for nobody
knows how it came here. In the chancel is an ancient engraved
figure of a priest; and one of the county's three sanctus bells
hangs here, apparently old enough for the unknown priest to have
set it ringing.

On a wall in the nave are traces of a painting the old priest may
have seen; and it is possible that a beautifully carved priest's door,
with four regal portraits and an angel trampling Satan underfoot,
opened to let him in and out. There is also grand old oak in the
chancel screen, the altar table, and the wonderful reredos.

Moorland Capital

LEEK. It lies on a hillside slope near the head of the Churnet
valley, a delightful town in a setting of natural grandeur. The
Capital of the Moors, it is faced on the north by the rugged group of
sinister-looking heights called the Roches, like the turrets and
battlements of huge forts raised by a race of Titans.

The Five Clouds, 1500 feet high, outsoar the rest, but the Hen
Cloud, solitary and apart, is by its isolation the most impressive in
its stark mass and mystery. The form of a section of the range is
responsible each midsummer for apparent double sunsets, a rare
phenomenon. On three successive June evenings the sun disappears,
eclipsed by a flank of Bosley Cloud, and then, having continued its
western way, reappears beyond another flank, and, slowly vanishing
again, seems to set a second time.

With what awe the first people here must have witnessed this seem-
ing miracle as they watched from where we find the remains of their
prehistoric camps at Tittesworth Farm. Still more marvellous to
them, perhaps, would have appeared the fine lake-like reservoir

which modern engineering has constructed near the site of the ancient homes.

The camps are silent; and the homes of a long line of owners have vanished. Until the Dissolution the town belonged to an Abbey founded in 1214 by Ranulph, the famous sixth Earl of Chester, who figures in Piers Plowman.

He carried the sword at the coronation of Lionheart, was present at the crowning of King John, and stood by his deathbed and witnessed his will. He was at the coronation of Henry the Third. As a Crusader he built Chartley Castle, and was a national leader in war and statecraft. At first the foe and then the saviour of Hubert de Burgh, he died in 1232 and sleeps at Chester, but his heart was buried here in the abbey he built.

Only fragmentary ruins of the abbey remain, but in the walls of a farm and its outbuildings are finely carved stones, bosses and gargoyles, long dear to the abbot lords of Leek. Near the farm is a fine timbered house of 1612; and in the same area is a rocky hermitage with traces of a fireplace, chimney, and doorway, where an anchorite once kept his solitary vigil.

It is believed here that but for the development of its industries Leek must have outrivalled Buxton as a health resort and beauty spot. Health and beauty it still has, and fortune has blessed it with famous silk manufactures, introduced by Huguenots in the 17th century. There are broad streets, a fine public square whose markets have been noted for centuries, and five parks and recreation grounds, among them one of the most beautiful public enclosures in England. There are quaint 17th-century almshouses, some more modern, and an 18th-century grammar school. The 19th-century Nicholson Institute, with its domed tower, has a library, art gallery, and museum with a rich array of fossils, birds, animals, and fantastic figures, and a magnificent collection of Burmese carving.

A low gabled house of yellow stone, with round-headed windows, makes a fascinating picture, but the most interesting of the old houses has become a shop, that in which was born, in the year of the Great Fire, Thomas Parker, first Earl of Macclesfield. The son of a lawyer, he was Chief Justice and Lord Chancellor, but in 1725, two years after founding the grammar school here, he was impeached for corruption and fined £30,000. He retired into private life ut was allowed to be a pall-bearer at the funeral of Sir Isaac Newton.

One of the most beautiful modern additions to the town is the lofty clock-tower in the cattle market, the peace memorial raised by Sir Arthur Nicholson in memory of his own son and all the sons of Leek who fell in the war. Of white stone, it looks, as we catch sight of it from the top of Derby Street, like a smaller edition of the Campanile at Venice. The fine Butter Cross, 20 feet high, now in the cemetery, has an inscription telling that it was the gift of J. Joliffe in 1671.

St Edward's, the mother church of the town, is a splendid building, with eight pinnacles crowning the noble 14th-century tower, in which ten silvery bells make the town ring with their 14 tunes.

In the churchyard, with its 17th-century arched and pinnacled gateway, is the magnificent 12-foot shaft of a cross supposed to be Saxon but possibly Danish. A smaller Saxon cross still reveals its ancient knotwork, and in the church when we called were fragments of carved Saxon stones from the original building lying on the floor. Resting against an outer wall of the chancel we found a coffin lid, inscribed HQCC 1180, said to be part of the coffin of the father of Ranulph, builder of the abbey. The churchyard is famous for another stone with a story. Raised to the memory of William Trafford, who died in 1697 at Swythamley Hall, it is carved with a man, a flail, a sheaf, and the words "Now Thus," the legend being that Trafford, an ardent Royalist, when discovered at his home by Commonwealth soldiers, feigned idiocy, and, beating his corn with the flail, answered every question put to him with "Now thus, now thus," so escaping capture. A man with a flail and sheaf, and the motto Now Thus, make up the coat-of-arms of the de Traffords, a family of Saxon origin.

Approached by a 17th-century porch, the church has a fine 14th-century rose window in either aisle. Scenes from the Bible are carved on the fine modern font, which has a richly-wrought metal canopy. The oldest treasure is a 16th-century brass with portraits of John Ashenhurst, his four wives, and ten children. In rich modern glass in the sanctuary are fine figures of Christ, the Madonna, Ezekiel, Isaiah, and the Four Evangelists; and the oak and walnut pulpit has the Twelve Apostles in canopied niches.

127

St Luke's Church, with a splendid tower and a richly fitted chancel is 19th century. Its fine woodwork includes splendid panelling, two angels guarding the screen, prophets and kings on either side of the reredos, and musical angels on the choir-stalls.

All Saints Church, built in 1887, has a charming wall mosaic of Peter, and, round an aisle window, a beautifully painted Annunciation by Gerald Horsley. In the modern windows are Christ in Majesty, the Madonna and Child, many angels, Adam and Eve and 12 other figures from the Old Testament.

Beauty and craftsmanship have been gathered at the 19th-century Roman Catholic church, with its lofty spire, elaborate stone reredos, and rich windows. One window, with a charming figure of Christ at a bedside, is in memory of Mother Mary Joseph, 49 years mistress of St Mary's School.

The parish church and some of the old houses must look much as they did when Charles Edward, the Young Pretender, came marching into the town, gay in his silk tartan and blue feathered bonnet, as Thackeray pictures him in Esmond. Failing to gain followers here, he marched the next day for Derby, returning in haste four days later to plunder the town on the retreat northwards.

It is interesting to remember that it was 34 ladies of Leek who made a wonderful copy of the famous Bayeux Tapestry. Beginning in 1885, they worked on it for 12 months, and their copy shows all the detail of the original tapestry—the life of the Conqueror, with 1512 embroidered objects (623 people, 202 horses and mules, 55 dogs, 505 other living creatures, 37 buildings, 41 boats, and 49 trees). The tapestry was bought by Alderman Hill in 1895 for £500 and given to Reading Museum, where we found it. It has since been exhibited in every big town in the country and shown in South Africa. The value of this remarkable work is reckoned to be £3000.

Treasure Old and New

LEIGH. Several neighbouring hamlets share the same name and the same new church with its medieval tower. The lovely vaulted chancel has treasure in its windows both ancient and modern. Among the old glass are figures of Christ and saints, kings and queens, and a quaint Crucifixion. In the modern glass is a picture of the Transfiguration, and figures of Enoch and Elijah, David and

Ilam   The Modern Cross

Ilam   The Old Church

Lichfield   The Sleeping Children, by Chantrey

Ilam   The David Watts Memorial, by Chantrey

Walsall .   Miserere Seats in St Matthew's Church

olomon, all designed by Burne-Jones. There is a grand altar tomb
with figures of Sir John Aston in the armour he wore 400 years
go, with his wife Joan in a tight-waisted dress and 14 battered
children below. On the wall of the porch is a coffin lid engraved with
cross seven centuries ago.

Hidden from the gaze of passers-by about a mile away is a fine
example of the moat of a vanished homestead.

The Town of the Ladies of the Vale

LICHFIELD. Almost in the very middle of England, this cathedral city has much for us to see that is lovely and of deep
interest. It has the smallest yet perhaps the most graceful of our
cathedrals, standing on one of the earliest English sites of a Christian
church. From its 16th-century grammar school has gone out into the
world a group of boys whose names are famous in literature, law,
the church, and the stage; and in one of its 17th-century houses
was born our illustrious Samuel Johnson, most famous man of
letters of his day, creator of the first adequate Dictionary of our
language.

Far back in the remote days of history the city was called the Lych
Field, Field of the Dead, from the tradition that thousands of Chris-
tians were martyred here by the Roman emperor Diocletian; and the
first church we know in the diocese was built in Saxon days by St
Chad at Stowe, on the farther side of the pleasant pool which borders
the Close. He came from Northumbria in 669 on a mission to
Mercia, and by his preaching and his saintly life reconciled the
Angles and Britons then living at enmity in the Mercian kingdom.
He was the first bishop of Mercia, and died at Stowe in 672. As a
shrine for the body of the holy man, his successor built a church
where the cathedral now stands, consecrating it in 700.

Bishop Roger de Clinton, who also founded Buildwas Abbey in
Shropshire in Stephen's reign, built a Norman church on the site,
and his successor, Roger Langton, completed it, putting walls and
towers round the Close, and building the cloisters and the bishop's
palace, the ruins of which are still in the palace garden.

By the middle of the 12th century the native genius of our race
was freeing itself from Norman influence in art, and to this time of
emancipation we owe the lovely conception and proportions of Lich-

field's cathedral as we see it. First the English builders replaced the Norman choir and transepts, in 1239 they raised the chapter house, and with the transformation of the nave and west front the whole building had changed its severe and massive Norman character and assumed the lofty grace and elegance familiar to us all.

The lady chapel and presbytery were added in the 14th century, and thus the church remained until the unhappy days of the Civil War, when the cathedral was held by the Royalists and besieged three times before it was taken by the Roundheads. The interior was sacked and cruelly laid waste by the blind zeal of the victorious besiegers. It is sad beyond words to know that this gem of 13th-century art, the first cathedral taken by the Parliamentary party, suffered more terribly than any other at the hands of wanton wreckers, who broke up the ancient carvings in wood and stone, destroyed or defaced the statues and monuments, and even carried away the roofs and the central tower, so that the first service here after the Restoration was in the chapter house, the only part sheltered from the weather.

But with the need came the man. The name of Bishop Hacket, appointed in 1662, should live as long as the stones are left standing. He threw himself devotedly into the work of restoration, he toiled night and day to get subscriptions, he lent his carriage-horses to help in carting away the rubbish and bringing stone for repairs, and in seven years he saw the triumphant completion of his labours. For two and a half centuries little care was taken of this priceless building, but from 1856 each part was strengthened and restored, so that in 1908 it stood in its pride again, an almost perfect revival of its medieval beauty.

Lovely as it is, its charm is enhanced by its natural setting, for, though in the heart of the city, it is protected and isolated by its two pools, and in the quiet waters of the Minster Pool, just below the Close, are reflected the graceful proportions of its crowning beauty, the Three Spires known affectionately in all this countryside as the Ladies of the Vale.

The west front is its greatest glory. Within its arcades and panels are 113 statues, a wonderful gallery of carvings, all modern but five. Above the figures of the Apostles is a group of English kings with St Chad in the middle. Above them are prophets, archangels, and figures from the Old Testament. Statues of saints and bishops adorn the towers, and on the gable between them is a figure of Our Lord.

The doorways are equally rich in ancient and modern work. The porch of the central doorway has a 14th-century figure of Christ, and here is set out in carved detail the genealogy of Christ in two lines, one from Abraham to the Virgin, the other from Adam to Joseph. In the north-west doorway are the Christian kings and queens of Saxon England, and on the other side is pictured the coming of Christianity, from the North with Aidan and St Chad, and from Rome with Gregory and Augustine. Much of the early ironwork of the doors was done by Thomas Leighton, the craftsman who made the exquisite grille of Queen Eleanor's tomb at Westminster.

The transept doorways have also a wealth of carving; in the north transept are the figures of a Tree of Jesse dating from the 13th century. Over the chapter house are the statues of famous churchmen: George Herbert, Richard Hooker, Bishop Ken (holding a scroll with the words of his great hymn, Glory to Thee, my God, this Night), Archbishop Laud, Izaak Walton, and Christopher Wren, who all had a share in Bishop Hacket's restoration. Among the figures on the buttresses are some of Lichfield's famous sons, including Samuel Johnson and Elias Ashmole, who is holding a model of his Ashmolean Museum. Groups of Latin and Greek early Christian Fathers complete this unrivalled collection of statuary.

As we enter we read this record of Christian worship through the ages that has hallowed this place:

Remember that you are standing on holy ground, since here for 1200 years God has been worshipped and 40 generations have confessed their faith in Jesus Christ.

The first impression of this fine place is of its extraordinary beauty. It extends 370 feet from the west door to the lady chapel, in a fascinating series of arches. As we look at the fine proportions of the nave arcade, the exquisite capitals of the slender pillars, the delicacy of the carved triforium and clerestory rising to the rich vaulting of the roof, we understand Sir Gilbert Scott's words: "I always hold his work to be almost absolute perfection in design and detail."

Detached from the great columns which support the central tower, 13th-century pillars spring like slender trees from floor to vaulted roof. The north transept dates from the early 13th century and the south is slightly later.

The nave pulpit and the choir screen of iron, brass, and copper were designed by Sir Gilbert Scott and are decorated with coloured marbles and enamels. The craftsmanship is very fine, especially the carved fruits of ivory, onyx, and precious stones. The design of the pulpit is Peter preaching on the Day of Pentecost, and there are angels in bronze playing musical instruments on the screen.

The choir and aisles are 13th-century work. In the 19th century many layers of whitewash were removed from the walls, the built-up arches were opened out, and the plaster taken away from the stone carvings. The choir vaulting with seven-ribbed shafts is very fine. Three of the bays date from 1200 and one pillar shows the blended influence of the 13th and 14th centuries.

There are six modern figures of saints in the spandrels of the arches where earlier figures once stood; they are Peter, Mary, Philip, James, Christopher, and Mary Magdalene.

The stalls and the bishop's throne were carved in 1860 by Samuel Evans, George Eliot's uncle, the original of Seth in Adam Bede. The carving is of delicate work enriched by wreaths of natural leaves; there are Bible scenes in the panels, and figures of the Apostles at the ends of the stalls. The work on the throne is specially fine, showing the Madonna and Mary Magdalene with angels above. The pavement is laid in engraved tiles illustrating the life of St Chad, and kings and bishops who have had some connection with the cathedral.

Two beautiful parts of the choir were designed by Scott, the reredos and the altar screen of alabaster and marble. The reredos shows the Ascension with exquisite angels holding ivory trumpets. In the side arcades are 12 alabaster figures representing the noble army of martyrs in pairs of different ages, the last two turned to face the lady chapel instead of the choir. In the canopied sedilia are remnants of the vanished loveliness of the great 15th-century screen, which we imagine must have been comparable with the masterpiece of Winchester Cathedral.

Beautiful and appropriate in the lady chapel is the series of modern statues of ten saints under ancient canopies. They are of exquisite workmanship: Cecilia with her organ, Werburga holding a model of Chester Cathedral, Priscilla with a lion at her feet, Faith with sword and rack, Catherine with her wheel, Margaret subduing a dragon, Lucy and her lamp, Agnes with a lamb, Agatha bearing a palm, and Ethelreda with a model of Ely Cathedral. The triptych on this altar was carved by the peasants of Oberammergau.

The 13th-century chapter house, with its finely vaulted roof, is octagonal, and the elaborately carved capitals of the central column show a different design on four sides. One whimsical old sculptor has introduced various animals, including a cat and a rat, into the decoration over the chief seat.

In the library over the chapter house are valuable books and manuscripts. There is a copy of the Treacle Bible and of the Breeches Bible, a vellum manuscript of Chaucer's Canterbury Tales, and Dr Johnson's marked copy of South's Sermons, from which he quoted in his Dictionary. A carefully guarded treasure is the illuminated 7th-century manuscript known as St Chad's Gospels, a unique copy consisting of 110 vellum leaves. At the sacking of the cathedral it was taken away for safety. Photographs of some of the pages of this precious work are in the lady chapel.

We find a picture book in stone in the wall arcade of the north choir aisle, where the artist has let his imagination wander as the strange medley of figures, foliage, birds, beasts, and grotesques came into being beneath his tool. There are joyous music makers on the bagpipe, harp, dulcimer, clarionette, and the pipe and tabor. St Christopher is over the doorway as the patron saint of travellers, to whom suppliants waiting for audience outside the chapter house would offer a prayer for a safe return home.

One of the oldest bits of the cathedral is St Stephen's chapel, built about 1230, long used as an organ loft but now worthily restored. There is a record that Bishop Pattishull, who died in 1240, was buried before the altar, and in the restoration a stone coffin was found there.

The simplest and perhaps the most charming of all the restored work is the little chapel of St Chad's Head, which was left in ruins after the Civil War. It is reached by a narrow stair, and a 15th-century stone gallery before the entrance was doubtless used for the exhibition of relics to pilgrims in the aisle below.

The County Roll of Honour, containing 20,000 names, is kept in a chapel of the south aisle, a printed copy lying on a desk for reference.

The aumbry is here in which St Chad's relics were preserved. The restored work is perfect in its simple dignity, and wherever possible the stone vaulting and the ancient wood and iron have been used. The story of St Chad is told on the bosses and corbels; we see him sheltering the hart which fled to him for refuge, and in his cell surrounded by ministering angels at the hour of death. The alabaster reredos, of unusual and primitive beauty, was carved by Mr Kempe; it has tall canopied niches for the Crucifixion, with St Mary and St John. Two local craftsmen, Mr Culwick and Mr Bridgeman, have carried out the iron and stone work.

To all who love the cathedral and its story the recovery of this small chapel has seemed to crown the work which has preceded it. Within its walls is a sense of tranquil reverence, as if the benediction of the saintly bishop had left a hallowed memory.

Remembering the glory of the old glass here we grieve that none was left from the years of desolation, but the famous 16th-century Herkenrode windows are the glory of the lady chapel. These were the gift of Sir Brooke Boothby in 1803, who brought them from the Belgian Abbey of Herkenrode near Liége. The precious glass had been taken out and stored during the troubled days of the French occupation of Belgium in Napoleon's time, and Sir Brooke is said to have paid only £200 for the whole collection, some of the most beautiful glass in England.

The figures and groups are small and at first sight appear too crowded, and in these tall narrow windows it is difficult to trace the scenes and characters; but the wealth of colour is enough. Particularly lovely is the deep blue of the glass in the upper tracery. The subjects of the seven windows are: The foundation of the abbey with national saints; the abbey church, Madonna and Child; the Annunciation and Scourging; the Journey to Emmaus and the Ascension; the Entry into Jerusalem, the Last Supper, and the Betrayal; the Day of Judgment, Pentecost, the Rebuke of Thomas, and Christ delivered to Crucifixion, the Descent from the Cross, and the Resurrection.

Two windows in this chapel are filled with other Flemish glass brought from the Low Countries after the French Revolution, lying forgotten for many years in Christie's cellars. It had belonged to the Marquis of Ely, and, beautifully restored by Mr Kempe, has a worthy place by the Herkenrode windows. One has a strangely beautiful design of the Fountain of Pity, in which the guardian angels of little children await them as they rise from the waters of baptism. The other, of equal mythical charm, shows the Falling Asleep of the Madonna, lying on a canopied bed surrounded by Apostles, who have assembled to watch the flight of her soul to Heaven.

Two other fragments of the Herkenrode glass are in the choir aisles. In one, a crude medieval conception of the Trinity, the Father, an old man in a tall hat, is holding the Son, and a weird kind of dove represents the Holy Spirit. The other fragment is a little figure of St Christopher.

There is much fine modern glass. The Martyrdom of Stephen in St Stephen's Chapel is in memory of Canon Lonsdale, Chancellor of the cathedral for 51 years, who died in the beginning of this century. There is an alabaster figure of him. The west window of the nave is in memory of Canon Hutchinson; it shows Michael, Joseph, the Madonna, and the Wise Men in the upper part, and below is a scene connected with each figure. A little window of the Presentation is in memory of Bishop Lonsdale.

The men of the North Staffordshire Regiment who died in the Dongola Expedition and in the South African War are remembered in a window by Mr Kempe, beautiful in design and workmanship; it has incidents from the lives of St Martin, St Edmund, and St Maurice. Another window by the same artist, in memory of Canon Curtis, has scenes from the life of Samuel, Paul, and St Catherine. A fine restored window with a Jesse tree by Clayton and Bell has taken the place of a poor 15th-century window; by using many of the head stones which were founded in the wall a beautiful reproduction of the original 13th-century five-light lancet has been given to the cathedral. The chapter house windows have scenes and figures connected with the early history of the Church. Another window is to the memory of William St George Patterson, a chanter here, with David in the Temple teaching the songs of the Sanctuary to the Chief Musicians.

Two of the finest Kempe windows are in the south choir aisle, one to a mayor of Lichfield who was a doctor, depicting the healing of the cripple at the Gate Beautiful, and one showing the Defence of Stephen before the Sanhedrim. The wealth of detail, the architectural

135

setting, the number of figures, and the brilliance of dress and colour make of these two small windows a masterpiece of painted glass. The artist has chosen the moment of Stephen's trial "when all that sat in the council saw his face as it had been the face of an angel," and the transfiguring radiance on the face of the martyr as he sees his Lord in the heavens is not to be forgotten.

Above the sleeping figure of the good Bishop Hacket, carved in stone and painted, a small window shows the damaged building in the 17th century when the central spire had fallen and the roof was riddled with cannon shot. The lovely lancets of the perfect little Chapel of St Chad's Head are filled with Kempe glass, showing the saint as the central figure among choirs of angels.

The magnificent Window of Sacrifice in the south transept to some of the Staffordshire men who fell in South Africa is striking in design, with Christ on the Cross with angels around, and soldier saints below who have laid down their lives for truth and faith. A David and Goliath window is to the memory of Staffordshire men who fell in the Indian Mutiny.

When we think of the monuments of Lichfield thought flies at once to the fairest of them all, Chantrey's lovely masterpiece of the Sleeping Children. More than a hundred years ago this group was placed here in memory of the daughters of Prebendary William Robinson, who lost both these little ones by fire in 1812. It has been aptly called the Snowdrop Monument, for the chaste beauty of the rounded limbs and girlish forms lying clasped in sleep, cut off in life's Springtide, reminds us of those fair and fragile flowers of the early year. Who can read unmoved the touching words which tell the loss of the widowed mother, who "in fond remembrance of their heaven-loved innocence consigns their resemblance to the sanctuary in humble gratitude for the glorious assurance that of such is the Kingdom of God"? We can well believe the story that Chantrey came here every year of his life to look again upon these sisters, one of his earliest inspirations.

Another of his fine carvings is the stately kneeling figure of Bishop Ryder, who died in 1836; the perfect moulding of the head and hands clasped in prayer are of rare beauty.

The sleeping figure by G. F. Watts of Bishop Lonsdale lies on a table tomb with canopies which were part of the old screen of the

The beautiful West Doorway of Lichfield Cathedral

The Magnificent Choir

The North Arcade   Bishop Ryder's Monument

LICHFIELD CATHEDRAL

The Spires seen from the East

The richly carved West Front

THE SPLENDOUR OF LICHFIELD CATHEDRAL

St Chad's Church

West Door of Cathedral

Dr Johnson's Birthplace

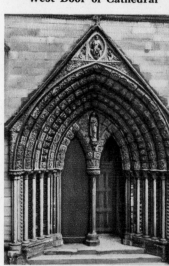

North Doorway of Cathedral

SCENES IN OLD LICHFIELD

ady chapel. Among the earlier bishops who lie here is the 13th-
century figure of Bishop Patteshull and the 14th-century figure of
Bishop Langton, which was once jewelled, as the holes in the
marble show. Bishop Selwyn's alabaster figure is in a little chantry
off the lady chapel. He died in 1878, first Bishop of New Zealand
and 90th of Lichfield. He was much loved in both parts of the
world where he laboured, and on painted tiles behind the tomb are
scenes from the story of his life. The canopies over the tomb where
Dean Howard lies were part of a dismantled altar screen.

There are here three of those curious medieval monuments in
which the head and feet were carved in a niche in the wall and a
plank stone surface represented the part where the body should be.
They are often nameless, but one of these is to the memory of Canon
Strangeways. Another strange memorial is the 15th-century tomb
of Dean Heywood, only the lower part with his skeleton being left.
The custom of the skeleton on the tomb was no doubt akin to the
skeleton at Roman banquets, to remind mankind of the final decay
of human life.

Several monuments are here to distinguished soldiers. One of the
earliest is a stone to Colonel Richard Bagot, one of the most gallant
defenders of the cathedral against the Parliamentary troops. He
died fighting at Naseby. A table tomb to Archdeacon Hodson has
alabaster panels of the Crucifixion, Burial, Resurrection, and
Ascension; and near to this is an elaborate memorial to his son,
Hodson of Hodson's Horse, who in the Indian Mutiny with a force of
100 men opposed 10,000 natives. It has a panel of the King of Delhi
handing his sword to Major Hodson, with figures of David, Joshua,
St Thomas, and St George, and the virtues of Justice, Fortitude,
Temperance, and Mercy. Lances carried by his troops form part of
the decorations.

An iron screen in St Stephen's Chapel is a memorial to men who
fell in the Zulu War of 1878, Zulu shields, assegais, and Indian corn
being introduced in the design. Admiral Parker, the last survivor of
the captains who fought with Nelson, is remembered by an altar tomb
of fine workmanship, inlaid with rare and beautiful pieces of lapis-
lazuli, jet, and porphyry, and with a gilt cross resting on a jasper stone.

Many of the famous names of the city are remembered here. There
are busts of Dr Johnson and David Garrick; there is a medallion of

Dr Erasmus Darwin, who lived here for many years; and a tablet to Dean Addison, father of the poet. He lived in the house which is now the deanery. Anna Seward, known through her poems in the 18th century as the Swan of Lichfield, is recalled by a tablet in the cathedral to her father, mother, and sister, the verses on it being written by her friend Sir Walter Scott, who ends his tribute to the dead with this tribute to the poet:

> Her worth, her warmth of heart, our sorrows say:
> Go, seek her genius in the living lay.

On the wall near is a grateful tribute to Lady Mary Montagu from a lady saved from the horrors of smallpox by Lady Montagu's introduction of inoculation into England. There is a tablet to Gilbert Walmsley, a friend of Johnson and Garrick, registrar of Lichfield and a man of much benevolence, of whom Johnson wrote:

> He was one of the first friends that literature procured me. I am not able to name a man of equal knowledge. He was of an advanced age and I was only a boy, yet he never received my notions with contempt. I honoured him and he endured me.

In the peaceful little Close a soft grass setting separates the Cathedral from the dignified 17th- and 18th-century houses which lie about it as a frame. Here in the bishop's palace lived Canon Seward and his daughter Anna. She was much admired for her poems in the literary circles of her time, and also wrote a life of Dr Darwin. Gilbert Walmsley lived at the palace before the Sewards, and Garrick is said to have given recitals in the hall. When Bishop Selwyn came here on his return from New Zealand he built the palace chapel and placed in it some stained glass. One little scene is connected with an incident in the Maori wars. It shows three of David's men bringing him the water he had desired from the Well of Bethlehem, then held by the Philistines. There is no inscription, but we are told that Bishop Selwyn intended it as a memorial to Henare Taratoa, a Maori warrior who fought against the British but who tried to fight in accordance with the Christian spirit he had learned. He drew up rules for his soldiers, and the effect of these was seen particularly at the battle of Gate Pa in 1864, when a Maori woman risked her life to take a drink of water to a wounded British soldier. When Taratoa was killed a month later he was found to have with him the text, If thine enemy hunger, feed him; if he thirst, give him to drink.

The quiet part of the Close known as the Dean's Walk was much loved by Johnson. A pleasant walk from the Close by the side of the 17-acre Stowe Pool, passing a willow descended from the tree Johnson loved so much, brings us to St Chad's church, where the Saxon bishop set up his monastic cell in 669. Most of the present church we see was built in the 14th and 15th centuries, but there is a charming 13th-century doorway. Here lie two friends who were closely linked with Samuel Johnson's life in Lichfield, his stepdaughter Lucy Porter and Catherine Chambers, the faithful servant of the Johnsons for many years. The tenderly worded inscription now on her stone was written about her by Dr Johnson to a friend:

My dear old friend Catherine Chambers—she buried my father, my brother, and my mother, I humbly hope to meet again and part no more.

There is a tradition that the tenor bell here, which has a Saxon inscription, dates from 1033; the actual date is unknown, but it was probably made in the middle of the 13th century.

From a little window just within the doorway look down Elizabeth of Hungary and St Christopher (in memory of the mother and grandson of the first Lord Charnwood) and St George and St Alban, set against a lovely background of green and blue, remind us of those who never came back.

In a cottage garden separated from the churchyard by a narrow stream is St Chad's Well, built over the little spring where no doubt the saint came to drink and to baptize his converts. It is roofed with heavy stones, a triangular archway heading the narrow doorway and five stone steps leading to the water. Three narrow loopholes in the massive walls show the solid work of the rounded interior and the stone on which he is said to have stood for baptism. The initials C.E. and E.P. and the date 669 in Roman figures are above the entrance.

St Michael's churchyard is one of the oldest and biggest in England. It was the central burial-place in Saxon times of the kingdom of Mercia, and there were burials here when there were only five other burial-places in the country. The church has gone through many changes, but has kept its 14th-century east window, its 15th-century tower, and its 17th-century font. Here sleep the father, mother, and brother of Dr Johnson, who wrote to his mother in her last illness:

You have been the best mother, and I believe the best woman in the world. I thank you for your indulgence to me, and beg forgiveness of all that I have done ill, and all that I have omitted to do well. God grant you His Holy Spirit and receive you to everlasting happiness, for Jesus Christ's sake, Amen.

Dr Johnson wrote his great work Rasselas to pay for her funeral and her few debts, and he composed this long Latin inscription on "the deep, massy, and hard stone," which lies in the aisle of the church.

St Mary's, the chief parish church of Lichfield, is in the market-place, practically rebuilt in the 19th century but still keeping its 14th-century tower arch. Opposite is the bookseller's shop of Michael Johnson, who was churchwarden here, and so it is thought that he may have brought his two sons here for baptism, although the famous Samuel was only a day old when he was baptized, and the ceremony may possibly have taken place at home.

The church contains the burial-place of the Dyotts, prominent in Lichfield history for centuries; the most famous of the sons was deaf and dumb and known as Dumb Dyott, but he was one of the stout defenders of the cathedral in the Civil War, and a shot from his musket killed Lord Brooke, the Parliamentary leader. When asked by Charles Stuart to name his own reward, he requested that all his descendants of the name of Dyott should be brought by torchlight from the family estate at Freeford, three miles away, and buried at midnight in the chapel of St Mary's, and this custom was observed until the last few years of last century. This Dyott Chapel has a fine oak altarpiece with some 14th-century panels.

The sanctuary of St Mary's is lined with oak painted and gilded, and on it are the names of those who fell in the war. The altar panels in blue and gold show Our Lord in majesty, the enthronement of the Madonna, the Nativity, the Presentation, and the Wise Men. Archdeacon Scott, brother of Sir Gilbert, was vicar here, and in a fine window to his memory are the angels at Bethlehem. Another vicar, William Baker, was here for 51 years in the 17th and 18th centuries.

St John's Church and Hospital were founded in 1252. The 15th-century hospital is one of the earliest English houses built after chimneys were introduced into domestic architecture. The eight tall chimneys form deep recesses rising from the pavement to the chim-

STAFFORDSHIRE

ey-tops. Within the gates is a pleasant little garden tended by the
old men, who rest in the sunshine on the seats of the stone terrace.
The little church has a stained window of St Philip in memory of a
warden of the hospital for 42 years, and there are fine old Corpora-
tion seats brought from St Mary's church over two centuries ago.

Three buildings in turn have stood on the site of Lichfield's old
grammar school; the first from 1497 to 1577, the second till 1849,
the third till 1903. Lichfield boys now go to a new and finely-
equipped school in the outskirts on Borrow Cop, a hill where legend
tells us that three kings died in battle. The curiously maimed bodies
of these kings form part of the city arms. The school and school-
house have been carefully preserved as civic offices, the playground
delightfully planted as a garden. The date 1680 is over the school
door and on the stone walls and mullions, on the woodwork of the
panelling and on the black oak spiral staircase, are the initials of
many generations of boys who have played their part and passed on,
leaving a noble school tradition to those who came after.

The school has a great record. It was the earliest provincial school
founded after Eton, Winchester, and Wainfleet; and few small schools
can show such a distinguished list of scholars. Three of the boys
who sat on its benches sleep in Westminster Abbey: Johnson, Garrick
and Addison. Two became Bishops of Bristol, George Smalridge and
Thomas Newton. Five contemporary judges had their first lessons
in these walls—Chief Justice Willis, Chief Baron Parker, Mr Justice
Noel, Chief Justice Wilmot, and Sir Richard Lloyd. John Hewlett,
musician and antiquary, was a boy here, and another famous
Lichfield scholar, Dr Richard Garnett, was Keeper of the Printed
Books in the British Museum.

Another son of Lichfield who was to win renown, both as traveller
and archaeologist, was Henry Salt, born here in 1780; by a strange
chance he went to the school at Market Bosworth in Leicestershire,
where for a short unhappy period Dr Johnson had been a tutor half
a century before.

As Shakespeare's memory is honoured in Stratford-on-Avon so
is Johnson's in Lichfield. In the marketplace are the statues of its
greatest son and his biographer Boswell, who must always live through
his admiring and faithful record of his friend's sayings and doings.
Three scenes from his life are pictured on Johnson's statue: we see

him as a little child taken to hear the preacher Dr Sacheverell in th
cathedral, as a schoolboy so much honoured by his mates that the
carried him on their shoulders, and as a man during a visit t
his birthplace, when with the touching humility that only a grea
soul could possess he stayed bareheaded in the rain for three hours o
the spot where his father's bookstall had stood, to atone for hi
youthful pride when he refused to take his father's place at the book
stall in Uttoxeter market.

This marketplace has seen strange and tragic sights. Thre
martyrs were burned alive at the stake in Mary Tudor's reign, an
here a hundred years later came George Fox, founder of the Quakers
he was released from prison in 1651 and stood like a prophet on th
snow-covered stones of the marketplace bareheaded and barefoote
to denounce the city and its inhabitants.

It is to the generosity of an alderman of the city that Lichfiel
owes the preservation of Dr Johnson's birthplace. It was the bool
shop of his father, and is kept as a museum and a memorial. The ol
shop window looks out on to one corner of the marketplace and th
small rooms with high narrow windows are fitted with relics and re
minders of the clumsy form, the mighty intellect, and the kindly hear
of the man who spent here his early days.

We see his three-legged mahogany breakfast table and the bi
armchair in which he passed his last days on this earth. In the littl
panelled parlour with deep window seats is the desk on which h
wrote Rasselas to pay for his mother's funeral. We climb the staircas
of wide oak boards and balustrade black and polished with age, an
pass from silent room to room haunted by a thousand memories
Here is a collection of editions of his works, many of his manuscripts
some of his letters, and portraits at various times of his life. In th
room in which he was born are some of the treasures he loved
his silver bib-holder, his teaspoons, and the silver pen which Edmun
Burke gave him to celebrate the completion of the Dictionary
there are his shoe-buckles, his wife's wedding-ring, the walking-stic
with which he used to tap the lamp-posts, and a precious teapo
which gave him his countless cups of tea.

We spend hours in wandering through the old town, where, b
means of an admirable series of inscriptions, the places of interest ar
identified and described. At the Three Crowns, next door to hi

irthplace, Johnson stayed with Boswell in 1776. We smile to see the ouse which was once Dame Oliver's school; she might well claim to e the grandmother of the famous Dictionary, for here little Samuel earned to read and spell.

At Redcourt, the home of his stepdaughter Lucy Porter, he often tayed. There was a sincere and tender affection between them; he deeply mourned his death and died here two years later in 1786. towe House, beyond the Pool, was in turn the home of Thomas Day, who wrote the edifying story of Sandford and Merton) and of Richard ovell Edgeworth, father of Maria Edgeworth.

The Parchments, now converted into two cottages, was the factory tarted by Michael Johnson for the manufacture of parchment, in which venture he lost much of the profits he made as a bookseller. At Stowe Hill lived Sir Thomas Aston, the father of three daughters ohnson much admired.

There is an inscription on the old home of Elias Ashmole describing him as " the greatest virtuoso and curioso that ever was known n England." He was born here in 1617; he went to the grammar chool and sang in the cathedral choir. He was a devoted student of hemistry, astrology, botany and other sciences. He gave a wonderful ollection of rarities to Oxford, on condition a suitable building was provided for it, and this was the origin of the Ashmolean Museum.

On the site of the Probate Court was the house where Captain Garrick lived, father of the celebrated David. The son was born at Hereford, where his parents were visiting, but the first twenty years of is life were spent here, and his mother's father was a lay singer in he cathedral.

Part of the walls of a 13th-century friary and a Tudor fireplace have been preserved in the building of the modern Girls High School. t was converted into a house by the Sheriff of Lichfield in Queen Mary's reign, and here Johnson and Boswell visited their friends Moll Cobb and Miss Adey.

Erasmus Darwin lived in the city from 1756 to 1781. He was a doctor and scientist much in advance of his times. Among his friends were Rousseau, Watt, Wedgwood, and the Sewards, but unhappily he was never on friendly terms with the " 18th-century's greatest conversationalist," for it was said that, "wherever Dr Johnson was, Dr Darwin had no chance of being heard."

At Edial Hall three miles away Dr Johnson started a school with "Little Davy Garrick" as one of his scholars. It had no success, and master and pupil started off to London to seek their fortunes with fourpence—twopence-halfpenny in one pocket and three-halfpence in the other.

The Guildhall is on the site of the old Guild House which stood here in the reign of Richard the Second. It has some early 19th century glass which was formerly in the cathedral and the cartoons from which they were designed. It includes figures of St Chad, Oswy King of Northumbria, Offa, King of Mercia, and King Stephen. Next door is a well-preserved timbered 16th-century house.

In the pleasant little park near the cathedral is a life-size statue of our King Edward sculptured by Robert Bridgeman, Sheriff of Lichfield in 1907. Facing it is a statue by Lady Scott of Edward John Smith, the captain who went down with his ship the Titanic, in the bitterest sea catastrophe of our century. He was a Staffordshire man, and we read on this statue that "he bequeathed to his countrymen the memory and example of a great heart, a brave life, and a heroic death."

The museum in this park has many reminders of the early days of the city, including one of the old scold's bridles and the stocks from the marketplace. The suits of armour have an annual air when they are worn in procession on Whit Monday, a survival of the old Guilds. One of the daintiest things here is the tiny pipe organ built by Father Smith for the cathedral in the 17th century, after its destruction in what is queerly called "the Oliverian Usurpation." On the short keyboard of four octaves the black and white notes are transposed and it has six little stops. It has suffered much since its first days of harmonious prosperity, for it was broken and cast out in the '45 Rebellion and humiliatingly used as a clothes press; but some lover of music rebuilt it in the 18th century and here it has found a quiet resting-place, the faded gilding of its pipes like a plaintive echo of its lovely tones in days of old. In a fine case of Copeland ware given by Mr. W. T. Copeland, M.P. for Lichfield in 1859, is a series of miniature busts of great Victorians, including Daniel O'Connell, Wellington, Jenny Lind, Sir Robert Peel, Queen Victoria, the Tsar Nicholas, and General Havelock. An extremely fine collection of rare and medieval ironwork has been presented by

Leek   **The Peace Memorial**

Longton   **Queen's Park**

Longnor   **Church Tower and Market Hall**

Croxden   Abbey Walls   **Biddulph**   Old Hall

Mr John Culwick, a local craftsman of wide fame, some of whose modern work and restoration is seen in the cathedral and the city.

One case has fascinating examples of beadwork and needlework from many parts of the world, and in another is the magnificent collection of silver plate and trophies of the Fourth Staffordshire Regiment. There are portraits of local celebrities and a masterly painting by Robert Spence of George Fox in the marketplace, with groups of smiling or scornful citizens about him and the snow-covered spires in the background.

In its Garden of Remembrance Lichfield has one of the most original and beautiful peace memorials in England. The stone balustrade has a curious history. It was removed from Moxhull Hall in Warwickshire to Shenstone Court, Lichfield, and was bought by the town for this garden. When it was being set up one of the stones was found to be marked with the letter V, the mark used by the mason Vinrace who had built the bridge crossing the water at this very spot. The city arms are on an old stone built into one of the piers of the entrance gates. The garden is laid out on the city side of the Minster Pool below the Close, and from its pleasant paths we have perhaps the finest view of the Three Ladies of the Vale. Wide stone steps lead down into the sheltered space of smooth lawns and flower-beds where two oak trees, already of fair size, have been grown from acorns picked up in the Great War at Verdun. A stone screen bears the names of those who never came back, and when we called at Eastertide the promise of life renewed was flashed like sunshine from the beds of primroses and daffodils.

One of Bede's Heroes

LICHFIELD owes its original glory to St Chad, who died here in 672. His beautiful story comes down to us from Bede, who had his information from a monk trained here by the saint.

Chad was one of four brothers in the priesthood, two of them becoming bishops. The Saint was partly educated in Ireland, which was then a sanctuary of learning, a light shining in the dark night of Europe's Dark Age. Wilfred, on being appointed to the see of York, went to Gaul for consecration, but was so long absent that Oswy, King of Northumbria, nominated Chad in his stead.

Mild and obedient, Chad went to Canterbury for confirmation in his office, but, the Primate having died, he was consecrated by two British bishops. He discharged the duties of his see with loving humility for the next three years, Wilfred approving his appointment and retiring to a monastery.

A new Archbishop of Canterbury deposed Chad because of the irregularity of his appointment, and reinstated Wilfred, but, delighted with the scholarship and saintly goodness of Chad, he appointed him bishop of Mercia, which then comprised an immense area.

He established his see here, building a home not far from his church for himself and a small number of monks. Their time was devoted to prayer and good works. When he travelled about his diocese Chad went modestly afoot, until the Primate, recognising in him a holy man, begged and even commanded him to ride.

Bede had a vivid pen, and in his picture the saint moves and lives after 13 centuries. Chad died in 672, having predicted a week earlier the day and time of his death. The prophecy is attributed to divine revelation, but Chad was probably helped to his calculation by observing the course of the pestilence that was thinning out his little community, to which he himself had fallen a victim.

His body was first buried in his own church of St Mary, but in 1148 his bones were transferred to the present cathedral. While Bede was writing miracles were said to be wrought at Chad's tomb. His body lay in "a wooden monument, made like a little house, covered, having a hole in the wall, through which those that go thither for devotion usually put in their hand and take out some of the dust, which they put into water and give to sick cattle or men to drink, upon which they are presently eased of their infirmity and restored to health."

So the legend ran and grew and led to the good man's canonisation. Chad clearly impressed his age as a man of great virtue, piety, and learning, and was an immense influence for good in a land still barbarous and largely pagan.

Bringing Old Egypt to England

ONE of the sons of whom Lichfield has reason to be proud is Henry Salt, who helped to unveil Egypt's past. A doctor's son and trained to art, Henry Salt, born here in 1780, turned his gifts with brush and pencil to account by making a series of drawings for

Lord Valentia, whom he accompanied to India, Ceylon, and Abyssinia, as secretary and draughtsman.

At 29 Salt was sent on a Government mission to Abyssinia to carry presents to the King, to promote friendly relations, and to bring back data. This led to his appointment, 13 years later, as British consul-general in Egypt. There, among the immemorial antiquities, he found the work of his life. Not only did he himself excavate as far as time would allow, he set others to work, among them that giant of strength and ardour, Belzoni.

The immense bust of Rameses the Second, now in the British Museum, was one of the finds; the splendid sarcophagus from the tomb of Seti the First, today the chief treasure of Sir John Soane's House in Lincoln's Inn Fields, was another. He caused temples to be unearthed, and the Sphinx and Pyramids to be investigated. He deciphered inscriptions, and brought to light precious papyri, bronzes, jewels, and many sculptures.

He sold to the British Museum for £2000 a collection that had cost him £3000 to obtain; and a second collection to France for £10,000. He was a pioneer in days of slow transport and inefficient implements, and it is his abiding glory to have been the first modern man systematically to re-open the book of Egypt's past and reveal its wonders to the present. He died on the scene of his labours in 1827, and was buried at Alexandria.

LONGDON. It straggles along the road near Lichfield, true to its name and to the ancient rhyme which tells us

> The stoutest beggar that goes by the way
> Cannot beg through Longdon in a summer's day.

A charming avenue of old yews leads to a church venerable with the marks of many centuries. The nave, its two doorways, and the chancel arch with its chevrons, are all Norman; the chancel is 700 years old, the tower 600. The south transept was built by John Stonywell, a 16th-century abbot of Pershore whose symbols of mitre, lamb, and dove are carved on three of the buttresses. In this church John was baptised, and back to it the monks of Pershore carried him to rest.

The Norman font is carved with foliage, and there are fragments of ancient glass with figures of two golden-haired monks and an angel's head. Cherubs guard the bust of Thomas Orme, a follower of Charles Stuart who died in the year of the Great Plague.

He'll March Again

LONGNOR. Amid lovely scenery between two rivers lies this small town with a stone market hall. After more than 250 years it proudly remembers old William Billinge, who took part in the capture of Gibraltar, fought under Marlborough, and died in 1791 at an astonishing age (said to be 112), having escaped death perhaps oftener than any other man of his day. The original inscription on his gravestone in the churchyard has faded and is replaced by a new one, which says:

> Billeted by Death, I quartered here remain,
> When the trumpet sounds I'll rise and march again;

but we think this is not so fine as the old epitaph, which said:

> Conquests I shared in many a dreadful scene,
> With matchless Marlboro and with brave Eugene.
> To peaceful quarters billeted am I,
> And here forgetful of my labours lie.
> Let me alone awhile, asleep, not slain,
> And when the trumpet sounds I'll march again.

The church was made new in his day, and all it has of the old place is its font, on which is a head carved 800 years ago.

LONGTON. It is one of Arnold Bennett's Five Towns, now famous for its everyday pottery, the world's greatest centre for cheap china, and linked with some of the earliest attempts to produce English porcelain. It was at Longton Hall that William Littler made the first Staffordshire porcelain about 1750. The fine building of the Sutherland Technical Institute has a frieze showing potters at work. Among many modern churches here is St James's, with attractive window portraits of Old and New Testament women.

The Zaccheus of London

MADELEY. Izaak Walton has made it famous wherever English is read. Here he walked and talked and stayed with a man he loved, visiting the fine old church and, we may be sure, viewing with wonder Heleigh Castle not far away, which had suddenly acquired a new character.

Demolished by the Commonwealth to prevent its being garrisoned for Charles, when Izaak came visiting his "most honoured friend" Sir John Offley, lord of the manor, the great castle had become a ruin, though it is still a noble picture among the trees above a farm.

A modern manor house has succeeded that to which Offley welcomed him; the actual scene of their meetings is a ruin concealed by mounds, with only an old gateway standing in a field. But we can picture the two old cronies here. Sir John had just founded his almshouses and endowed his free school for the village, and Izaak immortalised his name and his manor by dedicating to him the Complete Angler.

Sir Thomas Offley's grandfather went to London as a boy, made a fortune as a merchant tailor, and became Lord Mayor. There is a picture of his rowing to Greenwich, where Elizabeth waited to knight him. "Ring the bell, watchman!", the cry of children at play, dates from Sir Thomas, for it was he who appointed bellmen to rouse sleeping London in time of fire or burglary. He was a frugal man, of whom it was written:

> *Offley three dishes had of daily roast,*
> *An egg, an apple, and (the third) a toast,*

but Fuller called him the Zaccheus of London, "not for his low stature but for his high charity," for the half of his goods he gave to the poor. His tomb and monument are in the church of St Andrew Undershaft, London, the church in which Old Stow keeps him company, Old Stow the historical and licensed beggar of London and Offley the Lord Mayor.

Inscribed on a wall of the fine timbered old hall in the village is a challenge which must have startled gentle Izaak; with the date 1647 it reads, "Walk, Knave; What Lookest At?"

With a marble pedestal and an urn to tell of him, Sir John Offley has been sleeping in the church since 1688; and a window with the miracle of the fishes links his memory with that of his friend, for the window is Madeley's tribute to Izaak Walton. We found the church lit by candles as it was in their day.

Although its pinnacles are modern, the church tower was 200 years old when the two friends were here, and afforded them an opportunity of climbing one of the few outer stair turrets in the county.

The porch by which they would enter is here still, and here are the 13th-century arcade and chancel arch, the 15th-century arches and chapel and transepts, they would know; the finely carved Jacobean pulpit from which they heard the sermons, and the traceried oak screen they must have often looked at.

There are two fine 16th-century portrait brasses, one of John Egerton in a long cloak, and his wife in a flowing dress; the other with the reverent figure of Robert Hawkins kneeling in a cloak, gown, and ruff, before a prayer desk.

The oldest monument (1522) is the great altar tomb on which are engraved the figures of Randolph Egerton and his wife, she in a girdled gown and a pedimental headdress, he in armour, with a misshapen dog at his strangely-distorted feet. The worn panels round the tomb have impressive canopied figures of men and angels.

MAER. It is said to be named after a mere from which the River Tern rises to flow through Shropshire to the Severn. Near by is the hall, a fine grey house, and the little 17th-century church at the end of a yew-fringed path, in company with tall sycamores and four yews, one perhaps 300 years old.

The chancel and the nave have been greatly changed, but the south doorway keeps its Norman capitals, and there is an old round font. On an altar tomb under an arch in the chancel lie the figures of Sir John Bowyer of 1604, and his wife, he in armour and she in a long dress and ruff. Sir John was the builder of the Elizabethan vicarage near the churchyard, its walls still very attractive with their red brick and yellow stone.

Giant Oak and Great Chest

MARCHINGTON. Only a little way from Derbyshire is Marchington, in the lovely Dove Valley. There is still something to see of the ancient Needwood Forest, and in the neighbouring Forest Banks stands the finest oak of all the thousands hereabouts, with a waist of 22 feet.

An avenue of limes brings us to the churchyard with a hollow yew nearly 12 feet round. The modern church has a small domed tower and a door under a sculpture of St Michael, a peace memorial. An old chest, said to be Spanish, is one of the treasures of the village, eight feet long and strongly bound with iron. There is an alabaster monument with engraved portraits of Walter Vernon in his Elizabethan armour, and his wife looking like Mary Queen of Scots in her full-sleeved dress and ruff. At their feet are two dogs, and in front of the tomb are figures of their eight children, three of them babies.

Dangerous Neighbours

MAVESYN RIDWARE. One of the three Ridwares, it has memories of turbulent baronial days, of a bitter feud ending in battle, and of the coming of Cromwell to plan the capture of a city. The village takes its distinctive name from the Mavesyns, who in their Norman days were styled Mal-voisins (dangerous neighbours). Of their castle little evidence is left, and of their Tudor manor house which succeeded it there remains only the splendid gatehouse, with its ancient dovecot. Above is a chamber with great timbers.

It was in such a chamber of this gatehouse that Cromwell held his council of war on pausing for the night before setting out for the attack on Lichfield.

From the castle here in 1403 Sir Robert Mavesyn rode out at the head of his retainers to join the forces of Henry the Fourth at Shrewsbury, and at the same time his enemy Sir William Handsacre set forth to fight at the same place for the rebel Hotspur. The rivals met near here, where two ancient oaks (Gog and Magog) are said to mark the site; they fought till Handsacre was slain by Mavesyn, who then continued his way to Shrewsbury to die in battle.

The church has its massive low tower, on which grim gargoyles have been keeping watch 500 years. Only one aisle remains of the church which rose with them, the remainder being an 18th-century rebuilding from old materials faced with brick; but the Norman font, after a century of exposure in the manor garden, is back in its place. Keeping it company in a chapel are beautiful floor tiles from the Conqueror's palace at Caen; it is fascinating to think that he may have trodden them before he and the Malvoisins set out for Hastings.

The church is famous for its monuments. The oldest is the canopied 12th-century armoured figure of Hugo Mavesyn, founder of the church and father of its first rector; the next in age is a 13th-century Crusader, Sir Henry Mavesyn, who served in Holy Land. His body has been found wrapped in lead.

Two engraved 15th-century figures show Sir John and Elizabeth Cawarden, he in armour with huge elbow plates, she in a belted robe and a quaint round hat. Elizabeth was a daughter of the slayer of Sir William Handsacre. Her sister Joanna married the victim's son, and their daughter became the wife of Sir Hugh Davenport, who lies in a chapel in engraved armour, with a big crested helmet and wearing long pointed shoes resting on a queer heraldic creature.

A bareheaded 15th-century John Cawarden lies in armour with a lion at his feet; and David and Maud Cawarden rest under a 15th-century canopy, he in a robe with wide fur collar, she in a girdled gown. Below are their four children.

An interesting alabaster relief shows the redoubtable Sir Robert Mavesyn, first slaying Handsacre, and then as he was on the day of his death at Shrewsbury; and another has John Mavesyn, who was killed while hunting.

A Quiet Corner for Tom Moore

MAYFIELD. Here amid a romantic countryside of glorious woods and fields the five grey stone arches of the medieval Hanging Bridge cross the River Dove to link Staffordshire with Derbyshire. It started life as a packhorse bridge; was widened for carriages 200 years ago, and again for motors in our own day; but still the 500-year-old arches stand.

The tall chimneys of Mayfield Old Hall peep charmingly above its grey gables, and the tower of an ancient church soars triumphantly above the limes by the churchyard gate. The church tower was built in 1515 by Thomas Rolleston and its door is scarred by bullets fired, it is said, by straggling Jacobites who came this way in 1745. The chancel and the aisle windows are 14th century, but the nave is far older, for its arcades and its finely moulded doorway are Norman. There are pews, altar-rails, and a pulpit carved by craftsmen of Charles Stuart's day.

In the churchyard is a pathetic link with Thomas Moore, the grave of his daughter Olivia who was laid to rest here by her sorrowing parents in 1815. Not far off is the grey stone cottage where the poet lived for four years about the time of Waterloo, the home where he and his young wife Bessie spent many of their happiest hours. Here came the dawn of many of his hopes and fears. Here is the small garden where Bessie would pick the flowers to give away, and from these windows, with little Olivia in her arms, she would look across the road and watch her husband romping in the hayfield with little Barbara.

"I could not possibly have a more rural or secluded corner to court the Muses in," Moore wrote to a friend, and the Muses responded, for it was here, with his library of Eastern books massed round him, that he wrote his Oriental romance, Lalla Rookh.

It was in this quiet spot that he listened to the chimes of the Cathedral of the Peak across the river at Ashbourne, and immortalised their melody in these famous lines:

> *Those evening bells! Those evening bells.*
> *How many a tale their music tells.*
> *Of youth, and home, and that sweet time*
> *When last I heard their soothing chime.*
>
> *Those joyous hours are passed away*
> *And many a heart that then was gay*
> *Within the tomb now darkly dwells*
> *And hears no more those evening bells.*
>
> *And so 'twill be when I am gone;*
> *That tuneful peal will still ring on*
> *While other bards shall walk these dells*
> *And sing your praise, sweet evening bells!*

The memory of those bells was both sweet and sad to him in after years, for they reminded him of Barbara, once frolicsome as a young kitten and now no more, and of the day when small Olivia closed her eyes for the last time, only a few months old.

MILTON. A little place with a great name, it has a modern church and something of an old abbey. Traces of the abbey are near a small farmhouse with old stones built in the walls, but there is little to see of its ancient splendour. Excavations made in 1883, when several carved stone coffin lids were found, showed that the church was 200 feet long and half as wide across the transepts. Once known as Hilton Abbey, and said to have been founded in 1223 by Henry de Audley, it is now little more than a name, though in 1718 stone from the ruins was taken by the cartload to Bucknall for building a church there.

Unfinished for Seven Hundred Years

MILWICH. Its chief possession is a bell which was ringing here for Agincourt. It is the oldest dated bell in Staffordshire with the date 1409.

The old bell swings in an old belfry, for the tower is 15th century and has shields and an ornamented border below the parapet. The remainder of the church is of 18th-century brick, and shelters an old oak chest and a battered font with arcading unfinished round its bowl, perhaps the work of a 13th-century sculptor who grew tired of his task before it was finished.

A Cradle of Methodism

MOW COP. Its splendid hill, nearly 1100 feet above the sea with magnificent views far into Wales, belongs to us all, for it has been given to the National Trust. It is marred by a mock ruin of the 18th century, but is famous as the birthplace of Primitive Methodism, which, now merged in the parent body by the union of the church in 1932, began here in 1807 as the result of the first English camp meeting, summoned by Hugh Bourne, a wheelwright of Stoke-on-Trent. Ten thousand Methodists held a service in 1937 to mark the handing over of Mow Cop to the National Trust.

An earnest local preacher, Bourne, who built a chapel at Harriseahead from his own resources, had kindred spirits in a brother and in William Clowes, the champion dancer of Burslem. Seeking a return to a simpler form of worship, they called their sympathisers into the open air. Their first meeting was held on a May Sunday on this hill, and lasted 14 hours; similar gatherings followed elsewhere, and led to Bourne's dismissal from the denomination.

It was then that he and his friends formed the Primitive Methodist Church. Bourne continued to labour at his trade, but found time to conduct meetings all over the kingdom and in the United States, and before his death at Bemersley, an old man of 80, he saw over 5000 chapels established, with a membership exceeding 100,000. He sleeps at Englesea Brook in Cheshire. It seems not a little surprising that the chapel here has no mention of this remarkable man.

Beauty on the Slag Heap

MOXLEY. It has a shining example of how beauty may come from ugliness. With mines and ironworks, slag heaps and chimneys filling the air with smoke and chemicals, Moxley is not an attractive place, but a few enterprising men with vision have shown us what can be done with our commonplace towns. Here, in an unlovely setting, is a wood of 30 acres round a hospital. Sir Oliver Lodge planted one of the first trees in the days when no one thought a tree could grow in this vitiated atmosphere. These trees have grown year by year, hiding the ugliness with rich foliage and even bringing music back to the Midlands, for the birds have come to the wood: *the slag heaps have become a sanctuary.*

The modern church is in 13th-century style, its tower crowned with a small spire seen far off. In the east window are shining portraits of saints, and under the lofty chancel arch is a beautiful and pathetic figure of Christ nailed to a wooden cross.

A Queen Sees a Battle

MUCKLESTONE. It is near the Shropshire border, a good hour's walk from Market Drayton, where Clive of India went like a snail unwillingly to school.

Fragments of Staffordshire's unknown past have been revealed here from time to time, for at a farm are two stones called the Devil's Ring and the Devil's Finger, both pierced in prehistoric days, and in the River Tern an ancient dug-out canoe was found not long ago.

Old yews shade the gate of the church, which, though much rebuilt, has its finely proportioned 14th-century tower and many ancient fragments in its windows and walls. Within are three finely carved modern screens and a gallery of glass. One of the windows of the tower has figures of St George and the hapless Henry the Sixth with his queen, Margaret of Anjou. From the battlements of this very tower Queen Margaret watched the rout of 10,000 loyal Lancastrians in the Battle of the Roses at Blore Heath 500 years ago.

NETHERTON. Standing on a hill of 500 feet, its century-old church is seen for miles round and seems to have risen above the smoke of a black country. Here are made many things of metal, from spades to boilers and gasometers. One of its special industries is making chains, and there is in this place one of the eight depots of Lloyds, where anchors and chains must prove their strength before they may be used at sea.

The Midland Newcastle

NEWCASTLE-UNDER-LYME. Although its years have been peaceful, it rose by the river as a place of defence. Eight hundred years ago the new castle was built by the great forest of Lyme to replace the ruin at Chesterton. Castle and forest vanished long ago, and survive only as memories.

With Simon de Montfort and John of Gaunt among its ancient lords, the town sent two members to Parliament for 500 years, and from Shakespeare's time was a famous educational centre. Within recent years it has greatly increased in size, doubling its area by joining hands with Wolstanton, Silverdale, and Chesterton.

The old town hall by the market cross was made new last century, but the affairs of the town are transacted at the handsome civic buildings, where, under a clock tower with a lantern and a pinnacled dome, and enriched by statues symbolising Architecture, Painting, Music, and Literature, are the library and art school. There is a good covered market. During the construction of the cattle market last century remains were discovered of the ancient priory from which Friars Street takes its name.

The oldest thing in the town is the buttressed and pinnacled 13th-century tower of St Giles's Church, which has seen more than one building at its side. The present church is the work of Sir Gilbert Scott, who, finding ancient tiles in the course of his work, had them copied to form the tessellated pavement here. There are two relics from the church of long ago, the worn stone figure of a man wearing a gauntlet and holding a sword, and the splendidly carved pelican lectern.

St George's, one of the younger churches, has completed its century; with its fine buttresses and pinnacled tower it forms a splendid picture in its spacious, tree-shaded churchyard.

The town has cradled notable men in widely different fields. One of the most remarkable was Sir Nicholas Bagnal, son of a tailor-mayor, who educated him so well that he was admitted to the court of Henry the Eighth, and sent to fight in Ireland. A different career awaited Philip Astley, a cabinet-maker's son born here in 1742. Joining the Army as a youth, he became a magnificent rider, captured a standard at the battle of Ensdorff, and at the completion of his service received from his commanding officer a beautiful white charger, which he taught to perform. Developing into an unrivalled horse-breaker and showman, he opened the first circus in England, which was for many years famous as Astley's Circus, Westminster Bridge Road.

Paying yearly visits to Paris, he lost his property there during the Revolution, but was compensated by Napoleon. In all he built 19 circuses in London, Paris, and Dublin. Of his many famous performers one was Belzoni, the strong man who left Astley to explore the Pyramids.

Two men closely connected with the fate of Charles Stuart were associated with this place. John Bradshaw, who pronounced the sentence of death, was Recorder here, and one of the judges at the trial was Thomas Harrison, a butcher's son who left this town to become one of the most redoubtable of Ironsides.

He Brought the King to His Doom

HARRISON was the son of a grazier and butcher at Newcastle. He received an excellent education and left the practice of the law in Clifford's Inn to join Essex's lifeguard at the outbreak of the Civil War.

Passing from one Parliamentary force to another he fought with increasing fame at Marston Moor, Naseby, Langport, Winchester, Basing; and in the second war at Worcester, where he conducted the pursuit of the flying Royalists with such thoroughness that few escaped. During Cromwell's absence in Ireland he commanded the entire military forces of England.

For posterity the chief interest in Harrison is centred on his action as one of the most rigid of the King's judges. It was he whom Cromwell entrusted with the dangerous task of bringing Charles from Hurst Castle to London. The two men grew intimate, even friendly on the way! Yet no one was more active in drawing up the indictment and urging on the trial of the King than Harrison, and he was one of the signatories of the death warrant. With the Restoration he, after three months in the Tower, was the first of the judges brought to trial.

Unshaken, he defended himself with courage and ability. He declared that what he had done had been " as out of conscience to the Lord." He had never turned aside, even though it had caused him to be separated from wife and family and to suffer imprisonment. What had been done was done "in the name of the Parliament of England, by their power and authority," and "this Court, or any Court below the High Court of Parliament hath no jurisdiction of their actions." He maintained that the taking of the King's life had been ordained of God, that the King had "set up his standard against the people" and that his execution was no crime, but lawful. The sentence of death was unanimous, and on October 13, 1660, Samuel Pepys, who had witnessed the execution of Charles eleven years earlier, wrote:

I went out to Charing Cross, to see Major-General Harrison hanged, drawn, and quartered, which was done there, he looking as cheerful as any man could do in that condition. He was presently cut down, and his head and heart shown to the people, at which there was great shouts of joy.

The Canal Man

NEWCHAPEL. It is a mining village with a church on its hilltop looking south to the Potteries. Except for the east window with its picture of Christ in the clouds the church has little to show the traveller, but in the churchyard of this humble place sleeps one of our greatest engineers, the astonishing James Brindley.

Turnhurst, the house where he spent some of his last years, was unhappily pulled down in 1929, but his name lives on in the neighbouring hamlet of Brindley Ford.

Brindley was born at Thornsett in Derbyshire in 1716, son of a wastrel farmer. He learned how to write his name and do simple sums, and after a wretched childhood apprenticed himself to a millwright who was something of an engineer. His master at first regarded him as a slovenly workman, but was soon glad to resign the control of the business to him, and Brindley ran the place, supporting the old man and his family with unswerving fidelity. Then he started a business of his own, and became the general utility man of the neighbourhood. If a machine broke down Brindley was sent for, and he never failed.

The illiterate millwright's fame spread wide, and he was called to Lancashire to pump a mine. He did the pumping, but had to obtain his power by a water-wheel 30 feet underground, and to carry water to it from the Irwell through a tunnel of 600 yards bored partly through rock.

The great opportunity came to Brindley at last through another remarkable man, the Duke of Bridgewater, who heard of the untutored genius and called on him to build a canal, the first serious venture of the kind in England. It was to run from Worsley to Manchester, and to avoid waste from a system of locks it was to be on a level. This meant the boring of tunnels and the raising of embankments. Moreover, the canal had to be carried across the River Irwell.

Brindley thought matters out, formed his plans, and began. He went on, tunnelling here, embanking there, burrowing under Manchester at one end and under Worsley at the other, touching the coalfield at twenty points. The aqueduct was begun in July 1760; boats were crossing it in the next summer. Now the duke set him to link up Liverpool with Manchester, and Brindley did it—30 miles of canal carried over a course of infinite difficulty, including two rivers and two deep valleys, the first crossed by aqueducts and the second by broad and lofty embankments.

He had a genius for economy, for mastering difficulties by invention. It is impossible to follow him through all his works, which gave England 365 miles of canals, a marvellous means of transport in the days before railways. He stimulated industry enormously, for he opened up coalfields which had been inaccessible and manufacturing sites which had lain idle.

England has never produced another man like Brindley. All the complex calculations for his engineering feats he worked out in his head. He lived only for his work. Once he went to a play and it completely upset him, confusing his ideas, he said, and unfitting him for business. Why did people want to bother with such things when there were canals to build? Canals were his grand passion. He told a Parliamentary Committee that Nature had provided rivers to serve as feeders to canals.

When challenged by any specially difficult problem he would go to bed, and stay there wrestling with it. When he got up the problem was solved, and operations would begin. Rough and uncouth, he spoke like a genius, and Carlyle's picture of him is perfect:

The rugged Brindley has little to say for himself; the rugged Brindley, when difficulties accumulate, retires silent, generally to his bed that he may be in perfect privacy there, and ascertain in his rough head how the difficulties may be overcome.

The eloquent Brindley, behold, he has chained seas together; his ships do visibly float over valleys, invisibly through the hearts of mountains. The Mersey and the Thames, the Humber and the Severn, have shaken hands. Nature most audibly answers, Yea!

Here they brought James Brindley to rest after a lifetime of hard work which had brought enduring fame to him and a golden opportunity to his country.

The Poet Who Knew Shakespeare

NORBURY. Set in a beautiful countryside the village has records running back to a Saxon priest. It has an unlovely brick tower to its grand 14th-century church, but within is great compensation, for the nave with its fine pillars, and the chancel with its four stone seats, are splendid original work, and over all are the great beams which have borne the high-pitched roof for 600 years.

Two 14th-century possessions of the church are the founder's tomb and a brass portrait, the tomb showing Ralph le Botiller, cross-legged and in chain armour, with a red coat and shield, the brass showing his wife in a cloak and veil. The founder was the central figure of a grim story. In 1302 he summoned the rector on a charge of stealing fish from the manor pond, but failed to prove his accusation. Three years later one of his servants murdered the rector, and it is thought Botiller built the church as an act of expiation.

The broken 15th-century figure of a knight in armour, lying under the tower, is believed to be Sir Edward le Botiller, and one of the two stone women in the chancel is thought to be his wife. A slate memorial in the chancel to Robert Skrymsher records that his father was Adjutant-General to Prince Rupert.

The Skrymshers bought the Tudor manor and it passed in the reign of Elizabeth to Richard Barnfield by his marriage to the heiress. Their eldest son Richard, the poet, was born in 1574 at the manor house, which stood until the beginning of last century. Going up to Oxford at 15, Barnfield came to London, and, with wealth and scholarships to commend him, won the friendship of the leading

Newcastle-under-Lyme   The Iron Market

Burslem
The Wedgwood Institute

Newcastle-under-Lyme
A Corner of Bridge Street

Bagot's Bromley   Beggar's Oa

Rudyard   The Silver Lak

poets of the age. It is considered certain that he was for some time in close touch with Shakespeare.

By a strange stroke of destiny the young poet travelled down the centuries shorn of his chief laurels, which were added to Shakespeare's, for from 1599 until our own day his sonnet, "If music and sweet poetry agree," and the ode beginning

As it fell upon a day
In the merry month of May

were always included in The Passionate Pilgrim, and ascribed to his immortal contemporary. Barnfield himself sleeps at Stone.

NORTON CANES. It is sometimes known as Norton-under-Cannock, a mining village which saw its church burnt down and built again half a century ago. With its tower and its grey stone walls, all that was spared by the fire, the church has a red-tiled roof and a porch at the end of a row of dwarf yews. The fine east window, a tribute to heroes of peace and war in our own day, shows a radiant St James in a purple cloak, St John glowing in red, and a company of miners, some going down the pit and others dressed as soldiers. Here are two interesting memorials, a century-old monument of a beautiful woman with long hair mourning for Phineas Hussey, and a brass inscription to William Collis who was rector for more than the first half of the 15th century. A mile or so away is Little Wyrley Grove, a 17th-century gabled house with tall chimneys.

The First Cable Across the Atlantic

OAKAMOOR. A small place below a steep hill and amid the glorious scenery of the Churnet Valley, it is proud to have had a hand in one of the greatest engineering feats of the 19th century.

Here is the factory of Thomas Bolton to which Sir Charles Bright entrusted the making of the core of the first Atlantic cable. It was the people at Oakamoor who made the copper core, which was twisted in seven strands to be afterwards sheathed and armoured and fashioned into the actual cable laid down. It was the people of Oakamoor who made most of the 20,000 miles of wire which formed the copper conductor of the current and weighed 90 pounds to the mile. The factory produced this essential portion of the cable at a cost of £5 a mile, and we think the folk here, though the first cable was broken, must have been proud at that later day in 1858 when the first telegraphic message was flashed from continent to continent.

None could fail to be proud of being associated, however humbly, with what, at any distance of time, must be regarded as the tremendous feat of laying the Atlantic cable, a task accomplished in the face of heartbreaking disappointments and by the supreme resolve to gather every resource of discovery and invention to prevent their recurrence. The cable itself, begun in 1857, was finished in June and before the end of July was stowed partly in the British ship Agamemnon and partly in the American ship Niagara.

After the shore end of the cable had been landed in Valencia harbour the Niagara began the task of paying it out. For six days all went well, though slowly, and then, when 380 miles had been laid, the cable snapped and with it went £100,000, when the cost of preparations and postponement was reckoned. Next year, 700 miles of new cable having been made, the same ships renewed the attempt, meeting in mid ocean and intending to pay out from there in opposite directions. Again there were breaks followed by splices, but at last, in 1858, Newfoundland and Valencia were connected.

Then to everyone's dismay the cable, owing to mistaken ideas on the part of its electrical engineer, refused to work. Lord Kelvin was called in and managed to get messages through. Communication was established amid wild rejoicings on both sides of the Atlantic and altogether 732 messages were sent between England and America. But the damage done to the cable was now beginning to tell its tale, and at the height of the rejoicings communication failed altogether on the 20th of October and the first Atlantic cable fell silent for ever. Not till seven years later was the first successful cable laid.

The Strange Adventures of a Brass

OKEOVER. It has the beauty of the Dove and the ancient house of the Okeovers in their stately park, the modernised hall looking down on a beautiful avenue of limes and elms. King of the park is the magnificent Wishing Oak, with a trunk 29 feet round and a crown still green and vigorous.

In this park the Okeovers have safely traversed the centuries as one of the oldest families in England. Not since William Rufus has the village known any but an Okeover as its manorial lord. When

Charles Edward, the Young Pretender, came this way on his scurry to and from Derby in 1745, the head of the house was absent and the chaplain was in charge. A letter exists written by him to his master telling a rueful tale of outrages here by the Pretender's followers, who pillaged the house and church, picked the servants' pockets of their pence, robbed the parson of a treasured 1s 6d and his silver tobacco-box, and then, having threatened all with death, departed with the squire's horses and his saddles and bridles. Anything but a Bonnie Prince was Charles Edward to Staffordshire.

Near the hall is the church, with a 15th-century tower looking down on a 14th-century nave and chancel. It has a fine oak screen guarded by winged dragons, and memorials to the Okeovers, the most beautiful being a delightful angel holding a laurel for Mary Okeover, who died in 1764. Her husband soon followed her to the grave, and their inscription has the lines:

> *Thrice happy pair, in nuptial love so tied,*
> *Whom death but for a moment could divide.*

But the most famous of the Okeover memorials is a brass with a very queer story. Midway through the 15th century died William Lord Zouch, and his portrait was engraved on brass, showing him with two wives. When Humphrey Okeover died in 1538 this brass was stolen for him, the back of it being engraved with the 13 children of Humphrey and his wife. So matters stood for about three centuries, when the brass was stolen a second time, and in the end it came to light broken into 55 fragments. Mounted on oak these now hang in the nave, with a perfect figure of a woman in a big headdress and a sweeping gown, and with several childish figures, but as for Humphrey Okeover, with whose death the crime began, he has vanished for ever. Yet he is not entirely lost to knowledge, for his portrait is in a window, and there he surveys other windows with other members of his family, and looks down on the shattered brass that knows him no more.

The Six Princesses

OULTON. Six Saxon princesses are to be seen in this hillside village about a mile from Stone. Very lovely they are, all shining in one of the fine windows of the Pugin chapel of St Mary's Abbey, established here in 1794. An elaborate reredos has fine statues of Peter and Paul, and another lovely possession is a gilded iron screen. The grey buildings of the convent and the brick and stone walls of the 17th-century old hall with its low wall and yew hedge are pleasant features of Oulton, which has a modern church with a St George and five portraits of Our Lord in its windows.

The Fate of a Pitiless Man

PATSHULL. Church, great house, and cottages are all in its park of 800 acres, where we found pheasants and rabbits on the lawns, and rainbow trout gleaming in a stream which feeds two lakes.

The hall, made new in the 18th century, has been owned by three famous families, the Astleys, the Pigots, and the Earls of Dartmouth. Near the church are two pillars with gamecocks set up by a gambling squire to commemorate the fact that, having lost the estate by one wager, he won it back by another; and another curiosity of the park is a stone statue of a man in armour, with long curly hair, said to be the Duke of Monmouth.

The church, with its domed tower, comes from the 17th century, and has fine old yews about it. Near a wall is an ancient coffin lid; on the chancel roof St Michael slays his dragon.

Its founder, Sir Robert Astley, lies in armour on a 16th-century tomb with his wife and charming figures of their 15 children. The Richard who rebuilt the church is with his two wives on a finely sculptured 17th-century monument, he in Jacobean costume. He appears again in a panel at the head of his cavalry squadron, his wives on pedestals.

Here was born and here sleeps Sir Robert Pigot, who fought at Fontenoy; and here is a memory of the one ignoble Pigot, Robert's nephew Hugh. Baptised in this church in 1769, he entered the Navy, where his conduct was marked by an increasing severity which degenerated into tyranny. As captain of a frigate off the coast of South America he called to men up in the rigging that he would cause the last man down to be flogged, and in their haste two men fell to the deck dead at his feet. "Throw the lubbers overboard!" said Pigot, and that night the enraged crew mutinied and threw their pitiless captain overboard after them.

Framed on a wall is a wooden cross from the grave of Lord

Guernsey, killed on the Aisne in 1914. The graceful iron chancel screen is gilded and decorated with roses, and the oak pulpit has cherubs with urns on their heads.

There is a window with a trumpeting angel in memory of the famous Bishop Selwyn, and another to Bishop Lonsdale whom he succeeded, and in the sanctuary window is beautiful glass illustrating six of Our Lord's sayings.

The Golden Collar

PATTINGHAM. Here on a day of long ago a man found a treasure hid in a field, a gold collar about four feet long, that may have been lost a dozen centuries or more.

An attractive village on the Shropshire border, it has much beauty. In the churchyard is an old yew about ten feet round, a fine cedar, a weathered sundial on an ornamental pillar, and a Crucifix crowning an ancient cross. Above all rises the 14th-century tower of the finely placed church, its modern spire a lovely spectacle, unusual in Staffordshire. The massive north arcade was built by the Normans, and the spacious chancel is by our earliest English builders. The font, much changed, has been here about 800 years; at it George Greenstreet christened the children for 53 years of last century. On the south wall of the church are the oldest clocks in the village, two mass dials.

The Little Town of a Thousand Years

PENKRIDGE. A town of Saxon days, it gave the world a rare example of its love of progress by welcoming the coming of the railway and insisting that certain express trains should halt daily at its little station. Halt they still do.

Pillaton Hall two miles away, which has been the home of the Littleton family for three centuries, is now partly in ruins, and its moat is dry, but it has still its 16th-century gateway with four little turrets, and a medieval chapel. Near the chapel lies a quern, looking ancient enough to have ground corn for generations before the Littletons arrived.

A veritable gallery of monuments the stately church has, with its 14th-century tower and 13th-century arcades on lofty pillars. Nave and chancel are both 700 years old; the rest of the building is of the 15th and 16th centuries, the font from Cromwell's days. One of the most interesting things here is the 18th-century iron screen, given to a Dutch bride of the Littletons by a Dutch settler in South Africa.

In the beautiful sanctuary window is fine modern glass, with nine scenes from the life of Christ in memory of Edward Littleton, first Baron Hatherton, who has slept in the chancel since 1862. He was a warm advocate of reform, and Chief Secretary for Ireland.

In the chancel, which has a floor of fine coloured marble, are six grand old stalls with carved misereres. Eight angels from bygone days support the modern roof of the nave, and there is beautiful old carving in two choir screens.

The monuments show the last of the old manorial family, a 16th-century alabaster portrait group of William Winnesbury with his wife and daughter in girdled gowns, caps, and veils. The earliest of the Littleton monuments (1518) is the canopied alabaster engraving of Richard, with a pouch and dagger at his girdle, the heiress he married, and their seven children, all of whom worshipped in the chapel Richard built on becoming owner of the hall. He is the last of the Richards; the heirs for about a dozen generations after him are Edwards, the younger sons Williams.

Sir Edward Littleton, who lies on a tomb of coloured marble, is wearing armour and a necklace; and with him are two wives in close-fitting caps, and 10 children. The third Edward has an elaborate Tudor tomb showing him with flowing hair and beard, wearing armour and a ruff, his wife and their 16 children with him.

Most striking of all is the finely preserved double-decker monument in which a 17th-century Sir Edward and his wife kneel under canopies, with the next generation below them. The children of the two families are in panels, 26 portraits in all.

The only memorial to the Williams of the family is a 17th-century monument with a curious feature, for there are four Williams in the group. Father William kneels with his wife and their nine children, three of the sons called William.

On the monuments is verse of poor quality; but Penkridge finds compensation in the work of one of its own poets, Cecil James Tildesley, born here in 1877. His song on Cannock Chase has this joyous lyrical opening:

Oh have you seen, on Cannock Chase,
The Birches, queens of silver grace,
When Autumn's magic hand hath set
On each a golden coronet?

Truly there is something to charm the muse in this little town to which King Edgar issued a charter about a thousand years ago.

A Flaxman Sculpture

PENN. Across the common once part of the Royal Forest of Kinver we climb up to Penn tower among the trees. It is cased in red brick of the 18th century.

Two arches in the church are 13th century, and there is a fascinating collection of ancient tiles paving the sanctuary. Similar to some known to be 600 years old in Westminster Abbey, they show crowned figures, musicians, and bishops, all quaint and comical and marvellously preserved. A pathetic little memorial with no date was put on these walls by a mother "in memory of her lovely infant"; and the graceful sculpture of a woman by Flaxman is in memory of John Marsh of 1795, a Staffordshire magistrate.

One of the carved oak screens was put up by a man who worshipped here for half a century; and the other is in memory of Sir Alfred Hickman, a well-known ironmaster and colliery proprietor who died in 1910. He advocated the development of the canal system from the Midlands to the ports of London, Liverpool, and Gloucester.

RANTON. Here, on Vicarage Farm, is a house with a priest's room and timber said to be 800 years old, while Ranton Abbey is a modern house near a noble tower among tall trees. The tower itself is about 500 years old, all that remains of a priory founded here in the 12th century.

A yew about 14 feet round keeps company with the 13th-century church, which has been little changed except for some 18th-century brickwork. Two bells, which have a shed for belfry, are believed to have rung the monks to service in the great days of the priory.

The Ancient Cross

ROCESTER. It has lost a Roman camp and a Norman abbey. The camp was near a house known as Barrow Hill, and among the treasures found in its seven acres have been a brass spearhead,

coins, and pottery. Of the abbey founded in 1146 nothing is to be
seen except green mounds in a field near the church.

Though Rocester has lost much, it is proud to have saved what is
said to be the best-preserved cross in Staffordshire. It is about
20 feet high and has a beautiful clustered shaft on three steps. Ornamented with stars, the cross is thought to be 700 years old.

Although this small town near the meeting of the Dove and the
Churnet is very old, its church, which has a cotton mill for company,
has seen only two generations. The tower has a small spire; and
among the windows is one with ten beautiful scenes from the
life of Christ.

A Dovedale Village

ROLLESTON. Beautiful in the valley of the Dove, with Derbyshire but a stride away, it has woods and copses everywhere.
High above it all rises the fine spire of the 14th-century church.

Relatively a newcomer to the church is perhaps the oldest thing
visible in the village, the great head of a splendid Saxon cross, placed
by an outer wall of the tower. This rich treasure was found forming
part of the floor of a porch at Tatenhill Church, and an archaeological
gem despised in one village has come to be the cherished prize
of another.

Except for a modern aisle the church is 14th century. The most
surprising of the monuments is the alabaster figure in a chancel niche
of Robert Sherebourne, lying as if asleep in the robes he wore as
Bishop of Chichester for 28 of the most troublous years of the reign
of Henry the Eighth. There is a statue of him in his old cathedral,
but here he is, and above him in a glass case his episcopal seal has
been hanging since 1536.

The earliest monument shows the engraved figure of John Rolleston, a 15th-century lord of the manor, lying in armour such as was
worn during the Wars of the Roses, with a lion at his feet. By him is
his wife, whose close-fitting gown is crowned by a hat like a flower-
pot. At her feet is the happiest of little dogs. Below the parents are
their three children.

The strangest sculpture is the 16th-century alabaster Caldwell
group. At the top kneel Thomas in a cloak and a ruff and his wife in
a high-crowned hat and a ruff, and below, set between four columns,
are their three solemn little sons, clad exactly like their father.

The long reign of the Rollestons ended soon after James the First's began, when they sold the manor to the Mosleys, of whom Sir Edward, founder of that line here, is shown on a fine alabaster tomb, wearing the tunic, breeches, ruff, and long cloak of the period.

Fine old glass in the Mosley chapel shows the Baptism and the presentation in the Temple, and among modern glass is an appealing Annunciation by Kempe and a delightful Good Samaritan.

Four Churches in a Hundred Years

ROWLEY REGIS. A Black Country town set on a hillside rising over 700 feet. It has mines and industries of many kinds, and famous quarries yielding the very hard stone called Rowley Rag, much used in paving.

The red-brick church is very light and charming inside. In the east window is attractive glass of Our Lord and four saints, and in the chapel some excellent modern woodwork. A window and the finely carved font are in memory of a little boy of six whose jolly portrait is here in a medallion of the glass.

Misfortune seems to have dogged the church of Rowley Regis. For about 600 years there was a Norman building here, until it came to be rebuilt in 1840; 60 years later the rebuilt structure became unsafe and was condemned, a new church being built in 1904. After nine years this too perished, burnt down in the miserable Suffragette riots, and the present building was raised in 1923.

In the vestry we saw a portrait of a man who was baptised in the original Norman church, his lifetime spanning all four buildings.

The Name that Everybody Knows

RUDYARD. It gave the Empire a name known all the world over and it is in the heart of enchanting natural beauty, a tiny place at the end of Rudyard Lake, a reservoir of 400 acres and two miles long.

The centre of Staffordshire's little Lake District, it has glorious woods crowding down to the water's edge, and is a place of pilgrimage for lovers of beautiful things who come all the year round.

For some of us there is an invisible attraction, for here began the union which gave Rudyard Kipling to the world. Among the leafy paths of this wonderland a few miles from the drabness of the Five

Towns, walked young Lockwood Kipling and Alice Macdonald. Here it was that he asked her to be his wife, and here she said she would; and so happy were they that when their son was born in India they christened him Rudyard in memory of this corner of Staffordshire that had meant so much to them.

The Explorer of the Rocks

RUGELEY. A pleasant little town looking to the splendour of the hills of Cannock Chase, it has a town hall with a buttressed tower, a capital library, and a covered market. Two men have made it notable, a good one and a bad one; and it has two churches that look at each other, a new one and an old one. The town also has an impressive Roman Catholic church in Lichfield Street, built in the 19th century, with a graceful tapering spire 150 feet high.

The old church became ruinous last century, and was deserted for its successor, but something has been saved from the wreck. Although the 14th-century tower seems beyond redemption, here are still the 13th-century chancel, with a 14th-century window, a piscina, and the stone seats for the priests for whom the chancel doorway was built 500 years ago. There is a brass portrait of John Weston, wearing the long cloak and costume of Shakespeare's early days. Although reduced in size and with much of its glory vanished, the ancient church serves yet for worship.

The new parish church, which replaces the ruin, is chiefly notable for its fine oak pulpit, carved with grapes, roses, and acorns as a setting for a noble figure of St Augustine. In the churchyard are the ashes of Thomas George Bonney, Rugeley's most distinguished son, who left the rectory here for Uppingham and Cambridge, to distinguish himself in mathematics and classics. A born student of Nature, geology was his abiding passion, and during his vacations he explored practically the whole mountain systems of Europe, afterwards extending his investigations to the New World.

Entering the Church, he became lecturer on Geology at Cambridge and London and President of the British Association. He was one of the pioneers of the microscopical study of rocks. He fired his students with an enthusiasm matching his own, and led them to study the rocks in all parts of the kingdom. Retiring after a quarter of a century in London to study and write in the quiet of Cambridge he spent his last 22 years there, and died in 1923, leaving a record of work and discovery which had made him world famous.

Perhaps it is the bad man of Rugeley who is most widely known. His name is brought up by the most striking thing in the churchyard, a tombstone to John Parsons Cook, with the date 1855 and the statement that "his life was taken away." Behind that inscription lurks a terrible story. The man who took away the life of Cook was William Palmer, the Rugeley poisoner.

The Palmer Poison Case

WILLIAM PALMER, the Rugeley poisoner, born in 1824 and educated at the grammar school here, became acquainted with the nature of drugs as an apprentice to a Liverpool firm of druggists. He settled down as a doctor in a house opposite the Talbot Arms.

Five children were born to him, all but one dying in infancy. His practice being unremunerative, he took to betting and racehorse-owning, seeking extrication from money difficulties by forging bills. In 1854 his wife, whom he had insured for £13,000, died with mysterious suddenness; and within a year his brother, whom he had insured for a similar amount, also died. On this occasion, however, a suspicious insurance company refused payment.

Palmer was by this time deeply in debt to a bookmaker, John Parsons Cook. Attending Shrewsbury races with him, Palmer gave him poison and then conveyed him here, lodging him at the Talbot Arms. The poison did not kill him, and Cook summoned two other doctors, arranging that one should share his bedroom for the night. As Cook's medical attendant, Palmer was summoned from his house across the way, arriving immediately, ready dressed, as if he had expected a call. He gave the patient two more pills, and these effected his purpose, for his victim died in his presence.

The visiting doctor suspected no ill, but analysts from London declared that death was due to poison in the medicine Palmer had administered, and the coroner's jury returned a verdict of wilful murder against him. A hue and cry followed, for other people had died mysteriously after association with Palmer, but the police contented themselves with the exhumation of his wife and brother.

The case excited all Europe. The Times published an astounding article before the trial in London was reached, stating that Palmer had many partisans in Rugeley, adding: "The postmaster of the place is a spy in his interests, intercepts letters, and reports to him the contents. The very coroner of the adjacent county town, his judge, is for him as though he had been engaged as a solicitor for the defence, receives from him intercepted evidence from the other side, shrewd suggestions in his favour, and a present of game."

An astonishing feature of the 12-days trial was that, with all its resources, the prosecution was unable to identify the poison employed. Experts who attended the trial believed Palmer knew far more than his accusers about poisons, and had practised methods too subtle for them to penetrate.

Palmer staggered on hearing the verdict, but instantly recovered. The execution was carried out in public at Stafford.

A persistent legend tells how Rugeley sent a deputation to wait on Lord Palmerston, the Prime Minister, seeking permission to change the name of the town. "What name do you propose to substitute—Palmerstown?" he laughingly asked, and the deputation could not be sure whether such a name might be supposed to commemorate the Premier or the murderer; the subject was allowed to drop.

The Carnon Balls of the Civil War

RUSHALL. There were stirring scenes in this suburb of Walsall in 1643 when Prince Rupert attacked the old hall. It was bravely defended by the wife of Colonel Edward Leigh, but the Royalists made it their headquarters till they were driven out. A few of the cannon balls fired at the house can still be seen in the ruins of the medieval walls. The Harpers defended the house in the Wars of the Roses, and their arms are still on the gateway.

The last of the Leighs to live at Rushall Hall has been sleeping in the church since 1671. He was Edward Leigh, proud to his dying day of the way his wife had defended his house. He was a soldier, student of law, and a writer of books.

The church, which has been refashioned since his day, has a font 700 years old, and a fresco with daintily coloured angels. In the tree-shaded churchyard is the base of an old cross on three steps.

STAFFORDSHIRE

The Chapel in the Wilderness

RUSHTON SPENCER. It is a remarkable church we find here and a grim story that is told here. The story is of a young man buried alive—Thomas Meaykin, who has been sleeping under a stone in the churchyard since 1781.

"As a man falleth before wicked men, so fell I," we read, and the tale is that because Thomas was in love with his master's daughter her father had him drugged and buried alive at Stone. His friends, who are said to have opened his coffin and found him lying face downwards, brought his body to lie here in the place he had known as a child. He sleeps by the church on a wooded hilltop apart from the village, noble firs and old yews about him; one of the yews is probably 500 years old.

The church, once known as the Chapel in the Wilderness, is unique in the county for having been built almost entirely of wood 600 years ago; though Shropshire and Cheshire have their timbered churches, this is the only one we have come upon in Staffordshire. A quaint little building, it has a short wooden tower with an 18th-century belfry, a nave and chancel with timber walls inside, and a stone east wall. The north aisle and the Swythamley chapel are of stone about 300 years old, and there is a 20th-century porch and a west gallery of 1719. The pulpit is of 17th-century oak, and the massive font probably twice as old. In a beautiful modern window is a picture of the Sower.

Above the village rises the Cloud, a sombre hill nearly 1200 feet high, from which we look over Staffordshire and Cheshire.

The Story of the Five Hills

SANDON. It stirs our imagination by the beauty of the scene and the memories of the great. Its splendid 500-acre park, home of the Earls of Harrowby, with magnificent views of the Wrekin, of the Clent Hills, of storied Chartley, and of the famous spires of Lichfield, is a little kingdom of great interest, embracing the fine hall which replaces the Elizabethan house burnt down last century, the church, a lake, and at the end of an avenue of trees the moat, still wet, which long guarded the ancient manor of the Erdeswickes.

The Erdeswickes were famous people in their day, but this place has links with other names which have outlived them all. Sandon has reminders of two Prime Ministers. The monument to Pitt was raised by his Foreign Minister, the first Earl of Harrowby, who set up to his chief's memory a column 75 feet high, modelled on the famous Trajan column. The other monument to a Premier is a Gothic shrine to Spencer Perceval, who was shot in the lobby of the House of Commons by a demented bankrupt. Not far from these memorials is a notable example of the work of the man who built the House of Parliament: it is the summit of the tower Sir Charles Barry raised at Trentham Hall, brought here when that great house was taken down early this century.

The 13th-century church stands on high ground, with a 15th-century tower looking down on eight stalwart yews. The south aisle is believed to have been the original church; the nave and the north chapel are 600 years old. There is ancient glass in the sanctuary, a Norman font and a Jacobean one, and an altar table, and a canopied pulpit.

The most famous possessions of the church are the monuments of the Erdeswickes, descendants of proud Normans. Hugh Erdeswicke is in his 15th-century armour, with his wife in an ermine cloak, and their son Hugh, armoured but bareheaded, with his wife. Sampson Erdeswicke, who saw the red reign of Mary Tudor, lies with a dog at his feet, his wife in a long gown, and their five children. It was said of the next Hugh that he was "the sorest and most dangerous Papist in England"; here in this churchyard he struck a magistrate "upon the pate with his crabtree staff." On an immense monument is a second Sampson Erdeswicke in his red tunic and cloak, his two wives wearing long black dresses and white ruffs.

A pathetic story had the second wife, a Leicestershire heiress who first married Everard Digby and became the mother of a son who grew to manhood, a young giant in stature, full of promise. His widowed mother married Sampson and became a second time a widow, with only her son Everard Digby to comfort her. Everard turned Roman Catholic, and she turned too, and she had the agony of seeing him plunge into the murderous Gunpowder Plot which brought him to the scaffold. Sampson, with whom she kneels, settled down here to half a century of scholarly activity, the chief fruit of his labours being his treasured History of Staffordshire. He lavished time and fortune on this church, reglazing and restoring

building his own tomb and monument, and painting the chancel
alls with his family pedigree. His artistic record was lost, but in
929, bright as the day they were painted, out from hiding came the
ld scholar's proud proclamation of the glory of the Erdeswickes.
Iere are all his pictures as he had them painted in 1603, genealogical
ees rising from the tombs below, some of the trunks encircled with
oneysuckle and vine. The ancestral trees being too small for all the
eraldry of all the families he would commemorate, their shields are
ung on branches or painted like stained glass windows on the walls.

But the proud Erdeswickes are not all the pride of Sandon. There
s a white stone near the porch in the churchyard which tells us that
ere lies the old vicar Walter Carless. Little was known of him, but
much we know of his wife. She is dear to us because she was Dr
ohnson's first love, and a cherished friend of his old age.

Dr Johnson's Might-Have-Been

ANN HECTOR was a Lichfield girl, sister of one of Johnson's
choolmates. When the infatuation began and when it ended we do
ot know. Ann comes to knowledge late in the old scholar's life.

In the course of a visit to Birmingham, where Hector then lived,
ohnson, who was now 69, said to Boswell, "You will see, sir, at
Mr Hector's, his sister, Mrs Carless, a clergyman's widow. She was
he first woman with whom I was ever in love. It dropped out of my
ead imperceptibly; but she and I will always have a kindness for
ach other."

The same night he recurred to the subject as he and Boswell sat
lone. "If I had married her it might have been as happy for me,"
he mused. And then, challenged on the subject, he declared that it
was ridiculous to think that there was such a thing as only one
woman for one man; things might work out very well if the Lord
Chancellor, knowing all the circumstances, made marriages without
the parties having any choice in the matter. There, however, we may
assume that he was once more talking nonsense.

Ann's brother would have been proud of Johnson as his sister's
husband. In youth he and two other boys used to call at Johnson's
house in the morning, and, seating the young giant on his back, with
one boy on either side as support, would carry him in triumph to
school. He loved and venerated his old friend, and a few days

before Johnson's death he wrote him an account of all he coul‹
remember of their boyhood, when Mrs Carless was Ann Hector
the gaunt young scholar's heroine.

A Judge and a Poet

SEDGLEY. Set on high ground at the edge of the Black Country
its church is widely seen in this district where spires and chimney
stand out above all else. It is a dignified building, impressive as w
approach it and just over a century old, though it has preserve‹
memorials from an earlier church.

In the porch is a tablet to Michael Nickins and his wife, the onl‹
surviving great-granddaughter of Sir Matthew Hale, a famous lawye
in the time of Charles Stuart and the Commonwealth. He wa
counsel for Archbishop Laud in his impeachment, and prosper‹
under both Royalists and Roundheads. Cromwell made him ‹
Judge, and 18 years later Charles the Second raised him to be Lor‹
Chief Justice.

Hereabouts were born two poets of county fame who lived on t‹
our own time, David Bailey, a Shakespeare student long associate‹
with Sir Isaac Pitman, and John Cornfield, a Radical reformer, ‹
brickmaker, pawnbroker, and eccentric member of the Board o‹
Guardians which sat at Dudley. John Cornfield was found drowne‹
on his own estate, and left behind this verse among his writings:

> So man comes forth a peevish April fool;
> In vain pursuits oft wastes his life away;
> Fain would he take from heaven its sovereign rule,
> And have unclouded sunshine every day.
> Forgets that summer's bounteous crops depend
> On winter's rigour and the stormy blast,
> That they who sow in tears till life shall end
> Shall reap with joy in summer-land at last.

The Pictures Five Hundred Years Old

SEIGHFORD. Here lies a knight of the exciting Armada days
Sir William Bowyer, whose splendid tomb is one of the treasure‹
of the church. Sir William wears armour; his wife is in a long gow‹
and ruff, and with them are their six children, one in swaddling clothe‹

Other things to see in this church, rebuilt by the Normans on ‹
Saxon foundation, are the arches and massive pillars of the nort‹

The 13th Century Nave and Norman Font of St Mary's

The Handsome Norman Arches of St Chad's

STAFFORD'S OLD CHURCHES

Ellastone   Adam Bede's House

Shallowford   Izaak Walton's Cottage

rcade and the fine chancel arch, all Norman. The tower is 18th entury, but the chancel is 15th, and has a medieval window with ortraits of a Madonna and Child, St Christopher crossing the river, queen, a nun, a man, and a girl with golden hair, all nearly 500 ears old. The fine pulpit is Jacobean.

Seighford, three miles from Stafford, is pleasant with its charming hatched cottages, and a black-and-white hall with tall chimneys ising above noble cedars.

Izaak Walton's Farm

SHALLOWFORD. It is by the River Meece, and it should be a place of pilgrimage for all anglers, for here is Izaak Walton's arm, curiously named Halfhead. The brick-and-timber outbuildings re still much as he must have seen them, the black-and-white ottage still quaint and delightful. It was this farm that the kindly zaak left to his native town of Stafford, stipulating that the rent hould be used each year to apprentice two poor boys, provide a narriage portion for a servant girl, and buy coal for the needy.

His cottage was opened as a museum in 1924 and has unhappily een burned down twice since, but it has been built up again and efurnished carefully in a worthy effort to recapture the spirit of he angler's peaceful days.

Here are all kinds of things fishermen delight in, old pictures of Walton's day, pictures of a fishing house where he and his friend Cotton loved to idle, and the fireplace at which he sat long ago. How dearly Walton loved this corner of Staffordshire we know from one of his poems, picturing his life of contentment here:

> Here give my weary spirits rest,
> And raise my low-pitched thoughts above
> Earth, or what poor mortals love:
> Thus, free from lawsuits and the noise
> Of Princes' courts, I would rejoice;
> Or with my Bryan and a book,
> Loiter long days near Shawford brook;
> There sit by him, and eat my meat,
> There see the sun both rise and set;
> There bid good morning to next day;
> There meditate my time away,
> And angle on and beg to have
> A quiet passage to a welcome grave.

N

THE KING'S ENGLAND

Old Jack of Hilton

SHARESHILL. One of the strangest of feudal tenures is re
membered in this village, where an old hall and a church hav
the company of a windmill which, sailless and abandoned now, wa
grinding corn when Charles the Second was king.

Hilton Hall, home of the Vernons for the last four centuries, ha
still in it much that was familiar to the Swynnertons, lords of th
manor long before the Vernons arrived. In the 100-acre park stand
the lofty tower built in 1741 by Henry Vernon to commemorate th
capture of Portobello in 1739 by his Admiral kinsman.

In the hall is preserved a medieval hollow brass figure, a ma
leaning on his knee, with a hand on his breast, known as Jack c
Hilton. Under a feudal charter the lord of the neighbouring manc
of Essington held his lands on condition that each New Year's da
he brought here a live goose, and drove it three times round th
central fire of the hall. Filled with water through a hole which wa
afterwards plugged, Jack of Hilton was placed in the fire; the wate
boiled and issued as steam from his mouth. The promenade wit
the goose had to be completed while Jack steamed, after which th
bird was carried to a table, where its owner received from the lor
of the hall his title deed to another year's tenancy.

From the mound on which the tower stands an immense swee
of splendid country extending into Wales is visible. Near at han
is the medieval tower of the church, all that is left of the 15th-centur
building. It has a battered heritage of its ancient treasure in tw
sadly worn and broken figures, one said to represent Sir Humphre
Swynnerton and the other his wife. He wears his armour, with a chai
and pendant, she has her ruff; they are the last visible links wit
the ancient family from whom the hall passed to the Vernons.

Among the vicars here last century was William Havergal, on
of the most gifted musicians the church has produced. From boy
hood an organist, he was ordained when 23, but met with an acciden
which crippled him for years. During that time he found consolatio
in musical composition; he wrote anthems, services, and hymns
he brought about a re-birth of glory in church music. France
Ridley Havergal, writer of many famous hymns, was his daughter
and after his death in 1870 she edited and published his work.

SHEEN. For a lovely view of the famous Dove Valley we should climb Sheen Hill, and for a peep of a charming village we should come to Sheen with its gracious country by the river. Here is a delightful vicarage with grey walls and windows of all shapes and sizes, a 15th-century cross on five steps, and a church made new last century. The oldest stones are in the north wall, and outside the east window, exposed to the wind and rain, is the worn figure of a priest who ministered here 400 years ago. From the chancel arch hangs a wooden cross with a copy of Murillo's Head of Christ.

Nelson's Captain

SHENSTONE. On a windy hilltop, below two towers, sleeps the last of Nelson's captains, Admiral Parker. He was a middy at 12, commanded his own ship when he was 21 and took part in the famous chase of Villeneuve, the man who lost Trafalgar. By 1812 he was rich enough to buy Shenstone Lodge, where he lived for 15 years as a country gentleman, but he answered his country's call in 1827, and 14 years later sailed to China, where he captured many towns and won a knighthood. In the 30 years which followed he did much to establish a high standard of discipline in the navy.

The old church he knew was pulled down in 1852, but the 13th-century doorway and the old tower are here. In the churchyard, a magnificent view-point, is an old font. The new church has in its own tall tower an oak reredos with a panel of St George and the Dragon, and a wheel window in memory of the Admiral.

Neighbour of Birmingham

SMETHWICK. It is a neighbour of Birmingham and in the grip of great engineering works, as is right, seeing that James Watt's first engine was set up here and worked here 115 years before it was removed to Tipton, where it may now be seen. The town has fine open spaces in its two parks, one of them of 42 acres, given by Sir James Chance, whose lighthouse works are here. There is a bronze of him by Hamo Thornycroft inside the gates.

The name of Chance shines round the world. For nearly a hundred years this firm has been making lamps more wonderful than Aladdin's. Here was made one to cast a beam with an intensity equal to over a million candles; it has thousands of prisms for bending rays of light, every one set with focal accuracy so that not a scrap of light is wasted. In clear weather it has a range of about 100 miles over the Mediterranean. Here also we found working, in the works yard, an automatic light which lights itself when fog or darkness comes. Smethwick has little that is ancient, but it has a famous place in industry.

Two canals run through the town side by side, but with one at a much higher level than the other, and above them soars Summit Bridge at a place where nature is still rich and green along the water's edge.

There is a quiet corner at Holy Trinity church, ringed in with trees close by the schools. We enter through a lychgate built in our own time, both labour and material being a freewill offering of friends. The church is dark and spacious, with some pleasing modern glass in the big east window (a Crucifixion) and in a panel of St George dedicated to the memory of an artilleryman of the Great War.

In the old red brick Chapel, built in 1732, is a fine modern memorial window to Sir John Mitchell, with a beautiful picture of the Adoration as its centre panel. It came from the studio of Thomas Camm in this town, which has sent out so many splendid windows to our churches.

The Busy Capital

STAFFORD. Twelve hundred years ago began the story of Stafford as we know it. Here St Bertelin, prince of the Mercian kingdom, renounced that kingdom and built himself a hermitage. Here Alfred's daughter Ethelfleda built fortifications against the Danes. Here one of the Conqueror's own kinsman was feudal lord. Here came Richmond on his way to Bosworth Field to found the Tudor dynasty, and here came Elizabeth, receiving from the people the gift of a silver cup. We may still see a little of the town as Henry Tudor would have seen it, and a little more that Elizabeth would have known. Parts of it are little changed since Stuart days.

Old England lives on in Stafford's busy streets, Tudor days and the Twentieth Century side by side. We walk the crazy byways hedged with crowded buildings round St Mary's church, and above ancient doors and windows and modern shopfronts are blackened beams which have stood the rain and the wind 400 years and more. On one such beam above a shop at the corner of St Mary's Gate a rose is carved, not much less perfect than when Elizabeth came and may have glanced at it; on another beam is the date 1475.

Soon we are in thriving Greengate Street, where heavy traffic passes between north and south, but all the bustle of wheels, all the miscellany of modern buildings, cannot take away the dignity of Stafford's finest old dwelling, High House. Proudly it stands four storeys high, with sturdy gables and splendidly timbered sides, a challenge to the meanness of some of its neighbours.

In this house Charles Stuart stayed while on his way to recruit more men at Shrewsbury. Here Prince Rupert displayed his skill as a marksman. Standing in what was then the garden, he took a shot with a horseman's pistol at the weathercock of the church; the bullet pierced the tail and the hole was plainly seen by all below. The king thought it a chance, but Rupert, taking aim again, pierced the cock's tail a second time. The cock now here replaced Prince Rupert's victim.

It was in the Civil War, when the town was loyal to the Stuarts, that the Parliament troops brought the walls of Stafford's Norman castle to the ground, so that nothing of it remains. Close by High House, now a grocer's shop in its lower quarters, are several other old houses converted into shops, having heavily timbered walls and gables. Charming it is to see medieval architecture peeping out among the new. A few yards away is the Swan Hotel, an old inn with plastered front and an air of coaching days. Dickens stayed here one night and called it "the extinct town inn, the Dodo," but George Borrow found it busier. Here this strange genius came after parting with Isopel Berners in Mumpers Dingle, and he tells about it in some of the most fascinating chapters in Romany Rye:

The inn, of which I had become an inhabitant, was a place of infinite life & bustle.

Travellers of all descriptions, from all the cardinal points, were continually stopping at it. Jacks creaked in the kitchens, turning round spits on which large joints of meat piped & smoked before great fires. There was running up & down the stairs, & along galleries, slamming of doors, cries of Coming, sir, & Please-to-step-this-way, ma'am, during 18 hours of the four & twenty.

Truly a very great place for life & bustle was this inn. And often in after life, when lonely & melancholy, I have called up the time I spent there, & never failed to become cheerful from the recollection.

In the same street is Chetwynd House, where the Duke of Cumberland paused in his pursuit of the Young Pretender, and Richard Brinsley Sheridan, the town's M.P. for 26 years, often stayed. The making of boots and shoes was one of Stafford's chief industries then, as now, and Sheridan made this witty toast about it: *May the trade of Stafford be trod underfoot by all the world.*

But let us go by the narrow way from Greengate Street beneath the timbers of High House. In a few strides we are confronted by Stafford's noblest church. St Mary's has an immense octagonal tower, one of the few of its kind in England. The top is about 600 years old, the base older by a century. Very imposing is the doorway on the north side with its three orders of carving, ballflower and quatrefoil, carved six centuries ago. As we enter we pause to look round at the beautiful wall tracery, adorned with clustered faces of little cherubs, each no bigger than a man's hand.

In the north transept is a splendid 16th-century tomb on which lie the alabaster figures of Sir Edward Aston and his wife Joan. He has lost his head and hands, but the lady is complete and exquisite, her head resting on an elegantly embroidered cushion. Round the sides are their 17 children.

Near them is a small carved altar table with an odd bit of history. It is believed to have been used in an earlier church 500 years ago, but was lost for centuries, and about 30 years ago was found in a saddler's shop. The saddler used it for many years, and the beam where his feet rested as he sat making his harness is almost worn through. Now the table is reverently cared for again, and has for company a small carved chest nearly as old as itself.

Almost cathedral-like in its dimensions is this fine cruciform church. The tower rests on pillars of immense thickness. The fine nave and the aisles are probably 700 years old, the lofty chancel was built a little later, the clerestory windows are early Tudor. All the pillars in the nave differ in size and detail, and all the arches vary a little in width. The nave has a rich modern timber roof.

The font is one of the strangest we have seen, having survived eight centuries remarkably well. The great bowl is of irregular quatrefoil shape and has between its divisions four queer figures with a human resemblance in their faces and greatly attenuated bodies. Under the bowl crouch four massive lions, and round the base are four more animals grotesquely wrought.

At this font Stafford's most illustrious son, Izaak Walton, was baptised. There is a white stone bust of him against a wall of the nave, and the face has the gentle expression we should expect. It is the only memorial to him in the town where he was born.

In a corner of the west wall we discern a little filled-up arch, probably built long before the time of Alfred; it is the only relic of Stafford's Saxon church. Somewhere near this spot St Bertelin set up his hermitage, and around it the church would grow. It became famous and was the Royal Free chapel of the Conqueror's castle, of which not a trace remains. So powerful was it that it had the power to inflict capital punishment, and the dean and chapter had their own gallows near the church.

It is less than 200 years since the church of St Bertelin was pulled down and a few relics from it are preserved in a case near the chancel here. They include a fine black jack of 1750 with the names of the ringers of that year upon it, several small medieval seals, and a few fragments of ancient manuscript.

In the nave and chancel are hundreds of pew ends, and they are among the treasures of the church, all enriched with carving and all different, some with exquisite heads, others with elegant floral decorations. They are the work of last century. In one of the nave windows are a few fragments of 14th-century glass, and the west window is filled with 17th-century stories of the miracles. The clerestory windows are filled with heraldry. Above the chancel arch are two angels with trumpets, painted 200 years ago; and on a pillar facing the north transept is a group of 17th- and 18th-century brass tablets.

It is only a few steps, across Greengate Street again, to one of the greatest surprises in Stafford. Tucked away between modern buildings the tiny church of St Chad contains some of the finest Norman work in the county. The imposing arch over the entrance, with 16 grotesque heads and zigzag carving, is a modern copy of Norman, but inside we are in a building little changed since the Conqueror's day. The chancel arch is complete and practically perfect, an impressive sight. It has five orders of carving with hardly a blemish, and placed sideways down the columns are no fewer than 48 weirdly carved heads, no two alike. The nave with its massive pillars, the clerestory with its deep little windows, the arcade of simple arches and zigzag moulding, are all as their Norman makers left them. We look at the wall by the south-west pier of the tower and see a deeply cut inscription, made probably by the builder of the church; in it we read the name Odin, and the letters are almost as plain as on the day they were cut.

In the chancel is a series of small Norman arches with interlaced arcading, all finely preserved, discovered behind plaster some years ago. The men who made them may have made the splendid font, massively carved with grotesque heads in deep relief.

We leave this small place feeling that we have truly stepped through the centuries; there are not many churches in England which give us a more complete picture of Norman times.

Among Stafford's modern churches we are drawn to St John's at Littleworth. It was built a few years ago with much of the material from Tixall Hall, the ancient home of the Astons. The modern Roman Catholic church of St Austin has a west window filled with 15th-century Belgian glass showing four figures richly coloured. One figure, holding a sceptre, is probably intended to represent Jesus, two others are believed to represent St Hilary and St Gregory, and the fourth is a bishop.

If we wander through the town again we shall find in Mill Street a quaint little thatched and timbered dwelling, very old, wedged in between modern buildings and a row of almshouses built about 300 years ago. The peace memorial faces the fine bridge across Victoria Pleasure-ground, an area transformed from a swamp; on the handsome stone monument are bronze figures of a woman and a horse, symbolising Victory and Peace. In the Shire Hall, a modern stone building, is a bust of Sir Thomas Noon Talfourd, judge, poet, and friend of Charles Lamb. He died in 1854 while in the judge's seat.

Izaak Walton

BORN at Stafford in 1593, and apprenticed in London early in youth, Izaak Walton never forgot his birthplace, and was never more thankful to revisit it than when, after the Battle of Marston Moor, the party with which he was in sympathy sustained a crushing defeat. It was there, again, that he awaited the news of the Battle of Worcester, and was entrusted with the custody of Charles the Second's "lesser George" jewel.

The little shop in which he made his modest competence stood two doors west of Chancery Lane, in Fleet Street, hard by St

Dunstan's Church, where Dr Donne was vicar, and Izaak's friend. Through Donne he became acquainted with all the great Churchmen of the day. He married first a great-grandniece of Cranmer, and secondly the half-sister of Bishop Ken, author of such famous hymns as Awake my soul, and Glory to Thee, my God, this night. Walton was 19 when Shakespeare died; Michael Drayton was his "honest old friend"; he was familiarly acquainted with Ben Jonson; and he must often have encountered Milton, Pepys, and Evelyn, who, with Sir Thomas Browne, were among his contemporaries.

It was not until his sixtieth year that he published his Complete Angler. There has never been anything like it. Amid the crash and thunder of the great staggering sentences of the 17th-century rhetoricians come these quiet enchanting tones, musing aloud in melody: jocund, happy, charged with poetry, a prose poet singing late and lone.

What a world of wonder and delight he creates as with his two comrades he stretches his legs from Tottenham Hill to Ware, resting in the rain to fish and shelter beneath the great honeysuckle hedge; buying with his catch of fish the favour of a buxom dairymaid who ceases milking her red cow to sing, at his request, "Come, live with me, and be my love"; and of the milkmaid's comely mother to "sing the second part, an answer to it which was made by Sir Walter Raleigh in his younger days":

> If all the world and love were young
> And truth in every Shepherd's tongue,
> These pretty pleasures might me move
> To live with thee and be thy love.

And so on to the inn, where they find a clean room, lavender in the windows, and twenty ballads stuck about the walls; where the hostess instantly roasts the chub that Piscator has caught and proves it, when they have said grace, worthy of the praise, "Trust me, 'tis as good meat as ever I tasted."

But Hertfordshire, then as now, had birds to gladden the air as well as fish to grace its streams, and we see how the monarch of them all impresses honest Izaak:

The nightingale, another of my airy creatures, breathes such sweet loud music out of her little instrumental throat, that it might make mankind to think miracles are not ceased. He that at midnight, when the very labourer sleeps securely, should hear, as I have very often, the clear airs, the sweet descants, the natural rising and falling; the doubling and redoubling of her voice, might well be lifted above earth, and say, "Lord, what music hast Thou provided for the saints in heaven, when Thou affordest bad men such music on earth?"

Here is the prose challenge of the 17th century to the melody and imagination of Keats and Shelley.

Walton's Lives, biographies of Donne, Wotton, Hooker, Herbert, and Robert Sanderson are unrivalled in their era.

For more than 200 years scholars have been editing Walton and producing more and more sumptuous editions of his writings. He showers an added lustre upon historic Winchester, in the shelter of whose episcopal palace he passed his closing years and wrote his Lives. For all his apparent simplicity he was a punctilious artist; he gave two years to the writing of his life of Hooker, which runs only to some 20,000 words—a week's work for a journalist. His heroes shine the brighter from the spirit emanating from his personality and genius.

Stafford has made no richer contribution to the world than this gifted son of hers, who closed his creel and went to heaven in 1683, at the ripe old age of ninety.

The Little Stone Coffin

STANDON. Although its church was much restored about 100 years ago, it keeps its Norman doorway, and Norman stones in the base of its medieval tower, standing amid yews and sycamores. The arches in the nave have rested on octagonal pillars for 700 years, and in the vestry is the stone coffin of a child of those far-distant days. In a recess in the chancel lies the broken alabaster figure of a priest, and on an alabaster monument are portraits of Francis Rose who died in 1500, his wife in a long gown, and their ten children. Ten old stalls in the chancel have misereres with roses and grotesques; and on one of the stalls we found an inscription to William Thompson, who began singing here in 1860 and went on singing out of one century into another till he had been at it 50 years.

Benefactor of Oxford

STANTON. A tiny place above the Titbrook valley, it has a modern church looking out far over a lovely countryside, and a road taking us by a fragment that remains of Ouseley Cross.

The road by the cross brings us by a lovely dale to Ellastone, which gave George Eliot Adam Bede and Charles Stuart one of his truest friends, Gilbert Sheldon, who was born here in 1598. He was the king's chaplain and constant attendant during the Civil War, and at the Restoration became Bishop of London, then Archbishop of Canterbury, and Chancellor of Oxford. A relentless opponent of Nonconformists, he was generous and helpful to individuals. During the Great Plague he stayed at Lambeth Palace while so many fled, and heroically sustained the sufferers. He lost the royal favour by an act of great courage, for he denounced the gross immorality of Charles the Second and refused him the Holy Communion.

Although a poor man's son, Sheldon gathered riches and spent them nobly, his benefactions representing £350,000 of our money. His crowning work was the theatre at Oxford which bears his name. Built by Wren, it cost £125,000 in modern currency, and was opened in 1669. In addition Sheldon laid out £10,000 on lands to support the fabric from their revenues. He died in 1677 and was buried at Croydon.

STAPENHILL. Here by the Trent came Britons, Romans, and Saxons. About 30 skeletons were found in a Saxon cemetery 50 years ago, with urns, beads, iron knives, and spearheads, now in the museum at Burton.

The old church has been refashioned, but has one heritage from its medieval days, a much-worn alabaster monument engraved with the portraits of William and Mary Dethick, he in the armour he wore in the 15th century, she in a close-fitting hat. Their eight children are with them. The oak screen and pulpit are enriched with carving, and the east window has Christ and the Madonna with a company of prophets, saints, and angels.

Two Old Ladies

STATFOLD. A few houses and farms, a hall, and a church are almost all there is to see in this hamlet by the Warwickshire border. The hall, a big house which has been the home of the Wolferstans since the 15th century, has an octagonal turret said to have been built by Francis Wolferstan, a Jacobite and poet.

The small church in the hall grounds, long used as a mortuary chapel, has been restored for worship. The south door and two windows in the chancel are 14th century, and the west door and two little windows in the nave are 13th. The figures of two women have been lying under arches in the chancel for 600 years, one wearing a veil and one a bonnet.

The Five-Town Kingdom of the Potters

STOKE-ON-TRENT. The centre of the great china, porcelain, and earthenware industry, it has absorbed Burslem, Longton, Hanley, and Tunstall. Arnold Bennett's Five Towns are now one, the city of Stoke-on-Trent, with a lord mayor to direct its destinies.

In this area are hundreds of potteries, their great firing-ovens as characteristic a feature as the oasts of the hop-gardens of Kent. Here sleep potters who made English wares famous throughout the world, and the city seeks to be worthy of them. A fine building is the grey town hall with its stately columns, its law library and art gallery; the school of art and science is the city's tribute to the memory of Herbert Minton; the museum has a noble collection of pottery from the 17th century to ours, including examples of the finest work of Wedgwood, Spode, Copeland, Minton, and other local craftsmen.

Opposite the handsome King's Hall is the dignified peace memorial, modelled on the Cenotaph in Whitehall. Near it on a granite pedestal is a bronze statue of Colin Minton Campbell, three times mayor of Stoke and benefactor of his native town. But the proudest personal monument is that of the city's greatest son Josiah Wedgwood, who welcomes the visitor at the station. Proudly regarding one of his own vases, he stands, a lifelike figure in bronze, proclaiming to all comers that here is the kingdom of the potters, while his townsmen have made him declare that he himself is its chief.

The story of Stoke is the story of a long and stirring struggle with difficulties, and of a splendid discontent which has inspired its potters to better their best, and to maintain the progress first attained when Wedgwood's genius inspired them.

There are several churches, the oldest (St Peter ad Vincula) rebuilt last century. In its churchyard is part of a Saxon cross, decorated with knotwork. Here are erected two round arches on slender pillars, remnants of an arcade of the ancient church. Somewhere in the churchyard sleeps the father of the poet Joseph Fenton, and here is a tombstone with an astonishing inscription which

PENKRIDGE : The engraved stone Monument of William and Katherine Winnesbury, 1523

says that Sibil and Henry Clarke died in 1684, each aged 112. If i
is true, they were born before the Armada came, lived through th
days of Shakespeare's greatness, would shudder to hear of Charle
Stuart's execution, and would be amazed to learn that Londo
was burning.

With a beautiful reredos the church has a fine east window with
chained Peter among fine figures of Apostles and Evangelists. Th
chancel is a gallery of remembrance of the great potters. Here on a
alabaster tablet is a beautiful medallion of the prince of potters by
prince of sculptors, Josiah Wedgwood lovingly depicted by the maste
hand of Chantrey, a veritable portrait of the man who raised th
Potteries from primitive craftsmanship to a centre of high art
a noble figure, genius, philosopher, and true lover of his fellows
Above him are carved two vases symbolising his life's work. Her
he has lain since 1795.

There is a bronze medallion to his favourite pupil William Adams
a skilled potter who fashioned some of the choicest work of the age
and there is a simple memorial to William Taylor Copeland, th
commercial traveller who made known the works of Spode, was lor
mayor of London, and brought immense wealth to Stoke.

Three Josiah Spodes are remembered here. The first founded th
china works in 1770; the second revolutionised porcelain by intro
ducing bone into it, and made the famous willow-pattern ware; th
third has a marble monument with the graceful figure of a woma
weeping by a casket. Here also are memories of Herbert Minton
who, a child when Wedgwood died, was inspired by the example o
his great predecessor to surround himself with the most gifted artist
of his generation and to produce such porcelains, tiles, and mosaic
as had never before been seen. Beginning with a staff of 50 rough
and-ready potters, he made his works 30 times as large in as many
years, a veritable wonderland of art and industry.

All the interests here are associated with this staple industry
Men who made the Potteries wealthy and their name famous throug
the world came to this church to worship, and some at last to find
resting-place. All were disciples of Wedgwood, all lit a lamp at th
torch he had left burning. But for him there would have been n
Spodes or Mintons.

Of all the arts of England, none is more native to the soil than th work of the Staffordshire potter centred in the Five Towns we now know as Stoke. It has often a sort of childish innocence of design, which owes nothing to foreign influences and which makes it in its way as characteristic of its country as Chinese porcelain. It can in no way be compared to that incomparable ware either in colour, design, or workmanship, but in its products may be traced almost as clearly the story of generations, even of centuries, of discovery and invention in glaze, decoration, and material.

Staffordshire ware travels all over the world today. It would hardly be possible to find a civilised dwelling in any continent without some of its cups and saucers or dinner plates or other articles of domestic use, and most of these have the attractiveness which is based on adaptability to use and correctness of design. Of late years decoration and design, after a lapse in Victorian days, have greatly improved, partly owing to the search for new ideas and partly because many of the beautiful old patterns have been revived.

It would be hard to decide when this antique beauty was at its best, for the work of the Staffordshire potter has taken many forms. It seems to have always been present, ever since England exchanged vessels of wood or pewter for pottery, and was probably there long before that, for in the history of any country the clay turned on the potter's wheel has led the potter to seek for new elegance and distinction. We need not suppose that it was at Stoke or Burslem, or at any of the Five Towns, that English pottery was cradled. It certainly was made widely elsewhere, and one of its new departures can be traced to Fulham and to the genius of John Dwight, the greatest potter England ever knew.

Before then Staffordshire had its own particular pottery, known as slip ware, which, though not confined to the potteries, became identified with them because of the names of Ralph and Thomas Toft, who produced some of the finest pieces and left their name on their masterpieces. Any Chinese designer might be proud of one of the Toft dishes in the British Museum.

The new era in Staffordshire pottery came with John Dwight of Fulham who aimed at reproducing the substance and glazes of Chinese porcelain. His own researches never led farther than stone ware, one variety of which became known as the Staffordshire red clay, and in the hands of the brothers Elers, who set up a factory at

Bradwell Wood near Burslem, was fashioned into teapots and cups with stamped and raised ornament. It was altogether as different from the everyday pottery of Staffordshire at that time as Josiah Wedgwood's elaborate models and patterns differed at a much later date from that of the other factories about him. It gave new impetus to the Staffordshire Potteries. Thomas Astbury and Joshua Twyford continued to make the red ware, introducing the first of those small Staffordshire figures which through two centuries remained the most characteristic art of the Potteries, though both art and craft flowed into many other channels.

Staffordshire was not to be left behind in the revolution brought about by the manufacture of English porcelain, but for the greater part the county remained faithful to its own earthenware, and made an advance in it which it has never lost and which remains the practice today. The fine white biscuit ware was dipped into a fluid glaze and subjected to a further firing. As the glaze contained white lead the process was accompanied by danger to the dippers, such as modern factory legislation has sought to eliminate.

The Potteries were to win a new renown in the days of Josiah Wedgwood who, while the rest of the world was making porcelain, raised Staffordshire's cream-coloured earthenware to worldwide fame. The perfection of this earthenware was Wedgwood's greatest achievement, but he will always be remembered for his untiring experiments in producing new forms, new colourings, and new designs, and for his lavish expenditure in employing English artists to decorate his pieces.

Contemporary with Wedgwood was Thomas Whieldon, one of those rare inventive craftsmen from whom new methods naturally flow. He gave Staffordshire the Whieldon ware, enriched with mottled and coloured glazes, which is one of its dearest possessions; and with him sprang into life again those Staffordshire figures which, even more than those produced by Chelsea or Bow or Worcester, represent a native English art in inspiration and modelling. Dainty is the last word one would apply to most of them, but they have vigour and life and humour borrowed from nowhere else.

Last in the survey of the Potteries is the name of Josiah Spode, who came in with the bone ash porcelain, and whose Staffordshire factory was raised by his vigour and enterprise to a great position.

The Smoking Chimneys of the Five Towns

The Castle and the River Tame

The Ancient Castle Keep

Peel Statue and Town Hall

TAMWORTH, ANCIENT HOME OF KINGS

STAFFORDSHIRE

King of All the Potters

JOSIAH WEDGWOOD was born in 1730 into a family of potters, and owing to the death of his father was taken from school at nine and apprenticed to his brother. Illness maimed his right leg, and for the 25 years in which he was struggling for success he was constantly pained and hampered by his malady, which was not relieved until he submitted to amputation.

To a natural aptitude for his calling he added a passion for study and experiment, and by hard thinking and frugal living he was able to start a tiny business of his own and to apply art and science to the primitive methods then current. To improve his wares he had to revolutionise workshop practice, inventing new tools and teaching men to use them. In his quest of quality and beauty he nearly beggared himself with experiments in which his chemical combinations failed him, wrong temperatures ruined his pots, and kiln after kiln had to be destroyed.

Abundant success eventually rewarded his high courage and unflagging endeavour. He produced a beautiful cream ware which established him as the first potter of the age. It was used at Court; it was found in all aristocratic homes; it reached the continent; it crossed the Atlantic; and eventually the Empress of Russia ordered a dinner service of it, the cost of which was 50 guineas for the actual ware and 40 times as much for its decoration.

Staffordshire pottery now became famous throughout the world. Wedgwood loved to be known as a creator of beauty rather than a mere vendor of pottery, and he had the fortune to see beauty pay. Wisely he spent his wealth and energy. He had a great share in promoting the Grand Junction Canal, uniting the Mersey, the Trent, and the Severn; and in making Staffordshire roads fit for Staffordshire commerce.

He built great works and a great house for himself, made many families rich and happy, and became the father of Darwin's mother. He left a fortune of half a million and the proud record of having achieved something notable in developing a love of elegant things.

Storied Stone

STONE. It has a story which reads something like a Greek tragedy; it has been the nursery and sepulchre of saints; and in

o 193

its dust sleep a poet who knew Shakespeare, a sailor who saved us from invasion, and a bishop who helped to free Australia from a shameful chapter of its history.

It is possible that it might have averted the horrors of Culloden. When Charles Edward, the Young Pretender, burst into Staffordshire in 1745 the Duke of Cumberland, seeking to give him battle, made his headquarters here at Stonefield. Charles went to Leek and from there sent out a messenger to his friends. The messenger got drunk by the way, and the chance of an encounter and a swift decision between the rival forces was thus missed.

It is possible also that Motley Pits, an old entrenchment here, may be the relics of defences thrown up in the Civil War, but it is also possible that they are of Saxon origin. There is less doubt as to Bury Bank two miles away, which is an encampment of about four acres, the fortified palace of Wulfhere, the 7th-century Mercian king. Converted to Christianity, he married a daughter of Egbert and became the father of Werburga, over whose grave rose the cathedral at Chester.

Soured and shaken by incessant wars, Wulfhere reverted to paganism; and because his sons clung to their faith he murdered them. Filled with remorse for what he had done, he pleaded before St Chad, who bade him stamp out idolatry from his kingdom; and he was faithful to his pledge. He appointed the first Bishop of London. The scene of the tragedy is at the bottom of Abbey Street, where we may see the cellar of Priory House and the scanty remains of the ancient walls. They are all that is visible of the priory founded by Queen Ermenilda in memory of her murdered sons.

The new church, built partly on the site of the priory church about 1750, is the patriarch of the town, for the town hall and the market hall are both 19th century. In the churchyard is a relic of the older church; and where the old chancel stood, exposed to the weather, is a 17th-century altar tomb with Thomas Crompton in armour and his wife in a long dress and ruff.

In the family mausoleum lies John Jervis, Earl of St Vincent, Nelson's great leader, who by his victory over a Spanish fleet prevented its junction with the navy of France, and so averted the most serious threat of invasion of our shores since the Armada.

Born at Meaford Hall, not far away, he loved this place, and ordered that wherever he might die he should be buried here. As a token of his affection for the church he commissioned his friend Sir William Beechey to paint the beautiful picture which hangs on the chancel wall, of St Michael's triumph over Satan. With it hangs a fine copy of Raphael's Transfiguration. The sanctuary window of the Resurrection marks the centenary of St Vincent's great sea victory; another modern window has charming figures of the martyred sons of the Saxon king, Wulfhad and Rufin. The admiral's personal memorial is a fine bust by Chantrey.

The oldest things in the church are the worn sculptures of a priest and a woman 600 years old, and next in antiquity is the portrait brass of another Thomas Crompton, in Tudor armour, with his wife and their six children.

Sleeping here with the great folk is Thomas Bakewell, a poor weaver who gave his life to the study of insanity and established a private asylum where, by humane and rational methods, he effected astonishing cures. A poet as well as a reformer, he sang of the moorlands, of his weaving, of the sorrows of the poor, and tenderly of animal life. He died in 1835, aged 74.

In the richly decorated Roman Catholic church, with elegant arcades, is an altar tomb in which sleeps Bishop Ullathorne, with angels at his head. Humbly born at Pocklington in Yorkshire, he was first a sailor, next a monk, and then went at 25 as chaplain to New South Wales, where he worked heroically among depraved and desperate convicts. After five years he returned home to write a scathing exposure of the terrible convict system, and, though his criticism aroused the indignation of vested interests in the colony, he helped to kill the idea of transportation and to make Australia a land for free citizens of the Empire. As Bishop of Birmingham he laboured for 38 years, dying in 1889.

The most illustrious modern native of Stone was the landscape painter Peter de Wint, who, beginning his career under John Raphael Smith, the famous engraver, won lasting repute by his portrayal of the rustic beauties of the north and eastern counties. Although he died in 1849 his fame abides, and all may see his work in our National Gallery.

But of all the names that come to us in Stone is one perhaps more enduring than all these—Richard Barnfield, the poet who knew

Shakespeare, who wrote poems which have come down to us
erroneously attributed to Shakespeare himself. His home is gone and
his grave lost, but here somewhere sleeps this little-known immortal

Richard Barnfield and Shakespeare

FOR two centuries and more the world read and loved two
poems by this young squire, thinking Shakespeare himself had
written them. Even today we find Richard Barnfield's work in most
of the Complete Works of Shakespeare, in the group titled The
Passionate Pilgrim.

Few poems in that group, in fact, were written by the master
himself, though they were given to the world as his in 1599. Who but
the authors was to know of the theft? The sonnet, which begins:

> *If music and sweet poetry agree,*
> *As needs they must (the sister and the brother),*

is in the perfect Shakespearean style, and the ode is a lyric worthy
of Shakespeare both in its imagery and in its human touch.

The Ode opens with these often-quoted lines:

> *As it fell upon a day*
> *In the merry month of May,*
> *Sitting in a pleasant shade*
> *Which a grove of myrtles made,*
> *Beasts did leap and birds did sing,*
> *Trees did grow and plants did spring;*
> *Everything did banish moan*
> *Save the nightingale alone.*

The poet goes on to write about the sweet sad singer in lines which
stirred Swinburne to hail him as "the first adequate English laureate
of the nightingale" with none to take his place until Keats, who not
only wrote the famous Ode to the Nightingale but, like Barnfield,
was inspired by Spenser. The human note in the Ode reminding one
of Shakespeare is in Barnfield's description of the true friend, who, he
says, is not the flatterer whose words are easy, "like the wind," and
who is no friend but in misery,

> *He that is thy friend indeed*
> *He will help thee in thy need;*
> *If thou sorrow, he will weep;*
> *If thou wake, he cannot sleep;*

Thus of every grief in heart
He with thee doth bear a part.

This poem, which will keep Barnfield's name alive, was published with a few others in 1598, one being Remembrance, in which he praises his four favourite poets (Spenser, Samuel Daniel, Michael Drayton, and Shakespeare). Though Shakespeare, who was ten years older, had already published some of his plays, Barnfield only praises him for his Venus and Lucrece, perhaps because it was only Spenser's type of poetry that interested him. Though he was but 24 he had published two other books. The Affectionate Shepherd, an imitation of a poem by Virgil, and Cynthia, claiming that his Cynthia was "the first imitation of the verse of that excellent poet Master Spenser, in his Faerie Queene."

The fact is that he imitated too much and never for more than a line or two let his own imagination catch fire. He wrote smoothly and had an intense love for all flowers, birds, and beasts: the country-side of Staffordshire is always in the background.

Born in Norbury Manor in 1574, he went at 17 to Oxford. The last we know of him as a poet is from his third book in 1605, but we do know that he lived the life of a country gentleman at Darlaston, near Stone, had a son, nursed a granddaughter, and died at 52.

It is strange that his poetry ceased at 25, and that there are known only five copies of his books published during his lifetime; but the strangest thing of all is that his name is remembered because a pirate publisher stole two of his poems and gave them to the world as the work of Shakespeare.

The Hero of Cape St Vincent

JOHN JERVIS, who took his title of Lord St Vincent from the scene of his chief sea victory, was born in 1735, eight years the junior of James Wolfe, with whom he spent some time at school. They met again in 1759 on the eve of an immortal event.

The son of a flinty-hearted lawyer who kept him miserably poor, Jervis made his way in the Navy from the rank of seaman to that of acting commander of the little Porcupine, and as such was selected to lead the boats carrying the troops for Wolfe's night attack on the Plains of Abraham.

Before the flotilla set out Wolfe sent for his old school friend, and with a presentiment of impending death handed over to him his private papers and note-books, his will, and the portrait he always carried of Katherine Lowther, whom he loved but who was later to become Duchess of Bolton. In the event of his death the portrait was to be brought by Jervis to England, set in jewels and returned to her.

The part of Jervis in the little voyage to the spot appointed for the landing at Quebec was executed with skill and courage, and he and Captain Cook share with Wolfe the glory of the deed that that day made Canada part of the British Empire.

During the recurring wars that followed Jervis steadily advanced by intelligence, valour, and industry, entering Parliament during peace, and returning to sea to win fresh laurels for his country and himself. Trinidad and other islands of the West Indies were among his contribution to the Empire during these world-wide combats.

But we were then a little nation, impoverished by wars, and unable to maintain an efficient Navy in time of peace, so that ships and discipline alike deteriorated. The alliance of France and Spain made it necessary for us to quit the Mediterranean; a hostile fleet with 14,000 soldiers was prevented only by weather from invading Ireland; and plans were ripening for a descent by great French and Spanish forces upon our own coast.

That dream was shattered on St Valentine's day, 1597, when, in accordance with Jervis's expectations, a Spanish fleet of 27 ships of the line, heavily gunned, sailed from Carthagena with a view to joining the French fleet at Brest. Jervis was in the Victory, not yet famous; Nelson was in the Captain.

Nelson, to whom Jervis was ever a hero, wrote, as the battle drew near, "Of all the fleets I ever saw, I never beheld one, in point of officers and men, like Sir John Jervis's, who is a commander-in-chief able to lead them to glory." Battle was joined off Cape St Vincent, and Nelson himself made it a resounding victory, sending the shattered vessels of the Spanish fleet scurrying to harbour, from which they emerged no more throughout the war.

Nelson shows us what Jervis had done with his fleet before the battle; history tells how he improved it afterwards, sternly repressing mutiny, mercilessly purging the Admiralty of corruption and jobbery, and firmly pressing on reforms that redressed grievances afloat and bettered the lot of seamen's families on land. He built Nelson's victorious fleets.

A man of bitter humour but generous heart, he consistently defended Nelson's fame against the claims of Lady Hamilton and her creatures; and he was foremost in aiding Lady Nelson when she was in danger of being defrauded of her rights.

He died in his 89th year, and it was by his own desire that his body was laid to rest here, far from sea but in his native soil.

Constable of Warwick Castle

STOWE. The Normans gave the village its church, and their boldly carved chancel arch, a south doorway with flowers, a deeply-splayed window in the chancel, and a doorway by which a Norman priest came in and out, are still here to see. The tower is 14th century. The east window has lovely modern glass with Christ shining in majesty.

The most imposing monument is an alabaster tomb with figures of Sir Walter Devereux, grandfather of Queen Elizabeth's favourite Essex. He lies with his two wives. Sir Walter, who died the year Elizabeth was crowned, was Constable of Warwick Castle, saw hard fighting at sea, and served in Henry the Eighth's army against the French in 1544. He may have come to admire his monument, for it was made in his lifetime, showing him in his Garter collar, his head on a plumed helmet. His wives wear close-fitting hats, and round the tomb are six sons in armour and six daughters in the fashionable dress of the day. Over the monument hangs the helmet he wore. In the churchyard is a cross on an old base, and in the village are attractive cottages with old timbers.

STRETTON. It lies by the Roman Icknield Street. The fine church built in the last years of last century has a big central tower, and north and south doorways crowned by beautiful statues of a Madonna and St Chad.

Indoors the eye is drawn to the brightly painted and gilded roof, and the elaborate screen with flowers and fruit and 13 bosses, no two alike. The font cover, a fine example of modern craftsmanship, has niches with figures of Christ, Paul, John, Moses, Noah, Adam, and Abraham. There is a fine iron gate to a chapel, and the chancel has a striking east window with lovely tracery, and Our Lord in majesty designed by Sir William Richmond, whose mosaics are inside the dome of St Paul's.

The Canal Crossing the River

STRETTON. It is one of the two Strettons by the old Roman roads of Staffordshire; this one is by Watling Street. Here is the unusual sight of a canal crossing a river, the barges on the Shropshire Union Canal floating over an iron bridge of one arch built in 1832 by Thomas Telford.

The hall and the church are neighbours, the hall, in a park of tall and stately elms, sheltered from the churchyard by a row of old yews. Three great beeches are near the church, which was partly taken down and built up again last century. Though much of the church is new the chancel is old and has three deeply-splayed Norman windows, one over a niche with a stone head which may have come from the old church. The east window has fragments of old glass, among them a Crucifixion and a saint's head.

A Figure from a Cathedral?

SWYNNERTON. It has a great park of 800 acres, and high up in a wooded countryside a fair share of the treasures of our ancient past.

Standing by a fine chestnut tree is the tower the Normans began, crowned with a medieval belfry and entered through a doorway carved with beaks of birds. The nave arcades have been here 700 years, the south chapel 600, and the south aisle 500. The beautiful oak screen is by a Tudor craftsman. Under a canopy in the chancel lies a battered knight thought to have been a Swynnerton who was Constable of the Tower in the 14th century. A great sitting figure about eight feet high is so finely carved that it is believed it was brought to this church from Lichfield cathedral to escape destruction in the Commonwealth. It has lost an arm.

Shut In by Towering Rocks

SWYTHAMLEY. It has a modern church in the deer park round Swythamley Hall, and an old church with the sky for a roof.

In the new church, on an oak pedestal, is a beautiful white sculpture showing Judas about to give Christ the kiss of betrayal, an unusual piece of carving; and another rare possession is the font in the shape of an angel holding a scallop shell, a beautiful statue in gleaming marble.

What is known as the Lud or Lollard church stands in a wild and beautiful countryside with rocks and moors. The church is really a remarkable chasm shut in by towering rocks only 20 feet apart at the top. Here, in this natural cathedral, with its moss and fern-covered walls overhung by trees, the followers of Wycliffe are said to have gathered and on a ledge is a wooden figure supposed to be the grand-daughter of one of the Lollard leaders. Legend says that their singing betrayed a company of Lollards gathered here when soldiers were searching for them, and that Alice, a beautiful girl of 18, was killed. We are told that she sleeps in this lovely and lonely place.

The Talk of the Hill

TALKE O' THE HILL. Its queer name is said to come from a Welsh word meaning a high place, a good name for this mining village near the Cheshire border.

In the heart of the village is a modern cross on five steps of the 13th century; and in the modern church are two old treasures said to have come from Moreton Old Hall, the famous house over the Cheshire border. They are on brackets near the chancel arch, beautiful oak figures of Paul and John the Baptist.

The talk of the hill is often of tragic things, for the village has sad memories of four tragedies, two above ground and two below. In 1782 a disastrous fire destroyed many houses. Like a bolt from the blue came tragedy on another day in that same year, when nearly two tons of gunpowder which were being taken through the village exploded. Here one winter's day in 1866 a pit explosion took toll of over 90 lives, and another explosion in 1785 carried off 42 men and boys. Bitterly has this small place paid for our friendly English fireside.

The Ancient Home of Kings

TAMWORTH. Here flow two rivers, the Tame and the Anker, at the heart of a busy little town, the sound of their mingling waters running on like an ageless song. For a thousand years and more history has marched on the banks of these two streams, and we may stand on the castle walls built high on a mighty mound of earth and mark how the rivers join, and think of the pageant they have seen. Kings and queens come into it, a great statesman of modern times, and a boy who lived to find fame far beyond this town where he went to school.

The red roofs of Tamworth are below us as we stand on this proud height and look toward the massive tower of the church, imposing and a little grim without a spire. All around us lies the green and fertile countryside beloved by Sir Robert Peel. No one who looks on this district, he said, no one who sees the extent of its woodlands, the delightful rivers that water it, enriching the spacious meadows that border them, can be surprised to find that in the earliest times it was the chosen seat of those who were the conquerors of the country.

It was in Saxon times one of the most important places in the Midlands. Here Offa, King of Mercia, built a great palace where now the stalls of the market stand, and surrounded the town with a trench of which a few traces remain. For nearly a hundred years the kings of Mercia dwelt secure in Offa's palace, till it was destroyed by the Danes. Then for 40 years the place lay desolate, until there came a woman of good courage, Alfred's daughter Ethelfleda, to rebuild the defences and start the erection of the castle. She finished her work, and in five years was dead; she died here in 918, and from Tamworth her body was taken to Gloucester, where they buried her. She had seen this great mound raised to a height of 130 feet, with a space of 100 feet in diameter at the summit. She saw the great curtain wall rise, 10 feet thick and 20 feet high at the centre, containing some of the finest Saxon herringbone work we have seen. The passage of a thousand years had left its solidity unshaken, the regular precision of its stones unbroken, but most vivid is that chapter which saw Richmond encamped here four days before Bosworth Field, during his long eastward march from Milford Haven. The traditional site is two miles westward, not far from the village of Hopwas. In Shakespeare we read Henry's stirring speech heartening his soldiers on the plain near Tamworth:

> *Fellows in arms, and my most loving friends*
> *Bruised underneath the yoke of tyranny. . . .*

The walls of Tamworth Castle have work from Saxon to Tudor days. Most of the foundations are Saxon and Norman, and parts of the keep and the tower are Norman. Within the curtain wall is the Tudor and Stuart manor house of brick and stone. In the Tudor banqueting hall is a great window with oak mullions, one of the most striking features in this part of the castle. Overlooking it is the stone window of the minstrels' gallery. In the state drawing-room is a frieze of 55 panels of oak painted with the arms of the Ferrers family and other lords of the castle up to 1787; and in the oak room is a magnificent Tudor chimney-piece most richly carved, with heraldic pillars and Corinthian columns, human figures and small panels showing Jupiter in a chariot drawn by eagles, a dragon at the foot of a tree guarding the golden apples in the Garden of the Hesperides, the punishment of Prometheus, and the fate of Adonis. There is a splendid Tudor staircase with steps carved out of solid oak.

There are many pictures of historical interest and ancient arms and armour in these rooms. We see a collection of coins from Offa's Tamworth mint, and there are numerous mementoes of Sir Robert Peel. In front of the tower stands the Marmion Stone, a great weathered block, the base of a cross which stood perhaps six centuries ago on an ancient bridge across the Tame.

Tamworth's great church stands on the site where four other churches have stood since the middle of the 8th century. The north and south arcades of the central tower are Norman, and so is part of the south wall of the chancel. It has a 14th-century crypt, a chapel and tower of the 15th century, and a fine Tudor clerestory. The tower has a feature which has long been a fascination to architects, a curious double staircase mounting spirally, with 101 steps in one and 106 steps in the other. It is said to be unique in England. Both sets of steps are contained in a space little over six feet wide, and are so contrived that the floor of one is the roof of the other. One leads from an entrance in the churchyard to a landing on the roof, the other from inside the church to the same landing.

The nave arcade has fine 14th-century work, and the roof with its carved oak bosses is 15th century. The font is probably 500 years old.

Under 14th-century arches in the chancel are three table tombs with 14th-century figures. One shows Sir Baldwin Freville and his wife, another Lady Joan de Freville, and the third, Sir John Ferrers and his wife with their ten children. Under a pointed arch in the north wall lies a figure thought to be Baldwin de Witney, who rebuilt the church 600 years ago. In his dress the hood of the tippet is shown drawn over the head, and it is believed to be the only example in England of this way of arranging the vestments at that time. In the north transept is the mutilated figure of a warrior in chain mail, probably 14th century. Beneath the tower, in a pompous marble monument, we see John Ferrers and his son, both wearing Roman dress in the manner of 17th-century statues.

The church has a remarkable group of three windows in the clerestory of the chancel, designed by Ford Madox Brown and made by William Morris. They show the marriage of Editha, patron saint of the church, to Sithric; Editha as an Abbess with her nuns; the Conqueror giving Tamworth Castle to Marmion; and Editha striking one of the Marmions with her crozier in punishment for wrongs he did to the convent. In St George's Chapel are two windows designed by Burne-Jones, but not good examples of his work, though both were made by William Morris. One has the legend of St Christopher, the other St Martin, St Lambert, St Nicholas, and St George. A third window here shows Ruth and Naomi, from William Morris's workshops.

In the north aisle is a peace memorial window to the men of Tamworth and to Maurice Berkeley Peel, who was vicar here in the early years of the war. He became an army chaplain, and was killed in France while attending wounded soldiers. In a stone tablet below are carved the names of 265 men and boys of Tamworth.

Tamworth has lost its ancient deanery, of which we see the fragment of a ruined wall, and its old grammar school has a new home in which the tradition of 600 years is nobly kept. The town hall, on quaint weathered arches, was built in the first year of the 18th century by Thomas Guy, Tamworth's most famous schoolboy, founder of the London Hospital which bears his name. It is the only direct visible link with him that Tamworth has. The almshouses he built in 1678 were rebuilt in 1914, a handsome group of buildings round pleasant lawns. In front of the town hall stands a bronze statue of the first Sir Robert Peel, father of the great statesman.

A surprise awaits every visitor to Tamworth who seeks the Spital Chapel, half a mile outside the town. This little chapel of St James's Hospital, founded in 1285, is entirely hid by houses and we reach it through a small iron gate as if entering a house. Odd it is to find this tiny place, still used for worship, overlooked on all sides by the windows of 20th-century homes. We may come into it by a Norman or a medieval doorway, and it still has windows 600 years old. The best of all Tamworth's houses is perhaps the Moat, an Elizabethan house of brick with good gables on the Lichfield road.

The Child Asleep

TATENHILL. From the poplar at a corner of its churchyard, near a small waterfall, we look out on a delightful valley. We come into its 700-year-old church through its original doorway and find it much as it has been through all these centuries. All through them this font on six small pillars has been used. There is a sculptured monument from the days of Cromwell showing a kneeling woman in a close-fitting bonnet and a long dress with a quaint figure of a child fast asleep in bed. It is to Sir Henry Griffiths. Modern craftsmen have carved St Michael killing his dragon on the oak reading desk.

The Pride of the Wrottesleys

TETTENHALL. With Wolverhampton close by, it lies in beautiful wooded country, and, stretching from its brook up the hillside, is a picture of rural charm. Whoso reads the Anglo-Saxon Chronicle is familiar with it, for below Tettenhall Wood are barrows in which mingles the dust of Danes and Saxons slain on that day a thousand years ago when Alfred's son Edward defeated the invaders.

Tettenhall College, a fine modern building, crowns a hill; at Barnhurst are the Tudor gateway and the grey-tiled dovecot which were once part of the home of the Cresswells; Wrottesley Hall has gone but the site recalls the thought that here had been a home of the Wrottesleys for 800 years, the estate having passed from father to son without a break while 34 rulers have governed our land.

A Hugh Wrottesley suffered with Simon de Montfort, another Hugh was with the Black Prince at Crecy and was one of the first Knights of the Garter. Chief of the 19th-century Wrottesleys was John, second baron, a famous social reformer and amateur astronomer, who became President of the Royal Society and the British Association. George, one of his soldier sons, wrote the annals of four famous old Staffordshire families, his own, the Giffards, the Okeovers, and the Bagots. He has slept here since 1909. Many other

Wrottesleys lie in this grand old church, which, with two fine yews in its sloping churchyard (one 22 feet round and the other 18), stands where the Saxon King Edgar built his church ten centuries ago. Nothing of his work remains for us to see, but of the church raised by his Norman successors there are two round piers in an arcade, and leading from the chancel to the Wrottesley chapel is a Norman arch.

The massive battlemented tower, with a crucifix above it, is 600 years old; there are arcades from the 13th century, an aisle from the 14th, and a clerestory of the 15th. In the sanctuary is a splendid window of five lancets with detached columns, and there are fragments of ancient glass. Fifteen generations have been baptised at the sculptured font.

Fourteen old choir stalls have their misereres unspoiled, with carvings among which are a lion, a dragon, a grotesque, and two merry little gnome-like men. The oak screen between the chancel and the chapel was carved with grapes about the time the family sent a younger Wrottesley to act as squire to Henry the Seventh.

One Cresswell monument is to Joan, who lived to return thanks for the defeat of the Armada; she kneels at her prayer desk, wearing her ruff and a tight-waisted gown.

The other monuments are chiefly to the Wrottesleys, the earliest (1518) showing Richard in armour with a dog at his feet, his wife in a flowing dress, and their 16 children.

The armoured figure of John Wrottesley shows him wearing a ruff, with his wife in a belted black dress of Tudor days and their ten children. Painted on a wall of the chapel are 18 shields.

In the churchyard lies an unknown man with a famous name, a native, William Pitt, who wrote in prose on agriculture and the history of the county, made merry verse about money, and came to rest here in 1823, having lived through the days when his famous namesake was deciding the destinies of Europe.

On the outskirts of Tettenhall is the lovely black and white Wightwick Manor presented to the National Trust by Mr Geoffrey Mander, MP. It was built in 1887, and contains among its many treasures some fine stained glass of Kempe illustrating William Morris's Earthly Paradise, and the four-poster bed (from Moseley Hall) in which Charles the Second slept for two nights after the Battle of Worcester.

James Watt's Old Engine

TIPTON. In the midst of the Black Country, it is rich in coal and iron, and we found here, standing in an old building by the canal at Ocker Hill, a remarkable witness of the rise of the Industrial Era.

It is nothing less than the very first steam-engine made for sale by James Watt in 1777. It was set up at Smethwick on the premises of the Birmingham Canal Navigations, where it worked for 115 years, being then dismantled and set up at the Ocker Hill works of the Canal Company. Here it worked until 1922, and though this historic piece of mechanism is in complete order it has now been given a rest.

To some it will be Tipton's chief possession; to others that distinction will be given to the Parish Register, which is thought to be the oldest in the land. Much of it is beautifully written, and except for one gap it goes back to a day before Christmas in 1513 when (as we read) "Joane the daughter of Thomas Whitehouse was baptized."

This register (which the verger will produce if asked) had been kept for about 250 years when most of the old St Martin's was destroyed in a great storm. To get money for rebuilding the vicar of that time made use of a statute enabling him to apply through the Sheriff for aid from Parliament, and Parliament replied by authorising a levy. So towns from Brecon to Berwick-on-Tweed were made to contribute to the building of Tipton church as it stands today.

Two interesting men we come upon at Tipton: Ben Boucher, a collier who wrote topical rhymes and sold them at a penny a sheet until he died in the workhouse in 1851; and Joseph Davies, who brought honour to this Black Country town during the war, winning a VC for his share in the capture of Delville Wood while leading a company of Welsh Fusiliers.

A Queen Becomes a Beggar

TIXALL. With an abiding place in literature, it has stories to tell as sad, strange, and terrible as history affords. The village has a cross, 18 feet high, looking far more ancient than its date of 1776 suggests. On the heath are two barrows, Queen's Low and King's Low, burial-places of great antiquity. Much history is buried hereabout.

In the pretty yew-decked churchyard is a tombstone whose inscription must have stirred the imagination of many travellers. It is that of Richard Biddulph, who served at the hall as steward to four generations of Astons. He was here while Drake was sailing round the world and while the Armada was building and sailing to destruction. He saw the rise and decline of that marvellous literary era which eclipsed the writings of antiquity. Spenser, Marlowe, and Shakespeare played their parts and went their way while he was here. Including Lady Jane Grey, he lived under seven sovereigns, and, born in the reign of Henry the Eighth, he died with Charles Stuart on the throne. He was a young man when this superb gatehouse was built to guard his master's home.

Through this gateway passed many famous men, among them three great writers. One was Michael Drayton, who makes the hall live on by a couplet in Polyolbion:

> *Trent, by Tixall graced, the Astons' ancient seat,*
> *Which oft the Muse hath found her safe and sweet retreat.*

The patron by whom the old poet was welcomed was the distinguished ambassador Sir Walter Aston, to whom Fletcher dedicated his pastoral play The Faithful Shepherdess. Prejudice and the Plague having denied the dramatist success, he appeals to Aston, "that noble and true lover of learning":

> *Among the better souls, be you the best,*
> *In whom, as in a centre, I take rest.*

Izaak Walton was a visitor in his turn, and presented the Aston of his day with a copy of his Lives.

The house succeeding that to which these immortals came has followed its predecessor to destruction. The Georgian hall was pulled down in 1927, and much of its material was used for the new church of St John at Stafford. But the famous gatehouse is at last secure, scheduled as a national monument. A Tudor masterpiece with domed turrets at its corners, it is remarkable for the fact that the windows of its three storeys have Doric, Ionic, and Corinthian columns.

There was a startling scene before the gatehouse in 1586, when commotion and terror marked the arrival of a gay cavalcade. It was Mary Queen of Scots riding by to a hunt, lured here by a trick after the Babington Plot. She was forced into the hall, a prisoner without attendants or even a change of clothes. For 17 days she was detained here, and as she left, a captive, poor villagers collected before the gate-

A Corner of the lovely Grounds

The winding River Trent

THE GLORY OF TRENTHAM

The handsome Norman Front of Tutbury Church

house clamouring for alms. "Alas," she cried, "I have nothing for you; I am a beggar too; all is taken from me."

So the gatehouse saw its first tragic chapter of history while it was still young; before it had run its first century events occurred here which beggared the most fantastic plays. It was the boast of Charles the Second, when imprisonment and executions over the pretended Popish Plot were rife and the whole country panic-stricken, that from first to last he "believed not one word of what was called Oates's Plot." Yet he held his hand while an innocent man was dragged from here to the Tower, and his companions to the scaffold.

A Gateway of Tragic History

THE hall to which the great gateway led for many generations was a stronghold of Protestantism following the Reformation, but had become a centre of Roman Catholic influence during Stuart days, and the infamous Titus Oates had no difficulty in involving its owner, Lord Aston, in the wholesale accusations with which he induced the country to believe that Protestantism was in danger, that the Roman Catholics were about to rise, murder the king, invade Ireland, and perpetrate a general massacre.

Lord Aston and his friend Lord Stafford were concerned with other Roman Catholics in Staffordshire in a secret movement aiming at the peaceful conquest of Protestantism by their alien Church, but at the hall was an unjust steward, Stephen Dugdale, a Roman Catholic of 38, who, privy to his master's secrets, absconded with a sum of money and, arrested as a Roman Catholic suspect, sought to save himself by fabricating a tissue of lies. Oates found him an able ally, who swore that he had been present at conferences and had read letters implicating Aston and Stafford in a plot to murder Charles. He swore that he had been promised 1000 crowns and enrolment in the calendar of saints to secure the murder of the king. Aston was impeached and committed to the Tower, and not until seven years later, when Oates had been whipped at the cart's tail for perjury, did he regain his freedom. Afterwards he held Chester Castle for James the Second at the Revolution of 1688, then retired into private life, and died here in 1714.

Lord Stafford was less fortunate. Son of the Earl of Arundel, and a prominent Roman Catholic member of the House of Lords, he was accused by Dugdale of complicity in a Popish Plot, and finally Dugdale swore that in September 1678 he met Stafford as he came riding through the old gateway here, and that Stafford offered him £500 to assassinate King Charles. It was in vain that Stafford proved that Dugdale had originally sworn that there was no plot, in vain that witnesses swore to Dugdale's offering them heavy bribes to commit perjury against the prisoner, in vain that Stafford demonstrated that Dugdale's evidence was unsupported in a single particular. The panic-stricken country demanded victims, and the trial, lasting seven days in Westminster Hall, afforded the terrified capital a happy diversion. The aged prisoner was found guilty by 55 votes to 31, and in December 1680, protesting his innocence to the last, he was beheaded on Tower Hill, an outstanding sacrifice to mob terror.

Smitten with remorse, and imagining himself haunted by the ghost of the hapless viscount, Dugdale, the villain of the tragedy, sank into poverty and obscurity, and in 1683 died in a drunken delirium.

A Proud Park of the People

TRENTHAM. Eclipse and tragedy are written across the scene, for a great palace is gone. Its superb park has become a popular resort, one of the fairest playgrounds in the county; but the splendour of Trentham, home of the Dukes of Sutherland, is no more.

In this most beautiful corner of the Potteries, where the Trent flows by the site of a lost nunnery, stood the famous Trentham Hall of which there remain only the ballroom and one great hall, but with the grounds and their wonders open so that all who will may come. A Tudor house spoilt in the 18th century, and rebuilt in the 19th by Sir Charles Barry, architect of the Houses of Parliament, the hall was famous. It is the Brentham of Disraeli's Lothair, and has been described not only by our romantic Prime Minister but by a Shah of Persia, who came here on a visit and put Trentham into a book. The magnificence of the scene, the boundless hospitality of his entertainment, all that went to make for his ease and happiness, conjured up in the mind of the Shah the thought of a nobleman grown too mighty near the throne, and he drew the Prince of Wales aside and asked him if he would not behead this man when he came to the throne! With unshaken gravity the prince replied that there were many other great nobles in the land and he could not undertake so formidable a clearance.

The kings and captains have departed, for Trentham was pulled down in 1905. The two great apartments left standing are the sole relics of the home which had housed the Leveson Gowers for three centuries; but the grounds, converted in their time from a waste of meadow lands into Italian gardens with no rival out of Italy, remain a joy for ever. Here is a glorious park of a thousand acres, with velvety lawns, hanging woods mirrored in a winding lake, the forest trees beyond, boats on the water and games on the greens, and all that makes life joyous under the open sky. Once the pleasure-ground of royalties and nobles, scene of all that was brightest in English society, it is now a pleasure-ground of the people, a compensation to the many for the loss of one stately home unwanted. One reminder of the old family remains: a stone column with an immense bronze statue of the first Duke of Sutherland still crowns the hill.

The church has seen many changes. Built on the site of St Werburga's nunnery, it has the Norman pillars which supported the roof of a priory. The horses of Commonwealth soldiers were stabled here in the Civil War, and two holes in a panel of the royal arms are said to have been caused by bullets. On an alabaster tablet is a portrait brass of the armoured figure of Sir Richard Leveson, ancestor of the Dukes of Sutherland, with his wife and their children. There is the trunk of a headless and legless knight under a canopy in the nave, which has also, in a glazed niche, a fine sculpture of Christ sitting at table in the house of Mary and Martha. On a marble tomb lies the lifelike figure, in a bonnet and a long cloak, of the second Duchess; near by stands her husband in his ducal robes, and on an elaborate wall monument is a bust of Albert Sutherland Leveson Gower, who died in 1874. They lived in that proud place that is no more.

Waking Up the Sleepers

TRYSULL. Its best possession is the Tudor woodwork in the church. The screen, the pulpit, and the roof beams are all very good carving of this time. The nave is unusual for having clerestory windows on one side only, and a low Norman arch is blocked up in an outside wall. The old oak chest is a fine piece of work, very long,

with engraved iron bands; and some of the little heads and figures in
the east window are 15th-century glass.

It is recorded here that in 1725 John Rudge left a pound a year to
be paid to somebody who would send dogs out of the church and
rouse the people who were sleeping. The Sleep Rouser would carry a
long rod with a knob at one end and a fox's tail at the other; and he
would tickle the faces of sleeping ladies with the fox's tail but the
opposite sex he would deal severely with by using the knob.

From the woody ridge called Abbot's Castle Hill, about a mile
away, there are good views of the Shropshire countryside, the
boundary running along the crest of this hill.

TUNSTALL. One of Staffordshire's busy pottery towns, about a
mile from Burslem, it has a fine town hall and a museum with
a good collection of pottery. In Victoria Park is a clock tower in
memory of two men of the same name divided by a hundred years:
William Adams the potter, who finished his life-work in Trafalgar
year, and a namesake of this century who also distinguished himself
at pottery. On the tower are bronze medallion portraits of these two
master potters.

The 19th-century church has a tower and a tall spire, and an east
window with five brilliant pictures from the life of Christ.

The Castle's Storied Walls

TUTBURY. From the ruins of its castle to the ancient ford by the
five-arched bridge every yard is charged with history. With a
great Norman monument for background we seem to catch again
the trampling of warhorses and the clang of armed men on the walls;
we see men flee here for refuge and flee again to save their lives; we
see kings and princes come and go; we hear the sighs of a captive
beauty who has been Queen of France and Scotland, and was pro-
claimed by the Pope and the French as Queen of England too.

Like its busy manufactures, most of Tutbury's buildings are
modern, though a fine old inn has a timbered front which seems to
have known little change in 500 years, and in the churchyard are the
stocks. But imagination is content with the hillside church looking
down on the town, and the castle ruins looking down on the church.

Treasured and cherished as the gem it is, the church, with its
immensely strong low tower, rose as part of the priory founded

20 years after the Conquest by Henry de Ferrers. His son, first Earl of Derby, a great figure at the Battle of the Standard, completed the work, something of which is in the present church, the remains of the priory. The deeply recessed west doorway, one of the finest examples of Norman art in the kingdom, has seven depths of carving, the innermost believed to be the earliest use of alabaster for an arch in any English church. The whole is crowded with magnificent carvings of human figures, strange animals, and beakheads. Above the doorway is a Norman window flanked on either side by beautiful arcading.

There is a rich Norman south doorway under a tympanum carved with mounted men and dogs who for over 800 years have been hunting a colossal wild boar.

The interior does not disappoint our high expectations. Two graceful Norman arcades rest on columns about six feet thick, some of them clustered, some with scalloped capitals, and above these the pillared arches of the Norman triforium have become the clerestory. The west wall of the nave is a noble picture of Norman sculpture, with zigzag decorating the splendid doorway and interlaced arches, and there are three fine Norman windows in the 13th-century aisle.

Above the wonderful church, romantic on the skyline, the ruins of the castle are grouped about a three-acre enclosure bounded by an embattled wall and a deep dry moat. Here is what the fierce fighting of the Civil War left, with a 19th-century addition, a structure called the Julius Tower, tolerable only for its superb views. For the rest nearly all is the work of John of Gaunt, his great tiltyard, his ruined house, the remains of two halls with vaulted chambers below, and a splendid grey stone gateway.

The castle rose in Saxon days, but was rebuilt in the Conqueror's time by the founder of the church, whose grandson was punished for rebellion against Henry the Second by the destruction of his fortress. It was rebuilt soon after, but another Earl of Derby, fighting on the side of Simon de Montfort, was defeated and disgraced, and the castle again destroyed, when the estate passed to a son of Henry the Third, whose grandson, Thomas of Lancaster, raised the castle to its crowning military glory.

Thomas lost his fortune here and his head at Pontefract; and some 40 years later the most famous duke of Lancaster, John of Gaunt, built the stately castle whose remains we see today. Even he was not safe within its walls, but in 1385 had to fly for his life on hearing that Richard the Second was marching with murderous intent upon him. At Gaunt's death Richard seized Tutbury, and the estate has ever since remained Crown property. It was leased by Elizabeth to the sixth Earl of Shrewsbury, who brought here in custody Mary Queen of Scots. His wife, the redoubtable Bess of Hardwick, declared that there was a love intrigue between the lovely prisoner and the earl, but Mary wrote complaining of her accommodation, declaring that she was "in a walled enclosure, exposed to all the winds and inclemencies of heaven, the greater part of it rather a dungeon for base and abject criminals than for a person of my quality." Allowed £52 a week for the maintenance of his prisoner and her companions, Shrewsbury said the sum "did not pay for victuals alone," as may have been the case, seeing that her retinue included "5 gentlemen, 14 servitors, 3 cooks, 4 boys, 3 gentlemen's men, 6 gentlewomen, 2 wyves, 10 wenches, children, a number of good horses, and grooms."

Shrewsbury supplied her with plate and rich hangings, and a visitor, who described her as "wearing black hair though given to hair of other colours on other occasions," found her apparently contented with embroidery, and much at home with the Shrewsburys. In spite of the vigilance of her janitors, she maintained a busy correspondence in cipher with the Duke of Norfolk, to whom she was secretly engaged. After his arrest the letters she wrote here were conveyed to him in empty beer bottles with marked corks, which went in unsuspected with the full bottles carried into his cell in the Tower.

Mary's second departure from here, in November 1569, was taken in haste; she returned for five months in 1570; and she was here again in 1585, ill. Her lodging was an old hunting lodge of timber and plaster in the castle yard.

Little more than half a century was left to the castle when, in December 1585, Mary rode away for the last time. The Stuarts made it their headquarters when hunting in Needwood Forest, but the end approached with the Civil War. Here Charles came to hide and rest for the last time after Naseby; not until the following year, when his cause was hopeless, did the castle surrender. Then, warned by experience, the Ironsides destroyed it, leaving for us these old walls, and the gateway by which kings and princes, priests and soldiers, and a pitiless woman of bitter sorrows had so often come and gone.

STAFFORDSHIRE

The Remorse of Dr Johnson

UTTOXETER. With a Roman settlement underfoot, it looks down a sloping mile of Staffordshire to where the River Dove divides it from its neighbour, Derbyshire. Its revenues were given to Windsor and the chapel of the newly-founded Order of the Garter when the Staffordshire men came home from Crecy.

It has memories of a strange philosopher, of the surrender of a duke and his beaten army, of a gallant admiral, a famous lady, and our greatest talker. The philosopher was Thomas Allen, born here in 1542, and educated at Oxford, where he became one of the foremost mathematicians of the age, friend and correspondent of the greatest spirits of his era. But he was an astrologer, and men accused him of wizardry, declaring that he practised black magic to bring about the marriage of his patron Leicester to Queen Elizabeth. His servant asserted that spirits mounted the scholar's stairs as thick as bees, but in spite of this he escaped the perils of a credulous age and died in his bed at 90.

One of the most sensational scenes in the life of the town was in August 1648, when the first Duke of Hamilton, next in succession to the Stuarts for the Scottish throne, came here with all that was left of the army of 20,000 with which he had started from Scotland to strike a last blow for Charles. Always a muddler, never trusted by either side, he had rounded his luckless career by allowing himself to be hopelessly defeated by Cromwell, and fled here from Preston. He surrendered to Lambert, and while his soldiers were imprisoned in the church, where they played havoc, Hamilton was sent to Windsor. There he saw Charles leave for London for his trial and death, and his own execution followed three months after.

The town gave its name to the peerage conferred on Alan Gardner, its most illustrious sailor son, who left here in 1755, a boy of 13, to spend the greater part of the next half century fighting our battles at sea. The lady whose name is cherished here is Mary Howitt, a daughter of Uttoxeter folk, who married William Howitt in 1821. Although her mind was exercised in writing or editing about 100 books, she never forgot that on the day her Uttoxeter lover took her to the altar she wore her first silk gown, "a very pretty dove colour," with bonnet to match, and a soft silk shawl.

The parish church, still with the tower under which men came to thanksgiving for the victory at Crecy, has two alabaster tombs, one with the engraved figure of Thomas Kynnersley in armour such as he wore in the Wars of the Roses; the other with a nun in a flowing robe and veil, who died when the man who was to launch the Spanish Armada against us shared the throne of England.

A rare servant of this church was Thomas Lightfoot, vicar for 36 years of the 17th century. There is no memorial to him, but he lives on in the fame of his son John, the matchless Hebrew scholar. There is a memorial to Henry Abud, the iron chancel screen being in memory of his 48 years as vicar.

For centuries the town has been famous for its markets, and it is in the marketplace that we find the most appealing of all its monuments. Here, copied from a famous statue in Lichfield Cathedral, is shown an aged man with bowed head, the skirts of his coat swept by the wind, a picture of grief and remorse. It recalls one of the most moving events in a wonderful life, the penance of Dr Johnson.

Upon a bitterly inclement day when men in the full vigour of health were glad to seek shelter, an aged giant, strange in gait and given to convulsive shudderings and strange rolling of the head, lurched into the marketplace of Uttoxeter, came to a halt at a certain spot, bared his head to the storm, and stood like one transfixed. The time was about 1780, and the strange old figure in the marketplace had come from afar to make atonement for a petty rebellion against a father's will committed sixty years before.

It was Dr Johnson and he told the story of his pilgrimage on the occasion of his last visit to Lichfield, his beloved native city. True to his habit of recruiting new friends, he had this day taken to his heart a young clergyman, Henry White, who lives for ever in our literature merely because the Doctor talked to him on this day and told one of the strangest little stories of his strange and chequered life. Johnson discoursed of his boyhood and of his relations to his parents, and said that he could not in general accuse himself of having been an undutiful son. Then he went on in his inimitable easy-stately way to tell this famous anecdote:

Once I was disobedient; I refused to attend my father to Uttoxeter market. Pride was the source of that refusal, and the remembrance of it was painful. A few years ago I desired to atone for this fault; I went to Uttoxeter in very bad weather, and stood for a considerable time

bareheaded in the rain, on the spot where my father's stall used to stand.
In contrition I stood, and I hope the penance was expiatory.

A thousand visits to Uttoxeter could not dim the mental picture of that scene. All about this country old Michael and his son Samuel used to ride and walk intent on the sale of second-hand books. Perhaps shame rather than pride dictated the son's refusal to go to the Uttoxeter stall. The elder Johnson was a victim of melancholia, which could only be kept within bounds if the old man kept continually riding about the countryside, for he was a wrong-headed man, liable to mental breakdown during physical inactivity.

He had a workshop for the repair of his books and the making of parchment, a detached building which gradually became ruinous. Half of it, to the rear, fell down for want of money to keep it in repair, yet its owner was yet not less diligent to lock the door each night, although he knew that anyone who chose could walk in at the back, where the wall had fallen.

That was the father whom Johnson disobeyed and to whose memory he made reparation when he himself was 70 years of age.

The Lost City on Alfred's Boundary

WALL. The Romans built here a city and called it Letocetum. It flanked their Watling Street, crossed not far away by Icknield Street.

Then danger to the Eternal City called the legions home, and Letocetum, a prey to invading Saxons, fell into ruin.

Alfred used the road as a boundary between his kingdom and that of the Danes, but heeded it not as a place of strength and comeliness. The wonders we see here were as nothing to our ancestors. Not all was lost, not all fallen; Camden wrote of it in the 16th century as taking its name from its Roman walls; Plot, the 17th-century historian, described its Roman pavements; and there are 18th-century records of a military barricade of great oak trunks standing erect in close order.

Slowly the soil covered up the remainder, while much was carried away to make roads, houses, and farms. Less than a century ago the church with its tower and its little spire rose on the hill, a landmark in the beautiful country round. When this was completed the village bethought itself of the imperial city under its feet, and dug for it.

Three excavations were made last century, and a search resumed in 1912 was continued up to the time of the war. The results will be lost no more, for the site is scheduled as a national monument.

Here are Roman baths ranking with the best in the country, marvellously preserved by the soil which so long hid them. There is the hot bath, the tepid bath, and the cold bath. The furnace is perfectly revealed with its floor of splendid Roman cement intact, there are evidences of three floors having existed at different times in the Roman era. There is a wide step worn smooth by Roman sandals, and the remains of a niche in which was a statue. There are foundations of the walls which enclosed the exercising-grounds; and near by is the site of a Roman villa which, having been explored, is now again buried.

Here dwelt the Romans to whom Nero was lord of the world; here were Romans who trembled at the name of Domitian. Coins of both these tyrants circulated here. Not all is lost of the citizens of that proud Empire, for in the little museum is a black urn, still charged with the bones and ashes of some lordly Roman of that long ago. Roman tiles abound, and there is part of the flue which once conveyed hot air from the hypocaust, which we see still wonderfully preserved.

Shelters have been built over the remains now exposed, and security against weather and pillage is assured to the most impressive relics left of a Staffordshire ruled by the consuls and legions of Caesar. All trace of the Saxon is gone, but Rome remains.

Walsall's Pride

WALSALL. An ancient town on the edge of the Black Country, it looks north and east to scenes of unspoilt beauty, proud of its roll of fame and proud of its achievements. Bringing the country into the town, it is rich in open spaces and recreation grounds (it has hundreds of acres), chief among them being the Arboretum of nearly 90 acres beautiful with trees, shrubs, flowers, and lakes. Reedswood Park is an example for all time of what can be done to make an ugly country beautiful, for its 64 acres are a paradise won from the dumps of disused mines, one of the county's created wonderlands. It has also the county's first King George Playing-Field; it is at Bloxwich, and has fine heraldic gates.

Long the capital of the saddlery trade, where horses were bitted and buckled and harnessed in all the trappings of utility and splendour, it found its main industry menaced by the mechanical transport of our time and turned its leather-work to account in equipping cars, and its bit and buckle foundries into factories for steel structures of all kinds. With coal and iron at its door, and canals and railways to fetch and carry, we found it busy and thriving in spite of depressions.

There is honest pride in the wide main thoroughfares in the chief buildings of Walsall and in memorials to men and women who have served it or distinguished it. Twentieth-century Walsall seeks to better its streets as 18th-century Walsall bettered its manners. John Wesley recorded that he had an unhandsome reception here in 1743, but 20 years later found the town changed, for "God hath tamed the wild beasts, or chained them up!" A brass tablet reminds us that a hundred years later General Booth lived here with his saintly wife and his son Bramwell (at 5 Hatherton Street).

A missioner of a different type, Jerome K. Jerome, has a tablet at Belsize House in Bradford Street, where in 1859 he was born into the family of a preacher who was also a mine-owner, and a Nonconformist mother who remembered being pelted with mud and stones for going to chapel in Wales. Floods ruined Father Jerome's mine, and the boy suffered from miserable poverty, but he educated himself and made the English-speaking world laugh with his delightful story of Three Men in a Boat; and in his prime he thrilled it with a beautiful play, the Passing of the Third Floor Back. So it was with his autobiography, which is full of laughter and tears, and ends with the solemn testament of a Christian who has fought the good fight and is assured of his goal. He died in 1927, Walsall's most gifted literary son and one of England's merry gentlemen.

It was a younger son of the town, Lieutenant S. N. Webster, who won the distinction of being the first man to travel at more than four miles a minute. He won the Schneider Trophy for England by flying at 4.69 miles a minute, the greatest speed attained by a human being at that time. Walsall's proudest monument to warlike valour is the fine bronze bust (outside the library in Lichfield Street) of Seaman Carless, who won the VC in a naval engagement in the war while serving as a gunner. In spite of a fatal wound he helped to remove stricken men to safety and to lift a shell for his gun; then, falling, he struggled to his feet again, cheered on the men, sank down, and died. He looks here what he was, the happy warrior:

This is he
That every man in arms should wish to be.

The peace memorial is a white stone cenotaph in Bradford Place, but thought for the living has been blended with memories of the dead, and three playing-fields, an addition of 500 acres to the town's open spaces, are part of the gift of remembrance. In the fine town hall, with handsome pillars, beautiful gables, and a remarkable tower with a lantern and crown 150 feet high, are the records of the 2000 men who served, their names inscribed on eight panels, their story told in stately vellum volumes.

It is the valour of peace which is expressed in another monument at Walsall, valour which prompted a gentle woman to face death a hundred times. The monument is Mr F. J. Williamson's delightful statue of Dorothy Pattison, the immortal Sister Dora. She stands at the Bridge in white marble on a red granite pillar, with four panels of scenes from her work. We see her in nursing uniform, holding a roll of surgical bandages, her scissors hanging from her belt, her fine face a blend of courage, humour, and benevolence, looking as Walsall saw her last century, the Florence Nightingale of the town.

There are memories here of another brave but tragically mis-guided woman, Henrietta Maria, wife of Charles Stuart, who, when on her way in 1643 to join the king, then advancing to Edgehill, stayed at what is now the White Hart Inn, a fine Tudor brick house with a small hart's head in each of its lower windows.

High above the town, and seen for miles around, rises the lofty spire of St Matthew's Church on its hilltop, with superb views from its churchyard of the Wrekin, Barr Beacon, Cannock Chase, and of green fields stretching to the horizon. Nothing remains for us to see of the Norman church, for the present building with its many spire-like pinnacles was rebuilt in the last two centuries.

The oldest monument, worn and mutilated, is that of Sir Roger Hillary in 14th-century armour, who has come back to the church after being long lost. On an alabaster wall monument is a medallion bust of William Purvis, another of Walsall's heroes, who served for 24 years in the 17th Lancers, fought in the Crimea and the Mutiny, and returned to his birthplace, to tell of that marvellous ride in 1854 when he charged with the Light Brigade, and was one of that little host which came back through the valley of death.

Slender pillars carry the nave arcades, and there are two striking windows over the chancel arch, in which is a wonderfully carved modern screen, with a Crucifix between a pathetic Madonna and St John, reaching from the rood to the height of the arch. But it is the old woodwork which is most charming. There are eight splendidly carved poppyheads, among them an eagle with three bodies and a demon's head whose hair is like flames. There are 18 grand old choir-stalls, with richly chiselled arm-rests and misereres, a splendid series of carvings including an angel, grotesque animals, a jolly little man who might have sat for Lord Tom Noddy, all head and no body, a musician who has been cheerily blowing away for 500 years, a Centaur looking one way and shooting his arrow another, and an athlete who seems for ever seeking to leap over a pole.

We noticed that the parish clerk of this fine place was at his post for 54 years; he had the odd name of Hyla Archer.

Most appealing of all in the church is the sanctuary window, with its company of angels in memory of Walsall's good angel Sister Dora.

The Sacrifice of Sister Dora

THE daughter of a rector of Hauxwell in Yorkshire, Dorothy Pattison wanted to join Florence Nightingale in the Crimea, although at the time she knew nothing of nursing. But her father disapproved of her ideas, and not until she was nearly 30 did she leave home to teach in a Buckinghamshire village school.

Soon she joined the Sisterhood of the Good Samaritan, taking the name of Sister Dora. The Town Council of Walsall had asked the Sisters to open a hospital for industrial accidents; the Sister in charge fell ill, and Dora, with very little training, had to take over the work. Smallpox broke out. Epidemic followed epidemic, and she was taxed to the limits of her tremendous endurance. She spent her hours of rest nursing in their own homes those who had none to care for them.

The discipline of the Sisterhood could be strict to the point of inhumanity, as Dora found when she was refused permission to visit her dying father. In the end she left the Sisterhood, went on with her nursing, and took charge of the work of a hospital here. She did the work of an army, and always gaily. "Make you laugh?" said one of her patients. "She'd make you laugh if you were dying."

She studied anatomy, and could perform minor operations skilfully. As eye accidents were frequent in Walsall she went to the Ophthalmic Hospital in Birmingham to learn about their treatment. She was deeply religious, and combined her work with prayer.

"Sister, save my arm. It's my right arm!" pleaded a healthy-looking workman hurt by a machine. The doctor shook his head gravely, and said "Amputate," but suddenly Dora felt strength in her; she did what a nurse is supposed never to do—she opposed the doctor, who was furious. For three weeks she strove; the man's name was forgotten and to the whole hospital he became Sister's Arm. He was saved, and on every spare Sunday he had the workman would walk 11 miles to ring the bell and enquire after Sister Dora. "Just tell her that *her* arm rang the bell," he would say.

At last she was attacked by cancer. Nothing could be done for her, so she went back to her wards and continued dressing wounds, serving meals, washing up, cracking jokes, so that her patients, seeing her radiance, caught a new enthusiasm for living. To the end she hid her suffering from them.

WALTON. A little place by the county town, it has a fine thatched cottage for a Post Office and a church with a central tower and spire in which is the beautiful sleeping figure of Richard Byrd Levett in a soldier's uniform, and above him a bronze figure of a mother and a child under a canopy enriched with roses.

One Midsummer Night

WATERFALL. It is up on the lonely moors, taking its name from a queer trick of the River Hamps, which is not far off and sometimes vanishes underground through crevices.

Although the church has been made new, it has kept its wide Norman chancel arch and a Norman doorway, both adorned with chevron, and the windows have been refashioned in the Norman style. The plain screen and panelling in the chancel are Jacobean.

A mile or two south of the village is Cauldon Low, a hill Mary Howitt knew and loved. In her charming poem The Fairies of the

Caldon-Low she tells of the strange things little Mary saw at the top of the hill one midsummer's night.

> *Then take me on your knee, mother,*
> *And listen, mother of mine:*
> *A hundred fairies danced last night,*
> *And the harpers they were nine.*
>
> *And the harp-strings rang so merrily*
> *To their dancing feet so small;*
> *But, oh! the sound of their talking*
> *Was merrier far than all!*
>
> *And with that I could not help but laugh,*
> *And I laughed out loud and free;*
> *And then on the top of Caldon-Low*
> *There was no one left but me.*

The Temple Older than Christianity

WEDNESBURY. A large town playing its part in the age of iron and steel, yet with a memory older than Christianity in England still lingering in its name. It is believed that on this hilltop where St Bartholomew's church now stands was once a heathen temple to Woden, the great Norse god, the god who received heroes into Valhalla and had two ravens to keep him posted with the news of the day. It is thought, too, that Wednesbury is the place referred to in the Anglo-Saxon Chronicle as the scene of a fierce battle between Saxons and Britons in 592.

The modern Christian temple on the hill is a fine place. Its interior is enriched with a wealth of beautiful decoration, carved screens, alabaster panelling, and lovely stained glass. And there are ancient treasures too. The lectern is older than the Reformation and is believed to be unique in England. It is a gilded fighting cock made of plaster on an oak pedestal. The great picture shielded by curtains is a Descent from the Cross by Jean Jouvenet, a French artist of the 17th century. Several of his big canvases are in the Louvre, among them another Descent from the Cross. The carved oak pulpit of 1611 is one of the finest in Staffordshire.

On the sanctuary wall are the kneeling figures of Thomas and Eleanor Parkes of 300 years ago, with six children below them. Someone has written here of Thomas that he was

His country's lover,
His church's beautifier,
His poor's benefactor.

On an altar tomb lie the figures of Richard Parkes (who died a few years later) and his wife Dorothy who gave the church a beautiful chalice. Carved here with a huge head, Richard was "much wanted, and lamented when he died."

On the wall is a memorial to Isaac Clarkson, a 19th-century vicar who served for 35 years. We see his portrait again in the Art Gallery in Holyhead Road, where, as well as pictures, there are collections of ironwork, pottery, tapestry, and woolwork. Among the treasures of this museum we found the side of an embroidered silk waistcoat of the 18th century, a Buddhist prayer-wheel, a uniform, sword, and spurs worn at the charge of the Light Brigade, and a piece of the earliest gas-piping known, from the floor of William Murdock's house at Handsworth.

WEDNESFIELD. With the making of keys prominent among its present-day industries, it goes back in history a thousand years to the day of a fierce battle between Alfred's son Edward and the Danes. The Danes were heavily defeated by Edward with his army of Mercians and West Saxons, and their two kings Halfdan and Ecwils perished in the battle. The red-brick church standing today is the second rebuilding of an 18th-century ancestor.

The Village Carpenter

WEEFORD. Hereabouts in 1700 was born a forerunner of Sir Richard Arkwright. He was John Wyatt, a distant kinsman of Dr Johnson, and a mechanical genius who narrowly missed fame. In 1738 he patented the first machine to spin by rollers moving at different speeds. His machine, worked by donkeys, was set up in a cotton mill in Birmingham, where the first two hanks of cotton to be spun without hands are still preserved for us to see. Ingenious as his invention was, it was not as satisfactory as Arkwright's spinning-jenny, which quickly superseded it. Yet Wyatt was not entirely a failure as an inventor, for he first brought to perfection the compound lever weighing machine of the type still used at railway stations. He has been sleeping in St Philip's churchyard at Birmingham since 1766.

Looking down Lichfield Street

Sister Dora

The Town Hall

SCENES IN WALSALL

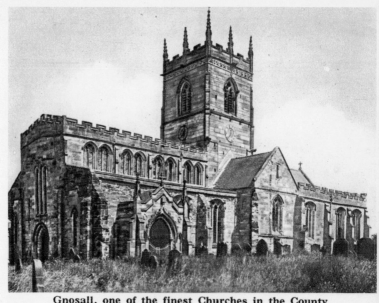

Gnosall, one of the finest Churches in the County

Wednesbury

West Bromwich

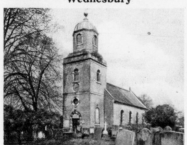

Marchington

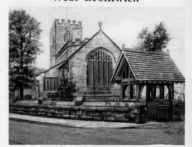

Cheadle

FIVE STAFFORDSHIRE CHURCHES

The village where he worked as a carpenter is in a hollow close by Watling Street. Its refashioned church is by a farmyard, and has interesting windows old and new. One has beautiful portraits of Christ and the Four Evangelists holding books and quills, in memory of Robert Cowpland, 46 years rector last century; the other has lovely old French glass showing Pilate washing his hands. It was brought from a chapel outside Paris during the French Revolution.

The Village Blacksmith

WEST BROMWICH. Any beauty in these parts must fight the grime of a thousand chimneys, yet West Bromwich has a possession of astonishing beauty as well as a church with much that is interesting.

Oak House, the town museum, is a treasure of which any Tudor gentleman would have been proud. How it escaped the slum-building century we do not know, but here it is, restored by Alderman Reuben Farley and given by him to the town for ever, a picture in black and white 400 years old, with lovely gables, a lantern turret, and clustering chimneys. In front is a charming flower garden, and behind (where the house is faced with Jacobean brickwork) is a rich lawn; and inside we can wander about its panelled rooms, upstairs and down, looking at the curious and beautiful things in the show cases, but enjoying the atmosphere of this wonderful old house. A marvel it is indeed for a Black Country town to possess in its midst. Out of gratitude West Bromwich presented Alderman Farley with the freedom of the Borough in a casket made out of some old timber from Oak House.

The church is on high ground away from the town and a good deal of its tower is 14th-century work. The oldest thing to see is a little Norman pillar built into the wall among some old tiles under the tower. The font is Tudor, and the sleeping figures in the chancel are Ann Whorwood of 1599 and her son Field Whorwood of 1658.

By the side of his mother Field looks a giant, yet he can scarcely have been as tall as another son of West Bromwich, of whom it is said that a hole was made in the ground for him to stand in so that he should equal his fellows. He was Walter Parsons, a blacksmith who became a porter of James the First and won fame as a strong man. Without undue exertion he could pick up two hefty yeomen of the guard, carrying them wherever he pleased, one under each arm, no matter how they struggled. The story is told that a foolish man who once insulted him in the street found himself almost immediately hanging by his waistband from a hook high up in a butcher's shop.

WESTON-ON-TRENT. Its oldest inhabitant is in the churchyard by a little brook, a yew which was a sapling when Queen Elizabeth was young. It has bells in its tower which have been ringing longer still, for both are said to be 15th century. The tower itself is 13th century and has on three sides a pair of lancet windows set between four small round arches. Most of the church is 700 years old, but the clerestory is modern and so is the oak pulpit with its flowers and angels. There is a silver paten engraved before the Reformation and a register record of the burial of Civil War soldiers.

Near by Weston runs the Trent and Mersey Canal, and there is a 17th-century gabled hall of grey stone.

The Friend of Disraeli

WESTON-UNDER-LIZARD. It is a delightful model village by Watling Street, near the Shropshire border. Its great house, the home of the Earl of Bradford, was built in the 17th century and has been enlarged. It is by a charming lake in a park, with a heronry.

The church, with old yews and old cedars about it, has long been famous for its monuments. Much restored in 1702 by Lady Wilbraham, it has 14th-century stones in the chancel and a 15th-century tower with three bells that were ringing before the Reformation. The finely carved oak pulpit is curious for its elaborate 18th-century ornament of flowers and vegetables, a rare combination.

In the Bradford chapel are several alabaster monuments to the Bridgemans, Earls of Bradford. There is a cherub with a laurel crown above a casket in memory of the first earl, a monument to the second, and one to his wife, who is lying on a couch with three angels hovering over her. It was this Lady Bradford who figured in the life of Disraeli after the death of his wife. He never seemed to be tired of the company of Lady Bradford, or of her sister Lady Chesterfield at Bretby in Derbyshire.

Once he wrote from Bretby to Lady Bradford expressing his

great regret that he was imposing himself as an invalid on the home of Lady Chesterfield. She was a dear angel, he said, who was more than kindness to him as he sat in silence musing over the past, and he added these human words in his letter to Lady Bradford:

I have had at least my dream, and if my shattered energies never rally, which is what I must be prepared for, I have at any rate reached the pinnacle of power and gauged the sweetest and deepest affections of the heart.

A painted marble monument with a ship in full sail is in memory of Richard Bridgeman, who served in the Navy and was killed in the air in East Africa in 1917; a wall monument has a weeping woman holding a portrait of the Lord Bradford of 1800; and there is a monument to the countess of 1894, shown on her bed, with angels kneeling.

In the chancel are two of England's small group of oak monuments, both showing cross-legged knights in armour with their feet on lions. One is perhaps Sir Hugh Weston of 1305 and the other his uncle Sir John Weston, who is thought to have accompanied Edward the First to Flanders. During the journey he is said to have been entrusted with royal jewels, and here he has a purse hanging from his belt.

The Westons lived here till about 1349, and among the old glass in the windows are fragments of 14th-century shields showing their arms. They are in the east window, with small kneeling figures of a Sir John Weston and his wife.

The Village Schoolmaster

WETTON. It has some of the loneliest country in Staffordshire round about it and glorious scenery everywhere. By it runs the River Manifold, but its romantic natural possession is Thor's Cave.

In the shadow of the ancient tower of the modern church lies a beloved village schoolmaster explorer of the cave in the Long Ago. He was Samuel Carrington, who shared with Derbyshire's antiquarian Thomas Bateman all his excavations on the moors. They found Roman remains at Borough Hole, they opened prehistoric graves, they sought and found rich treasure in Thor's Cave. The stone on the schoolmaster's grave has shells and fossils carved on it, and the Weston Park Museum in Sheffield has some of the things they found, part of a collection of Bronze Age, Stone Age, and Roman antiquities which is one of the best out of London. The old tower of the church is 15th or 16th century and the font in which the school-master would be baptised has been here several centuries.

A Boy's Famous Hymn

WHITMORE. Here was born a country boy who was to spend most of his days in the East End of London; he was Samuel Stone, born at the rectory in the year the Victorian Era began.

He would be baptised in the battered old font the Normans made, for his father was rector at this attractive church, one of only two half-timbered churches in Staffordshire. Though made new in 1676 it has its characteristic west window, a timbered porch, and one timbered wall; the bell-turret is borne on wooden posts.

There is an alabaster tomb on which are engraved the portraits of Edward Mainwaring in armour and his wife in the long flowing dress that women wore in the days before the Armada. With them are three children and their dog.

Very pleasant is this birthplace of Samuel Stone the poet, for the River Sowe flows through the village; and there is Swynnerton Old Park in the woods, and Whitmore Hall, reached from the church by a splendid avenue of limes. Samuel grew up to be a scholar and a poet, and it is the pride of this village that when it sings "The Church's One Foundation" on Sundays it is singing a hymn with a worldwide fame, written by one of its own boys.

The Flitch of Bacon

WICHNOR. Its flitch of bacon is not so well known as Dun-mow's, but everyone hereabouts has heard of it, and a wooden flitch still hangs in the hall of Wichnor Lodge, a house hidden by trees. It is said that John of Gaunt granted the manor to the Somervilles on condition that they would always give a man who had been married a year and a day a flitch of bacon if he would swear that he and his wife lived happily together.

By three firs on a little hill overlooking pleasant meadows stands the church with an Elizabethan brick tower, and walls perhaps a century older. Fragments of old glass are in the windows, and there is an old font.

George Borrow's Dingle

WILLENHALL. Lying between Wolverhampton and Walsall, it has a lock-making industry and iron and brass foundries; and amid all this is a modern church with much beauty and interest, part of it built in memory of a vicar, G. H. Fisher, who was here 57 years. A corner stone of the transept is inscribed to his memory.

There is attractive woodwork and a good east window of scenes from the Crucifixion, and there are two memorial tablets, each with its human appeal. One is to Dr Richard Wilkes of 1760, the last of a family who had lived here for 300 years, and the other to Mr William Hall, who died suddenly in a railway carriage. The tablet is placed over the pew he occupied for half a century.

But for those with imagination there is more than this in Willenhall. For those who can forget the new housing estate creeping towards it, and the Birmingham Canal running through it, there is the piece of waste land that was Mumpers Dingle in George Borrow, the Dingle where Lavengro fought the Flaming Tinman. It is a mile north of the town, and they still call the bridge over the canal Dingle Bridge.

Halfway between Willenhall and Walsall stood Bentley Hall, the home of that Colonel John Lane who sleeps in the family chapel in Wolverhampton church. Here on a September morning in 1651 a King of England set out as a humble member of a little procession, making an escape which was to change the course of England's history.

Bentley Hall was pulled down in 1927, but the historic site is marked by a cross set up by the father of the poet Harold Parry of whom we read at Bloxwich.

Jane Lane's Serving-Man

AT Bentley Hall lived Jane Lane whose quick brain and undaunted courage enabled Charles the Second to escape from his enemies after the Battle of Worcester. Charles, disguised as a yokel, had spent three days and nights wandering from hiding-place to hiding-place, including a whole day up an oak tree at Boscobel. On September 8, five days after the battle, Charles sent his devoted friend Lord Wilmot to Bentley to ask Colonel John Lane to help him to escape to London.

Now it so happened that the Colonel's sister Jane had arranged to

pay a visit to her sister Mrs Norton at Abbot's Leigh near Bristol.
She had already secured from the Governor at Stafford the necessary
permission to travel, which included a man-servant and her cousin
Henry Lascelles. Jane at once offered to take Charles as her servant
in order that he could reach Bristol and take a ship out of England.

That night Charles arrived and changed his green threadbare
coat and ill-fitting breeches for the grey suit of a serving man.
He had already shorn off his dark curls when he donned a very
greasy old grey steeple hat without lining or hat band at the beginning
of his flight.

Next morning at daybreak Charles, assuming the name of William
Jackson (one of Colonel Lane's tenants), brought Jane's horse out
of the stable and helped her on to the pillion seat behind him.
John Petre and his wife, her relatives but not in the secret, mounted
a second horse, proposing to accompany them as far as Stratford-on-
Avon, while Henry Lascelles, who was to escort them the whole
way, mounted a third.

The little cavalcade proceeded without any adventures until they
sighted some cavalry near Stratford. The Petres were terrified and
in spite of Jane's remonstrances turned aside. But Charles and Jane
and Henry quietly jogged their way through soldiers and town
without a challenge.

That night they spent at Long Marston in the house of John
Tomes, a kinsman of Jane, where the king was bullied by the cook
because he did not know how to wind up the roasting jack. On the
following night they stayed at Cirencester, and next day they rode
through Bristol to the Nortons' house beyond it. The first man the
king saw was one of his own chaplains watching a game of bowls
being played on the green before the door, but he was unrecognised,
and took Jane's horse round to the stable and waited events.

Jane, in the meantime, interviewed Pope the butler, told him that
her man-servant William was still weak from ague, and so secured
him a good bedroom. Now Pope had been a trooper in the Royalist
Army and recognised him, but he proved a real friend, trying to
find him a ship and meeting and warning Lord Wilmot, who refused
to disguise himself, not to come to the house, but to meet him at
Frank Windham's house at Trent, near Sherborne.

But Mrs Norton had fallen ill and it was difficult for Jane to leave. Her ready brain quickly devised a plan. She had a letter delivered to her purporting to come from home and stating that her father was desperately ill and needed her. So off they set again, William Jackson this time riding singly with the luggage, and they came to Trent where Jane and her cousin Henry Lascelles bade farewell to the king and returned to Bentley.

Jane's travels, however, had only begun. It somehow leaked out that a lady had aided Charles, and so, disguised as peasants, Jane and her brother tramped across England to take ship at Yarmouth for the continent. Charles went to meet her and sent her to live with the Princess of Orange. He gave her a gold watch and other presents and at the Restoration Parliament voted her a pension of £1000 a year. She then married Sir Clement Fisher, of Great Packington in Warwickshire, and lived until 1689, spending her pension freely.

WOLSTANTON. We come uphill to a church with a fine spire and a beautifully decorated west doorway, and meet a knight of Elizabeth's day. He is William Sneyd of 1571, lying in alabaster on a canopied tomb. Dressed in armour and a ruff, he rests his head on a helmet, his wife by him, and with them their 15 children, the five boys wearing armour as if to protect their ten sisters.

From the hilltop here we look down on Wolstanton, thought to be on the site of a Saxon settlement, and far over the busy Potteries.

The Fine Capital of the Black Country

WOLVERHAMPTON. The capital of the Black Country, the biggest town in Staffordshire after the Potteries, and the centre of an immense iron industry, Wolverhampton has a thousand years of history behind it and the remains of Roman iron furnaces not far away. It has on its ten thousand acres a multitude of workers in nearly two hundred trades, and it has all round it a delightful countryside in which its workers can take their pleasures. As he walks through its streets the traveller is probably set wondering by the sight of the name Fold—Blossoms Fold and Mitre Fold in North Street, Farm Fold in John Street, Pountney Fold in Dudley Street, Bennet's Fold in Salop Street, and more. It is the town's way of remembering the time when its situation in the middle of the Midlands made Wolverhampton the natural market for the sale of wool. Here the wool was gathered for sending to the Continent to be made into cloth, and the wool was stored in barns or warehouses, each warehouse having a yard into which the sheep were driven. Here came merchants from the ports of London and Bristol to make their bargains. The years have rolled on, and no more are the sheep in their Wolverhampton fold, but the names remain to remind the busy folk of this industrial town of the days when the world was a quieter place, and shepherds with their flocks were familiar figures in their streets. Now there is a change indeed, and Wolverhampton is among our most progressive towns, no longer with sheep in its folds, but with aeroplanes in its municipal airport.

To walk through the streets of this town is to feel that behind it is the spirit of moving forward; to go through its vast workshops and see the building of buses and cars, of locks and safes, of electrical machines and automatic devices, of tubes and boilers and tanks—and to see coming into being the countless things that belong to this age of wheels and cranks and pulleys and levers, is to feel that we are touching industry at a thousand points. To be taking a holiday here and running into the country round—into Worcestershire and Shropshire with all their charm—is to realise that Wolverhampton, though of the Black Country, is not in it. It has a marvellous range of lovely places within its reach; Cannock Chase with its thirty thousand acres of gorse and heather, fir trees and flowers, is only nine miles off, and the beautiful black and white village of Claverley is only ten. If the motorist has only half a day to spare he may run out to Broadway, or Evesham, or Warwick, or Shakespeare's Stratford, or the unique little town of Ludlow, or he may run to see Worcester Cathedral after lunch and be home after tea. The whole of this town is in the hands of a Planning Authority, and we have seen in Wolverhampton houses and gardens and residential roads as fine as any town could expect to have within its bounds. The grammar school built for girls in 1911 is worthy of the new home of the Grammar School founded for the boys in 1512, and the Technical College from which the industrial world of Wolverhampton draws so much of its skilled labour is a building stamped with the genius of our 20th-century architects.

For centuries before the Black Country was black this must have been a place of importance, and if there were nothing else to prove it there would be the splendid church of St Peter, this great centre-piece of a town, standing proudly on a hill where Christians have

Tutbury   John of Gaunt's Gateway

Wootton   The handsome Hall

The 19th Century Town Hall

The Lake in West Park

MODERN WOLVERHAMPTON

The Ancient Cross

St Peter's Church

The Art Gallery and Museum

WOLVERHAMPTON, OLD AND NEW

Abbots Bromley　　　　　　　　　　**The Horn Dance**

Uttoxeter　　**The Conduit and its Carving of Dr Johnson's Penance**

been worshipping for at least ten centuries. Reached by a flight of steps and set among trees, it is an attractive spectacle.

Something of the air of a cathedral it has, with a splendid 15th-century tower rising up from 13th-century arches. The lofty nave with its double clerestory windows is 15th century, and the chancel is a modern copy of 14th-century style. Wherever we look about us there are things old and beautiful to catch the eye. The oldest of them was already ancient when Christianity came, but we were told that until a few years ago men who had made a bargain still came to shake hands on it through this holed stone. Near it is the 12-foot shaft of a Norman churchyard cross. The porch has a vaulted roof, and a room above in which it is thought the priest slept, his duty being to say very early mass for merchants and travellers. The interior of the porch is finely carved in oak in memory of Sir Charles Mander. The western gallery of the nave is a good piece of Jacobean carving, put here in 1610 by the Merchant Taylors Company for the use of the Grammar School boys. The old oak miserere seats were brought here from the ruined monastery of Lilleshall in Shropshire.

Two remarkable examples of carving in stone are the font and the pulpit. The font bowl was brought here at the Restoration to replace one destroyed during the Commonwealth. Carved with flowers and foliage, it stands on a 15th-century pedestal with eight quaint little figures of saints under arches. The 15th-century pulpit is a veritable treasure, unique in Staffordshire and taking a high place among the stone pulpits of England; there are only about 60 of these old stone pulpits left. With all its sides beautifully decorated, the pulpit here is attached to a pillar of the nave. A fascinating lion sits guarding the step, and there is a tradition among the choirboys that the animal will yawn if the preacher goes on over half an hour.

The north chapel with its carved oak roof was built before the Reformation. In it are the 16th-century figures of Thomas and Katharine Lane, and the wall monument to Colonel John Lane of Bentley, who, with his famous sister Jane, helped Charles the Second to escape after the Battle of Worcester and hid with him in the oak at Boscobel. The nation paid the cost of this monument, Parliament granting £1000 for it.

Cut off by 15th-century screen work, a 14th-century chapel holds the Leveson memorials. John and Joyce Leveson have been sleeping here since Elizabethan times, and there is a fine bronze statue of Sir Richard of 1605, showing him in armour. It was carved by Hubert Le Soeur, whose figure of Charles Stuart at Charing Cross is one of the finest sculptures in London and has been called one of the three most impressive equestrian monuments in the world. As a boy of 18 Sir Richard Leveson fought against the Armada, serving as a volunteer in the Ark Royal, the biggest ship in Elizabeth's navy. In 1600 he was Admiral of the Narrow Seas commanding a fleet sent to look for Spanish treasure ships, and within two years he had destroyed Spanish ships in Kinsale harbour and engaged others off Lisbon, wrecking two galleys and bringing ten back to England. For his exploits they made him an admiral for life, but he passed away when he was only 35, a fine sailor of the breed of Drake. The Jesse Tree window in this chapel is in memory of other men who fought for the Motherland in the Great War.

On the walls of St Peter's are sculptured portraits of the first MP and the first mayor of Wolverhampton; and there is a tablet to William Walker, who as a chorister of St George's at Windsor sang before Queen Elizabeth; he was organist here. Most fascinating of all, an 18th-century tablet in the porch tells of another musician, Charles Phillips, "beloved by all for his absolute contempt of riches and inimitable performance on the violin." Born in Wales, he fiddled his way through Europe and met with both kinds of fortune, and on his death Dr Wilkes of St John's College, Cambridge, wrote for him this epitaph:

> Exalted soul, thy various sounds could please
> The love-sick virgin and the gouty ease;
> Could jarring crowds, like old Amphion, move
> To beauteous order and harmonious love;
> Rest here in peace till angels bid thee rise
> And join thy Saviour's consort in the skies.

Boswell tells us that Garrick once repeated this epitaph to Dr Johnson, who, with a shake of his head, said: "I think, Davy, I can produce a better." Then, stirring his tea awhile in a state of meditation, he produced these lines:

> Phillips, whose touch harmonious could remove
> The pangs of guilty power or hapless love;

Rest here, distressed by poverty no more,
Here find that calm thou gav'st so oft before;
Sleep undisturbed within this peaceful shrine
Till angels wake thee with a note like thine!

A generation after the death of old Charles Phillips there stood with his bride before the altar of St Peter's a man who had a remarkable career abroad. He was Button Gwinnett, who married a Wolverhampton girl, their three daughters being baptised at this ancient font.

This man with so queer a name came from Gloucestershire, having been born in the parsonage at Down Hatherley in 1732. He became a trader in Wolverhampton, but was of little account here and emigrated to America while it was still a British colony. He kept a shop in Savannah, was made a magistrate, and happened in 1776 to be elected one of the three delegates of Georgia to Congress, which in August of that year drew up the Declaration of Independence. His signature was one of the 55 on that historic document; it was one of the last times he signed his name, for in 1777 he fought a duel and died of his wounds, and for years no more was heard of Button Gwinnett.

But much more has been heard of him since then on both sides of the Atlantic, for he has become the most Immortal Nobody in the world. It may be said that everybody in the United States has heard of him, for one of the things most sought for there by autograph hunters is a complete set of the signatories to the Declaration of Independence. Every autograph hunter strives to get these 55 names, and one of them has proved to be the most tantalising thing an autograph hunter ever knew, for, because he was nobody, his name is hard to find. It has been searched for all over the world, and after many years it was found that 36 of Button Gwinnett's autographs had come to light. All but nine of them had come into complete sets of Declaration autographs and the other nine came into the market one by one. Somebody paid £520 for one, but the price jumped to £2800, from that to £5700, and at last it reached ten thousand pounds.

And what has all this to do with Wolverhampton? Only this—that when Button Gwinnett's name had so become the passport to fortune somebody thought of looking among the records of the

Bluecoat School at Wolverhampton, and found that within four months of 1761 Mr Button Gwinnett had attended three meetings of subscribers to the school and at each meeting had *signed the minutes*.

Most of us have thought the minutes of a meeting rather dull, but not so these, for the signatures were sold for a handsome sum. This Immortal Nobody's Bluecoat School, alas, is no more, but Wolverhampton still has its famous Grammar School, flourishing as it did in his day.

The Grammar School is now in its fifth century, for it was founded in 1512 by Sir Stephen Jenyns, a Wolverhampton boy who grew up to become a wealthy Merchant Taylor and Lord Mayor of London in 1508. His school was moved in 1874 from the heart of the town to a fine new home in the healthy western suburbs 400 feet above the sea. From time to time since then new buildings have been set up in its 20 acres of grounds, and now neither Lord Mayor Jenyns nor Mr Button Gwinnett would recognise the little grammar school in these fine buildings that have grown up.

St Chad's College, the Girls' High School, Wolverhampton and Staffordshire Technical College, and the School of Arts and Crafts are among the town's many educational centres, the technical college housed in a noble building, with a sculptured relief of Science and Industry on the front of one wing. The Central Library, with 60,000 volumes on its shelves, was a pioneer in providing students with a separate room where they may study in the utmost peace and comfort. The town has also 200 acres of parks and playing-fields, West Park being among the loveliest in the Midlands, with a great day every year when 60,000 people come to see its flowers and shrubs and trees, and the swans on its lake. Here, on a fine commanding site, stands the statue of Charles Pelham Villiers, one of the remarkable public men of the 19th century. He lived through the whole of it except the first and the last two years, and for over 60 years sat in the House of Commons for Wolverhampton.

But while Wolverhampton is zealous in its care of the citizens of tomorrow, it by no means forgets its citizens of today, and it has a group of public buildings worthy of any town of its size in the land. In Victoria Street a small black-and-white house with a big leaning gable has been allowed to remain as a worthy fragment of the past, but elsewhere ugly out-of-date buildings are constantly being replaced by new and better ones, and streets are being widened so that Wolverhampton's 140,000 people may keep moving with the times. The new public hall, with grand and dignified lines, set up by the builders of Bristol University and Truro Cathedral, has given the citizens fresh cause for pride. Queen Square, the recognised centre of the town with its banks, shops, and business premises and its equestrian statue of Prince Albert (by Thomas Thornycroft), seems to embody all the solid qualities of the Midlander; and it is certain that the practical-minded Wolverhampton man, who may claim that his manufactures are in every corner of the world, thinks first and foremost of utility. But that he has also a warm regard for the arts and crafts is shown by the splendid Art Gallery and Museum in Lichfield Street.

This fine building, given by Philip Horsman at the end of last century, is adorned outside with sculptured panels in which scores of figures represent Painting, Sculpture, and Science; and inside are seven galleries with collections of sculpture, crafts, pottery, and antiquities. Among the paintings are pictures by Romney, Gainsborough, Lawrence, Sidney Cooper, David Cox, and George Morland; and among the sculptors whose work is seen here are Chantrey, Sir Edgar Boehm, and John Gibson.

We have looked at the great church of St Peter's, and the town has other churches with something for the traveller to see.

St Mary's church has several treasures older than itself. The chancel windows have old Flemish and German glass, and the reredos is a vivid piece of 17th-century Flemish carving of the Crucifixion and the Ascension. The old wooden lectern is carved with an eagle holding a serpent, and there are three small lions sitting on its base. The decorated Norman font was rescued from a farmyard near Tettenhall.

A typical piece of 18th-century England is St John's, with a most attractive interior. There are two old carved chairs in the chancel, and the altar painting is a copy made by a Wolverhampton man of Rubens's Descent from the Cross. The organ is the work of that great 17th-century organ-builder Renatus Harris, and has a story of its own. In 1682 Temple Church in London decided to have a new organ, and commissioned both Harris and his famous rival Father Smith to set up instruments for trial. Both did so, and an exciting contest it must have been, for the immortal Purcell was one of the players. After some disagreement the Benchers decided in favour of Father Smith, and the rejected organ of Renatus Harris found its way into this church in Wolverhampton, where the richly carved case is well in keeping with its surroundings.

At a time when England was in a panic, and many atrocities were being committed, two priests of Wolverhampton were martyred for their share in the bogus plot discovered by the wretched Titus Oates. One, named Gavan, was beheaded along with two other priests and the aged Lord Stafford; the other, William Atkins, a poor paralysed man of 80, was dragged from his bed, taken to Stafford, and condemned to death. Someone relented, and the sentence was not carried out; the old man was shut up in Stafford gaol and allowed to perish there.

We may wonder if any coin of precious metal ever caused such strife as the rejected halfpence of William Wood of Wolverhampton.

William Wood and His Money

WILLIAM WOOD was a prosperous ironmaster of Wolverhampton, where he was born in 1671. We owe him gratitude for the preservation of our old woods and forests, for he was the first man ever seriously to attempt the substitution of coal for wood in the smelting of iron.

He had a stake in the country, mining iron and copper in 39 counties and receiving the exclusive right to furnish Ireland with halfpennies and farthings for 14 years.

At that time 23 pence were coined from a pound of copper for England, and Wood was allowed to make a pound of copper yield the equivalent of 30 pence for Ireland. That might have passed, but it was learned that the patent had in reality been granted by George the Second to the Duchess of Kendal, to whom Wood had had to pay £10,000, in addition to annual bribes to people about the Court.

All that Ireland needed was small change to the value of £15,000, but Wood was authorised to foist upon her over £100,000 worth, his reward being an estimated annual profit of £4000.

A fury of indignation was excited in Ireland; denunciation by the Irish Parliament; protests that the coins would involve Ireland in a loss of £150 on every hundred pounds of copper coined; declarations that the money as issued was debased even beyond specification. Then Swift took up the cudgels for Ireland in the famous Drapier's letters; and, in the character of a Dublin draper, predicted the ruin of his country by Wood's small coins. A grand jury refused to return a true bill when a prosecution was instituted against Swift; instead, the jury indicted the persons who had accepted the coins. All Ireland, led by Swift, the Chancellor, and the Archbishop of Dublin, was up in arms, and so fierce and protracted was the storm that Wood's licence had to be cancelled, and the patentee consoled with a pension of £3000 a year. This he received for only three years, for he died in 1730.

A literature collected about him and his ha'pence, and today the farthings Ireland refused are each worth some three thousand unquestionable English farthings.

The Incredible Jonathan Wild

IT was at Wolverhampton that one of the most proficient villains in history, the notorious Jonathan Wild, was born about 1682, his parents being worthy people. He grew up to the trade of a buckle-maker at Birmingham, married, deserted his wife and child, and left for London, a competent workman, with a mind of unusual audacity and organising faculties.

His life in London soon brought him to prison for debt, and during his four years' confinement he made the acquaintance and learned the secrets of many of the worst criminals. At length released he entered into an infamous partnership with a woman of notorious life, and converted an inn in Cock Lane, Cripplegate, into a depot for the reception of stolen property.

But he soon out-distanced all other criminals. He employed thieves of both sexes and sent to prison or the gallows those who would not work for him. He mapped the metropolis into areas and appointed thieves for every area—special depots for robbery with violence, pocket-picking, and burglary, down to petty thefts in houses by girls whom he had placed in service. His plan was to act as broker between thieves and victims, restoring the product of the robberies he had planned to the owners for handsome rewards, and paying the robbers a moderate commission. All the criminals were at his beck and call.

Advertising widely as a restorer of property and as thief-taker, Wild owned several warehouses for the storage of his plunder, engaged a staff of skilled jewellers to alter and disguise stolen jewellery and watches, and kept a sloop to transport to the Continent goods too dangerous for sale in London.

As self-appointed thief-taker he set up an office, wore a handsome livery, and carried a staff heavily tipped with silver. An Act of Parliament was passed to declare the receiver equally culpable with the thief, but he went triumphantly on, planning robberies, receiving the goods, and sending to the gallows those who rebelled or whom he feared.

He had a run of many years but was at last laid by the heels, and in May 1725 was hanged at Tyburn, with a record of villainy and treachery far transcending the wildest fiction.

The Little Scholar Saved From the Plague

WOMBOURN. Its grey 15th-century spire crowns a red sandstone tower a century older, the only church in England dedicated to St Benedict Biscop, who is said to have introduced glass windows into England. The rest of the church is modern, with two good possessions.

One is the alabaster tablet carved with the Good Samaritan and brought here from Italy in 1720 by Sir Samuel Hellier, very quaint in its perspective of the winding road from Jerusalem to Jericho. The other is the monument to Richard Marsh of 1820, a medallion portrait and an expressive weeping figure of a woman sculptured by Chantrey.

Half a mile away stands the Wodehouse in attractive grounds. It is partly Jacobean and partly much older, and has among its treasures a carving of an Elizabethan figure called the Silent and Good Woman, with these among the lines below her:

> Be frugal, ye wives, live in silence and love,
> Nor abroad ever gossip and roam.

St Benedict Biscop, whose memory is enshrined in this village, was born in 628, and at 25 renounced the world and went on a pilgrimage to Rome. Two years later he went again, and the Pope, knowing Benedict to be "a man of wisdom, piety, and nobility of mind," appointed him to conduct to England Theodore of Tarsus, the new primate.

After two years as an abbot at Canterbury Benedict was in Rome again, this time buying books. He brought them to his native Northumbria and showed them to the king. Perceiving his learning and zeal, the king gave him some land at the mouth of the Wear on which to found a monastery.

Here at Wearmouth Benedict started to build, and within a year there stood a church which was the wonder of all Britain. Benedict adorned it with the most beautiful pictures and ornaments he could find, and for the first time there was a church in this country worthy to be compared with those on the Continent. He was the first Englishman thus to consecrate art to the service of religion.

Ten years later he founded another monastery, this time at Jarrow, and made a last journey to Rome to gather together a library. On his return he found that the plague had carried off a great number of his monks, and the only survivors at Jarrow were the abbot and one little scholar. The little boy was the Venerable Bede, who, when he grew up, was to write a life of St Benedict, telling us most of what we know of him.

With his usual energy Benedict soon collected a new company of monks, but his end was near. In 703 he died, leaving behind him a tradition of vigour and beauty long to be felt in these islands.

The Wild Figure in the Long Black Gown

WOOTTON. A grey hamlet in the shelter of the Weaver Hills, its claim upon the traveller is its big house, Wootton Lodge, a stately Stuart mansion; it has lost its handsome Wootton Hall, where a book was written by a man who set the intellectual world on fire, Jean Jacques Rousseau.

Wootton Lodge, standing in a park rich with timber, was built for Sir Richard Fleetwood, who moved in here early in the 17th century, leaving the family house of Calwich Abbey (not two miles away) to his son. He was allowed to put on the escutcheon over the great doorway the heraldic symbol of the Red Hand of Ulster, for he was one of the squires to whom James the First sold baronetcies in return for money for the Ulster Army.

Sir Richard's old home, lonely in its state, rises abruptly from a wedge-shaped rock at the head of a wooded ravine, with magnificent views from its noble windows and from the flat roof with its delightful open parapet and chimneys which from a distance look like pinnacles. There are few statelier houses in the county than this, approached by a bold flight of steps on the only side that does not descend precipitately to the stream. Admirably placed for fortification, it was the boast of Sir Richard that none could take it, yet, when Parliament's guns were raised on the spot still called Cromwell's Battery, it surrendered in less than two days, and Sir Richard and his two younger sons and 70 other prisoners were roped together and taken to Derby.

Not far off stood Wootton Hall, the handsome house which was built as the home of the Davenports. It was to an older, smaller house of the Davenports on this site that there came in 1766 one of the strangest visitors entertained in this country, Jean Jacques Rousseau, who was then 54 and just entering on that phase of dementia which was to develop into madness and death.

The most famous man in Europe, Rousseau had already done his work, with books which had shaken Europe after centuries of slumber. Intensely gifted, but governed less by the head than by the heart (and a bad heart at that), he had attacked culture as the evidence and the cause of social degeneration. Putting into practice his cry for the defiance of convention, he had already deposited his five children in a foundling hospital.

His greatest work of all, the Social Contract, represented society as founded by agreement, with the head of the State as the people's mandatory, not their master. With gaps of obvious absurdity in his philosophy, he was nevertheless a new and thrilling voice, and is still regarded by many as having enunciated principles which constitute a Magna Carta for mankind. His teaching set Europe aflame; he was the prophet of the French Revolution, as Napoleon was its sword.

Then, Europe having become impossible for him, he fell in with his friend Hume's suggestion and came to England as a refugee, to be received like a prince and to have several houses placed at his disposal. He chose old Wootton Hall for its seclusion, insisted on paying £30 a year rent to its owner and his staunch admirer, Mr Davenport, whose servants were left to wait on him, and here he settled down with his French housekeeper, Therèse Le Vasseur.

For a time he delighted in the beauty of the countryside, but gradually the peace he had sought drove him nearly mad. He was filled with the embittered suspicions of a hunted animal, seeing enmity and treachery in his friends and deadly foes in his neighbours; even the servants (to whom he could express his wishes only by signs) he suspected of wishing to poison him.

The simple village folk of Wootton encountered with fear and wonder this wild figure who would walk their lanes in a long black gown and a gold-tasselled velvet cap, his arms often filled with wild plants, for his one absorbing passion here was botany. It is said that at a spot known as Twenty Oaks he would sit to write the unjust and bitter letters which estranged David Hume from him. The only neighbour he made a friend of, in fact the only one who could speak French with him, was the taciturn bachelor Bernard Granville of Calwich Abbey. Here that wonderful woman Mary Delany, Bernard's sister, met Rousseau and was alarmed at his gallantry to her favourite niece Mary Dewes.

It was when Bernard Granville closed his house for the winter that the lonely Rousseau sat down to write his detestable yet immortal Confessions.

But all the time his French housekeeper, hating the English solitude, continued to aggravate his fears of persecution, and when, after rather more than a year, she told him that she had found the cook mixing cinders with the food, it was the final straw. He rushed away, leaving his trunks with the keys dangling in them and his rent money on the table. He was next heard of at Spalding, where he wrote to the Lord Chancellor appealing, in this friendly country, for a cavalry escort to guard him to the coast. He fled to Dover, where a storm which delayed his sailing was regarded by him as the special inter-position of a malevolent Providence. He reached France in May 1767 and England knew him no more—except as all the world knew him, by his works, the influence of which has been abiding and profound. The house he stayed in has vanished, and all that is left to remind us of this strange visitor is an arched grotto under one of the terraces, still called Rousseau's Cave.

Friends of the Slaves

YOXALL. It was the home of a famous booklover and the scene of a campaign against slavery. Thomas Gisborne lived for 60 years at Yoxall Lodge, which has now vanished. A saintly man who wrote books and poems, he was a great friend of Wilberforce, who often visited him here. Wilberforce was here with his friend Thomas Babington in the autumn of 1790, both devoting their time to a report on slavery. Another visitor at the Lodge has given us this peep of the month they spent here:

Mr Wilberforce and Mr Babington have never appeared downstairs since we came, except to take a hasty dinner, and for half an hour after we have supped; the Slave Trade now occupies them nine hours daily. They talk of sitting up one night each week. The two friends begin to look very ill, but they are in excellent spirits, and at this moment I hear them laughing.

Over 50 years before Wilberforce came to Yoxall Lodge Thomas Astle, the famous expert in ancient writing, was born here. He wrote a valuable book on the Origin and Progress of Writing, and gathered an amazing library. From his relative Philip Morant, the Essex historian, he inherited a fortune and a library of old books and manuscripts, and for the rest of his life he went on adding to this collection till he had the finest private library of manuscripts in England. His books were bought by the Royal Institution for £1000, but he had thought too much of his precious manuscripts to allow them to be dispersed. They went first to the Marquis of Buckingham, who built a library for them at Stowe, and eventually they were sold to the British Museum for £45,000. Among the greatest treasures were King Alfred's Psalter, the Wardrobe Book of Edward the Second, and a beautiful volume of Anglo-Saxon charters.

The village, near the meeting of the Swarbourn and the Trent and once the home of Izaak Walton's grandfather, has an old vicarage with a tiny oak-panelled room thought to have been a hiding-place. The church was made new with the aid of Lord Palmerston, who helped to pay the cost. The tower is 17th century. There are two modern screens, one under the tower with old fragments. A beautiful peace memorial window has in it a battlefield with two Red Cross men carrying a soldier on a stretcher, and another wounded man looking up at a vision of Calvary in the glow of a glorious sunset.

There is a monument with marble figures of the Elizabethan Humphrey Welles and his wife, he in a long cloak, she in a close-fitting cap and tight-waisted dress. A handsome sleeping figure in the uniform of an admiral, a sword at his side, is Admiral Henry Meynell, whose memorial is here though he sleeps at Hoar Cross.

STAFFORDSHIRE TOWNS AND VILLAGES

In this key to our map of Staffordshire are all the towns and villages treated in this book. If a place is not on the map by name, its square is given here, so that the way to it is easily found, each square being five miles. One or two hamlets are in the book with their neighbouring villages ; for these see Index.

Seighford	C7	Talke	C3	Wednesbury	E10
Shallowford	C6	Tamworth	G9	Wednesfield	D10
Shareshill	D9	Tatenhill	G7	Weeford	F9
Sheen	F2	Tettenhall	C10	West Bromwich	E11
Shenstone	F9	Tipton	D10	Weston-on-Trent	E6
Smethwick	E11	Tixall	D7	Weston-under-	
Stafford	D7	Trentham	C5	Lizard	B8
Standon	C5	Trysull	C10	Wetton	F3
Stanton	F4	Tunstall	C3	Whitmore	B5
Stapenhill	H7	Tutbury	G6	Wichnor	G8
Statfold	H9			Willenhall	D10
Stoke-on-Trent	C4			Wolstanton	C4
Stone	D5	Uttoxeter	F5	Wolverhampton	D10
Stowe	E6			Wombourn	C10
Stretton	C8	Wall	F9	Wootton	F4
Stretton (Burton)	H6	Walsall	E10		
Swynnerton	C5	Walton	D7		
Swythamley	D2	Waterfall	F3	Yoxall	G7

INDEX

This index includes all notable subjects and people likely to be sought for, and a special index of pictures appears at the beginning of the volume.

INDEX

INDEX

INDEX

INDEX

251

INDEX